DEMOCRATIC REFORM IN NEW BRUNSWICK

DEMOCRATIC REFORM IN NEW BRUNSWICK

EDITED BY WILLIAM CROSS

CANADIAN SCHOLARS' PRESS INC. • TORONTO

Democratic Reform in New Brunswick
Edited by William Cross

First published in 2007 by
Canadian Scholars' Press Inc.
180 Bloor Street West, Suite 801
Toronto, Ontario
M5S 2V6

www.cspi.org

Copyright © 2007 William Cross, the contributing authors, and Canadian Scholars' Press Inc. All rights reserved. No part of this publication may be photocopied, reproduced, stored in a retrieval system, or transmitted, in any form or by any means, electronic, mechanical, or otherwise, without the written permission of Canadian Scholars' Press Inc., except for brief passages quoted for review purposes. In the case of photocopying, a licence may be obtained from Access Copyright: One Yonge Street, Suite 1900, Toronto, Ontario, M5E 1E5, (416) 868-1620, fax (416) 868-1621, toll-free 1-800-893-5777, www.accesscopyright.ca.

Every reasonable effort has been made to identify copyright holders. CSPI would be pleased to have any errors or omissions brought to its attention.

Canadian Scholars' Press gratefully acknowledges financial support for our publishing activities from the Government of Canada through the Book Publishing Industry Development Program (BPIDP) and the Government of Ontario through the Ontario Book Publishing Tax Credit Program:

Library and Archives Canada Cataloguing in Publication

Democratic reform in New Brunswick / edited by William Cross.
Includes bibliographical references.
ISBN 978-1-55130-326-0

1. Elections—Canada. 2. Elections—New Brunswick. 3. Legislative bodies—Canada—Reform. I. Cross, William P. (William Paul), 1962-
JL193.D445 2007   324.6'0971   C2007-900599-3

07   08   09   10   11   5   4   3   2   1

Printed and bound in Canada by Marquis Book Printing Inc.
Book design: George Kirkpatrick

Canadä

Contents

Acknowledgments • 7

CHAPTER ONE • 9
Democratic Reform in New Brunswick
William Cross [*Carleton University*]

CHAPTER TWO • 23
The New Brunswick Commission on Legislative Democracy
David McLaughlin [*Former Deputy Minster, NB*]

CHAPTER THREE • 39
Electoral Systems and Evaluations of Democracy
André Blais and Peter Loewen [*University of Montreal*]

CHAPTER FOUR • 58
The Effects of Differing Electoral Systems on Party Politics, Government Formation, and Voter Turnout
Alan Siaroff [*University of Lethbridge*]

CHAPTER FIVE • 90
The Government Life Cycle
André Blais, Peter Loewen, and Maxime Ricard [*University of Montreal*]

CHAPTER SIX • 103
Electoral Systems and Representational Issues
Joanna Everitt and Sonia Pitre [*University of New Brunswick and Canadian Policy Research Networks*]

CHAPTER SEVEN • 122
Candidate Nomination in New Brunswick's Political Parties
William Cross and Lisa Young [*Carleton University and University of Calgary*]

CHAPTER EIGHT • 145
Representation in New Brunswick: Capital and Constituency Concerns
David C. Docherty [*Wilfrid Laurier University*]

CHAPTER NINE • 170
Electoral Reform and Electoral Boundaries in New Brunswick
Munroe Eagles [*State University of New York, Buffalo*]

CHAPTER TEN • 204
Fixed-Date Elections under the Canadian Parliamentary System
Don Desserud [*University of New Brunswick*]

CHAPTER ELEVEN • 221
The Referendum Experience in New Brunswick
Chedly Belkhodja [*University of Moncton*]

CHAPTER TWELVE • 240
Voter Participation in New Brunswick and the Political
Disengagement of the Young
Paul Howe [*University of New Brunswick*]

CHAPTER THIRTEEN • 273
Defining and Redefining Democracy:
The History of Electoral Reform in New Brunswick
Gail Campbell [*University of New Brunswick*]

Copyright Acknowledgments • 301

Acknowledgments

THIS BOOK IS the result of the research program of the New Brunswick Commission on Legislative Democracy completed with the assistance of the Centre for Canadian Studies at Mount Allison University. The commission and the centre were partners in a research colloquium on the Mount Allison campus at which the earliest versions of most of these papers were presented. The authors benefited from comments then and at subsequent roundtables from members of the commission and other guests from the academic, government, and public policy communities. The University of New Brunswick in Fredericton and the Université de Moncton also hosted events related to the commission's research work.

The papers were completed prior to the commission issuing its report in January 2005. Subsequent elections and changes in electoral practice are noted where appropriate but are not fully considered in the analysis.

Debbie Hackett, Lisa Lacenaire, and Marie Joseé Groulx, all staff members with the Commission on Legislative Democracy, made important contributions to the commission's research program and to the academic conferences and roundtables.

The commission's co-chairs, Lorne McGuigan and Lise Ouellette, and the responsible deputy minister, David McLaughlin, were early and consistent supporters of this project. The research papers played an important role in informing the commission's Final Report and Recommendations.

Finally, we thank Premier Bernard Lord for his leadership in establishing the commission.

CHAPTER ONE

Democratic Reform in New Brunswick

WILLIAM CROSS

IN DECEMBER 2003 New Brunswick joined a growing number of political jurisdictions both in Canada and throughout the Western world that have launched democratic reform projects. The federal government and the provinces of British Columbia, Alberta, Manitoba, Ontario, Quebec, and Prince Edward Island have all been recently, or are currently, involved in considering reform of some of their democratic institutions and practices.[1] In some cases these have been relatively limited exercises (such as Manitoba's reform of its campaign finance laws and Alberta's attempts to empower backbench members of its legislative assembly), while others have been more wholesale reviews of the state of democracy. The New Brunswick exercise is probably the best example of the latter.

When Premier Bernard Lord announced the creation of the Commission on Legislative Democracy, he reminded New Brunswickers that "our democracy needs to be constantly nurtured and improved. As our society evolves, so too must our democratic institutions and practices. If we are to continue to make economic and social progress as a province, then we must ensure our legislative democracy is strong and vital so it can effectively support the prosperity we are together trying to create."[2] As Lord suggests, it is the duty of citizens from time to time to pause and examine their democratic life to ensure that it is keeping up with their changing values and meeting the policy demands of ever more complex social and economic arrangements. That this is going on across the country can only be an encouraging sign to those concerned about the health and vitality of Canadian democracy.

There are, of course, many reasons to be concerned about the state of our democratic institutions and practices in Canada. For more than a decade there has been evidence that Canadians are dissatisfied with the state of their democratic affairs. The 1991 Royal Commission on Electoral Reform and Party Financing concluded that "many Canadians are critical of their existing political institutions. Many are concerned that these institutions are not sufficiently responsive to their views" (Volume 2:229). That same year the Citizens' Forum on Canada's Future reported that:

> One of the strongest messages the forum received from participants was that they have lost their faith in both the political process and their political leaders. They do not feel that their governments, especially at the federal level, reflect the will of the people, and they do not feel that citizens have the means at the moment to correct this. (135)

Public opinion polling data throughout the last decade have consistently shown low levels of voter confidence in institutions such as parliament and political parties. At the same time, large numbers of Canadians believe that their elected officials are out-of-touch and non-responsive (Howe and Northrup 2000). The best, and most worrisome, evidence of this democratic malaise is the declining voter turnout that has occurred at the federal level and in almost every province during the course of the past two decades. At the federal level, turnout declined in each of the four elections held after 1988 before rebounding modestly in 2006. Participation in the 2004 election marked an all-time low and was some 20% lower than in 1988. In New Brunswick turnout in the 2003 provincial election dipped below 70% for the first time since accurate records have been kept. There is also considerable evidence that this decline in voter turnout is sharpest among young Canadians. According to some estimates, as few as one-quarter of eligible 18–25 year olds have participated in recent federal elections (Leduc and Pammett 2003).

Our political institutions are also far from representative. Too few visible minorities and women are elected to our legislatures. While considerable gains were made in the 1970s and 1980s, these seem to have stalled, and the proportion of female MPs has plateaued at less than one in four. The picture differs among the provinces, with some, like Quebec, performing considerably better than the federal experience. Others, however, like New Brunswick, are lagging far behind. The number of women elected to the New Brunswick legislature has actually dropped in recent years, and after the 2003 election only about one in eight members was female.³

Criticism of our legislatures is not restricted to their composition. Elected members have complained about the strict party discipline they are subject to, and voters have criticized this practice for failing to provide sufficient opportunity for their representatives to advocate constituents' interests that may differ from those of the member's party. Others criticize the extreme partisanship that characterizes our legislatures. Few voters believe that the party they support is right about every issue while the others are always wrong, yet this is the posture routinely taken by our elected representatives. Reasoned debate, aimed at learning and finding common ground, is almost completely absent from at least the public face of Canada's legislatures. All of these factors combine to produce low levels of voter confidence in both their elected representatives as a class and their parliamentary institutions.

It is, of course, also incumbent upon democratic citizens to pause from time to time to ensure that their public institutions and governmental practices are keeping up with their changing values and the changing socio-economic needs of their communities. Our society has changed dramatically in recent decades, and it is important to consider whether our democratic institutions reflect these changing realities and meet the contemporary needs of Canadians.

Given all of this—low levels of voter confidence in their democratic and legislative institutions, low rates of voter participation, the failure to make our elected legislatures more representative, and the changing democratic demands of a dynamic Canadian citizenry—it is not surprising that so many jurisdictions across the country are considering democratic reform. As suggested above, this has taken many forms. At the federal level it began with reform of the party and election financing laws in 2003, and gained strength with Prime Minister Paul Martin's talk of a democratic deficit among MPs and the resulting introduction of the three-line party whip system. Subsequently the project expanded under a democratic renewal secretariat in the Privy Council's Office, with consideration given to electoral reforms and other initiatives. British Columbia, Newfoundland, Prince Edward Island, and Ontario have passed legislation providing for fixed election dates, referendum legislation has been enacted in several jurisdictions, and several provinces are following the federal lead in exploring ways of empowering private members of their legislature.

The single most common reform being considered, however, is change to our first-past-the-post electoral system. At the federal level, the issue came on the agenda with a 2004 report to Parliament from the Law Commission of Canada calling for adoption of a mixed-member proportional (MMP) system.

The New Democratic Party raised the issue in the 2004 election and appears to have extracted a commitment from the government to consider the issue in return for NDP support of their minority government. The Martin government appointed a federal minister responsible for democratic renewal, and an all-party committee held hearings to consider the best process for consideration of reform. While its intentions are unclear, the Conservative government has shown signs (including a reference in its first speech from the throne) that it will continue the process.

In doing so, the federal parliament joins at least five provinces in considering electoral reform. Ontario held a citizens' assembly on electoral reform for the purpose of considering whether the single-member plurality (SMP) system should be replaced, and if so with what. The assembly's recommendation to adopt MMP will be considered by voters in an October 2007 referendum. Four other provinces are all well along with their reform projects, and in each case a recommendation has been made to replace the current system with a form of proportional representation (PR). In Prince Edward Island and New Brunswick, government-appointed commissions have recommended the MMP system. Islanders considered and rejected the proposed new system in a fall 2005 referendum. The Quebec government has released a draft bill also calling for implementation of an MMP system and is conducting public hearings on the subject of electoral reform. In British Columbia, a Citizens Assembly on Electoral Reform recommended adoption of the single transferable vote system (STV) and 58% of the province's voters supported the recommendation in a spring 2005 referendum. The provincial government, however, had set a 60% threshold for the referendum, so the measure was deemed to have failed. Nonetheless, Premier Gordon Campbell has promised a second referendum on the question for 2009.

The New Brunswick project has been the most expansive, encompassing a full re-examination of the province's democratic life. Underlying the New Brunswick approach are two principles: first, that it is not possible to reform one area of democratic practice without those changes affecting other institutions and practices; and, second, that the malaise infecting Canadian public life requires comprehensive assessment of the state of democracy and cannot be cured through a piecemeal approach.

Surely this is the correct approach. For example, changes to the electoral system should not be entertained without full consideration of how they might affect the nature of representation and the functioning of the legislature. Similarly, the electoral system cannot be changed without changing the way constituency boundaries are drawn, the way political parties nominate their candidates, and the composition and operations of our legislatures. And when we think about ways of improving our legislatures to encourage both more independence among members and cooperation across party lines, reform of the electoral system is a change worth considering. Likewise, increasing voter confidence and participation rates cannot result from one democratic reform, but rather can only be accomplished through a complete re-evaluation of our democratic practices. This argues for a full consideration of the role of elected members, of the way our legislatures and parties operate, and of our other democratic institutions and practices in any electoral reform initiative.

Other literature considers the effects of various types of electoral systems and of reform of individual institutions. For example, Henry Milner's recent books on the possibilities of proportional representation in Canada provide significant contributions to this particular debate (1999 and 2004). Similarly, works by David Docherty (2005) on legislatures, John Courtney (2004) on elections, Donald Savoie (1999) on governing, Graham White (2005) on the executive, and William Cross (2004) on political parties, all add to our understanding of questions of democratic reform, but do so by focusing on a single democratic institution. The current collection, however, differs from what already exists by providing a full consideration of electoral and democratic reform and drawing the connections among reforms of individual institutions. The expansive mandate of the New Brunswick Commission on Legislative Democracy provides a unique opportunity to consider the whole menu of reform possibilities, to identify linkages between individual reforms, and to consider how they might fit together in creating a more vibrant and citizen-centred democracy.

Considering these questions and situating them in the context of a particular jurisdiction should be of interest to all those interested in questions of democratic and electoral reform in Canada, and to those interested in the politics of New Brunswick. Situating these issues in the context of a particular province requires consideration of the links between the various reforms and highlights their interdependence. As several contributions to this volume suggest, analysis at the provincial level also highlights the ways in which democratic reforms in relatively small jurisdictions are likely to produce different results than those in larger national legislatures. The New Brunswick case is appropriate, as the province is often referred to as a microcosm of Canada. Canada's only officially bilingual province, New Brunswick has a similar linguistic and cultural duality to Canada as a whole. Similarly, the province has the same urban/rural cleavage that is found in much of Canada. Where it differs from some of the rest of the country is in its lack of a significant immigrant population.

This collection begins with an overview of the genesis and the work of New Brunswick's Commission on Legislative Democracy. The commission's deputy minister, David McLaughlin, provides us with an insiders' perspective of the rationale for the province's democratic reform exercise and an explanation of why the commission was given such a broad mandate. McLaughlin also explains the process the commission used in doing its work and he evaluates this as a form of democratic renewal. Different methods have been used in different jurisdictions, and McLaughlin assesses the strengths and weaknesses of the more traditional approach used in New Brunswick. Among his observations are the difficulties the commission had in energizing the general public to become engaged in the democratic reform discussion. McLaughlin sets the context for the discussion that follows by outlining the principal reforms suggested by the commission.

The chapters that follow are essentially research reports that the commission required in support of its mandate. Written by some of the leading students of democratic and electoral reform in Canada, these chapters address many of the central questions facing jurisdictions considering reform. The collection is somewhat eclectic, reflecting the needs of the commission. Some of the chapters consider generic questions of electoral reform, such as the difference in the average length of governments elected under different systems. This is crucial information for those considering reform, but is not tied to any particular geographic jurisdiction. Other chapters situate their analysis more fully in the New Brunswick context and reflect the democratic imperatives arising from the socio-demographic and geographic constraints that define the province. While this may at times seem uneven, it reflects the necessity that democratic reformers consider both types of information: structural changes that result from institutional design reform, and the unique democratic character—and particularly the representational needs—of the jurisdiction considering reform. Reform initiatives should ideally reflect both the best science on the generic effects of institutional change and the particular democratic needs and aspirations of the relevant jurisdiction.

The renewed interest in electoral reform in Canada is, to a significant degree, fuelled by elites' concern regarding the apparent decline in voter confidence in their democratic institutions and practices. Underlying this interest in electoral reform is a belief that the workings of the single-member plurality system are at least partially responsible for the perceived voter discontent. The potential culprits are many and varied, including design barriers preventing the election of adequate numbers of women and minorities, disproportionality in the translation of votes into seats in the legislature, "wasted" votes, lack of representation for small and non-territorial interests, and extreme partisanship in campaigning and governing. While there is evidence to suggest that, to varying degrees, Canadians are concerned about all of these things, we lack a systematic examination of the relationship between the type of electoral system in use and voters' evaluation of their democracy. This is a crucial question in the current Canadian context. If electoral reform is to have the desired effect of increasing levels of voter confidence and trust, then this should be observable through examination of this relationship in similarly situated countries with different electoral systems.

This is the question that André Blais and Peter Loewen tackle in Chapter 3. Making use of survey data from 19 Western democracies, they examine the relationship between the electoral system and voters' overall satisfaction with their democracy, the perceived fairness of their elections, and their views regarding the responsiveness of their democratic institutions. Their findings are encouraging for proponents of electoral reform. After isolating the effect of the electoral system, they find "a clear and systematic pattern: assessments of fairness and responsiveness are much more negative (or less positive) in countries where there is a poor fit between seat and vote shares." Their findings further suggest that overall democratic satisfaction may depend more on whether one-party or coalition governments are formed—with voters preferring the former. This finding is important as some forms of proportional representation, such as that being considered in New Brunswick—regional MMP with relatively high thresholds—are more likely to produce single party governments than, for example, the single transferable vote option being considered in British Columbia, or the party list systems used in much of Europe.

Closely related to the question of voter satisfaction is that of voter turnout under different electoral systems. Concern over declining turnout rates has been a driving force behind the current attention paid to democratic reform. In Chapter 4, Alan Siaroff considers the relationship between different types of electoral systems and rates of voter participation. He finds that there is no easy relationship but rather a complex one depending on many factors. Nonetheless, he does conclude that "shifting from a plurality to a PR system and/or lessening the disproportionality of one's elections will increase turnout, but presumably only by a single digit figure." Siaroff suggests that other components of the electoral regime, such as ease of voting, can have an important effect on turnout rates. His analysis supports the New Brunswick approach of viewing electoral system reform as only one part of an effort to attract more voters to democratic participation, along with better education relating to public institutions and practices, increasing the ease of voter registration, and decreasing the barriers to participation.

While reflecting the unique political culture and needs of each jurisdiction, the debate about electoral reform in Canada is routinely weighed down by a common set of concerns: that more proportional electoral systems will lead to increased fragmentation in the party system, difficulty in government formation, shorter-lived governments, and an increase in the frequency of elections. These concerns are tackled head-on by Siaroff, and by Blais, Loewen, and Ricard in Chapter 5. Siaroff adapts his analysis to the New Brunswick case by examining the effect of the electoral system on these issues in jurisdictions that have proportional electoral systems but are otherwise similar to New Brunswick in terms of form of government and size of the legislature. In considering the concerns about proportional representation, which are often seen to be the cost of greater proportionality, Siaroff concludes that "the good news here is that these trade-offs are not likely to be as sharp in small legislatures such as that of New Brunswick." And he suggests that what might be perceived as the negative side effects of proportional representation (increased party fragmentation and government instability) can be minimized by some combination of small district magnitudes (i.e., small numbers of seats in each constituency), high electoral thresholds, limited numbers of compensatory seats, and allocation of those seats on a regional rather than national basis. These findings should help inform those who are crafting new systems.

In an analysis that may surprise many critics and casual followers of the debate over electoral system change, Blais, Loewen, and Ricard find that there is little relationship between the type of electoral system in place and either the lifespan of governments or the frequency of elections. After isolating for other effects and considering cases from 35 countries, they find that governments in both proportional and plurality systems tend to last for similar lengths of time. Governments in systems with more proportional electoral systems last on average only seven months longer than those in plurality systems. Furthermore, they find that elections in democracies using either system tend to be held approximately every three years. This appears to result from the ability of legislatures in PR systems to identify and install new governments without need of an election. These are particularly important findings given that many critics of PR point to particular cases of an unstable democracy using a proportional electoral system and suggest that the former is the cause of the latter. The analysis in Chapter 5 challenges these easy assumptions.

Among the perceived benefits of adopting a system of electoral reform are more proportionality in the translation of votes into seats and greater diversity in the types of individuals elected to the legislature—particularly in terms of gender. Siaroff's analysis tackles the issue of proportionality and, not surprisingly, finds that in comparison with the single-member plurality system, "most any alternate electoral system will produce greater proportionality." Nonetheless, he does caution that the design particulars matter and points to district magnitude and the number of compensatory seats as key factors in determining overall proportionality. These considerations take on added importance when dealing with relatively small legislatures like those found in most Canadian provinces.

Joanna Everitt and Sonia Pitre tackle the issue of inclusiveness in Chapter 6. Through the prism of gender they examine the relatively poor record of inclusive representation in the New Brunswick legislature. They suggest that central to the under-representation of women are barriers imposed by "institutions such as the electoral system and the political parties that are involved in the candidate recruitment and selection process." While their examination considers much more than the effect of the electoral system, they do point to the single-member plurality practice as one of the traditional obstacles to equitable representation of women. Consistent with a large body of research, they find that women are generally elected in larger numbers in more proportional electoral systems. They point to the larger district magnitudes in these systems as one of the key reasons for this outcome and argue that engineers of electoral reform in Canada must be careful not to design systems with small district magnitudes if they wish to see a substantial increase in the number of women elected. Given the penchant for the single transferable vote and regional mixed-member systems in the provincial exercises to date, this is an important and timely caution. Beyond the influence of the electoral system, they consider the possible use of quotas and financial incentives as ways of enticing political parties to nominate more female candidates. This discussion is particularly important given that several provinces, including New Brunswick, are considering an increase in public financing for parties that nominate a significant number of female candidates.

The focus on political parties as crucial actors in the selection and recruitment of candidates is continued in Chapter 7, with a discussion on candidate nomination in New Brunswick's political parties by William Cross and Lisa Young. Cross and Young argue that party candidate nomination lies at the centre of Canadian democratic process, having a significant influence on "which individuals and groups have access to elected office." Cross and Young focus on both the impact of various electoral systems on candidate nomination and the possibility of public regulation of these contests. The issues they consider include the relative balance of power between local and central party authority, the openness and fairness of nomination contests, voter choice in candidate selection, and inclusiveness of the candidate pool. Arguing that electoral system reform offers opportunity for change in the way candidates are nominated, they suggest that what is key is whether the parties have the desire to take advantage of these new opportunities to make candidate selection more inclusive and participatory. Pointing to experiences in other jurisdictions, they suggest that while some systems of proportional representation may offer opportunity for a greater democratization of these processes, they offer no guarantees if the attitudes of parties are not supportive.

Finally, Cross and Young pick up on the recent discussion regarding state intervention in nomination contests, suggesting that these events are too central to our democratic practice to be left entirely to the whim of the political parties. Accordingly, they lay out possible regulatory scenarios involving different levels of state intervention in nomination contests. This discussion is timely in light of the federal government's regulation of the financing of these contests for the first time ever in the 2004 general election, the perceived widespread concern over the lack of fairness of these contests, and the New Brunswick commission's recommendations for significant state involvement in both the financing and conduct of the parties' candidate nomination processes.

The selection of candidates by parties is of such importance because it largely determines who gets into the legislature. In Chapter 8, David Docherty provides a wide-ranging investigation of the operations of the New Brunswick Legislative Assembly and the role of its members both in and outside the provincial capital. Docherty's analysis is cast in "the understanding that changes to one democratic institution will have an impact on other areas," and he considers the likely impact of a change to proportional representation on both the operations of the legislature and the role of the MLA. He does this through a thorough examination of the resources available to MLAs in both their legislative and constituency service functions, the way they fulfill their party and constituency representative roles in the provincial capital, and their career paths. Docherty's analysis is premised on the fact that the electoral system under which members are selected can potentially have an important influence on the way they subsequently do their job as MLAs.

While focusing on the New Brunswick case, Docherty situates it within a comparative provincial framework by drawing upon data collected from jurisdictions across the country and by considering experiences in similarly situated legislatures in jurisdictions with proportional electoral systems, particularly Scotland, New Zealand, and Wales. Among Docherty's conclusions are that New Brunswick's MLAs lack adequate resources and require additional support in both their constituency and capital work. He finds that New Brunswick MLAs favour a weakening of party discipline and are generally open-minded about the possible increase in minority or coalition governments as a result of electoral reform. Among the issues Docherty discusses is the potential difficulty of having two types of elected members under some forms of MMP—those with constituency responsibilities and those largely without. As he suggests, in the New Brunswick case this is made more complicated by the fact that approximately one in three voters lives in an unincorporated area with no municipal government, making the constituency demands on their local member of the provincial assembly all the greater. This is the kind of localized issue that illustrates the importance of considering democratic reform within the context of the democratic needs and realities of a particular jurisdiction and not solely in the abstract.

The adoption of any of the proportional electoral systems being seriously considered in Canada would necessitate the drawing of new multi-member electoral districts. This issue has particular saliency in New Brunswick, as prior to the work of the commission it was the only province in Canada without standing boundary-drawing legislation. Munroe Eagles considers both the process of boundary drawing and the principles that govern it in Chapter 9. Eagles also considers the unique challenges involved in drawing multi-member districts inherent in proportional systems, which, he reminds us, are not new to New Brunswick or, for that matter, many other provinces. New Brunswick had multi-member elections as recently as the provincial election of 1970. He suggests that these larger multi-member regions provide an opportunity to maintain many existing associational communities within single districts and lessen many of the challenges faced in drawing smaller single-member districts.

In terms of process, Eagles provides a historical overview of the changes to boundary drawing in Canada, moving from partisan gerrymanders (often based on protection of incumbents) to the boundary-drawing revolution of the late 20th century, which saw almost all Canadian jurisdictions move to a regularized, non-partisan exercise.[4] He notes that while the federal, officially non-partisan process has generally been perceived to be successful, "the last two federal electoral maps drawn in New Brunswick have been associated with considerable controversy, both within the boundary commissions themselves and more broadly among citizens, regarding the appropriate representation of the province's sizeable francophone minority." By contrast, he notes, in the New Brunswick provincial exercise of the early 1990s, all of the boundary commissioners had "clearly identified partisan backgrounds," but that "did not appear to compromise their independence and willingness to compromise in the interests of a fair map." Eagles's conclusions in this regard challenge the widely held consensus that only a non-partisan process, modelled after the federal practice, can succeed in producing fair and widely accepted maps.

Several provinces have enacted, or are considering, fixed election dates as a democratic reform. To a large extent, this reform is a response to criticism that governments manipulate the timing of election calls to suit their own political interests. As Don Desserud reports in Chapter 10, most people oppose the supposed "right" of the party in power to call elections whenever it wants, and instead prefer that elections be held at fixed times. In addition to considering the pros and cons of this reform, Desserud considers why fixed election dates have become such a popular reform with almost no one voicing opposition to this change of one of the basic principles of our traditional form of parliamentary government. In a refreshing change from the often single-minded chorus in support of fixed election dates, Desserud suggests it is an "inappropriate and overly simplistic solution to a more difficult and complex problem: the decline in public confidence in the parliamentary system and in civic engagement in general." He further suggests that fixed election dates may create new problems by encouraging governments to ignore the legislature even more than they currently do. They may, as well, be a difficult fit with more proportional electoral systems in which governments may be defeated on a more regular basis.

Of course, citizen engagement in democracy involves more than participation in elections and, for a select few, service in a legislature. In recent years, there has been increased interest in exercises of direct democracy, and much of this has focused on the possible use of referendums as a way of allowing voters to participate directly in policy formation, unmediated by the political parties and elected officials.

In Chapter 11, Chedly Belkhodja considers the use of referendums in the New Brunswick context, exploring the rise of populism in the province. Belkhodja considers why governments are showing increased interest in referendums, whether the use of referendums can diminish the current democratic malaise, and whether they are appropriate tools in "plurinational" societies such as Canada and New Brunswick. Belkhodja provides a nuanced analysis of this last point, acknowledging the common concern that referendums can result in a diminution of minority interests, but suggesting that this is far from certain and that "the outcomes depend more on the role of political elites and the political context...than on a general theory." Nonetheless, he illustrates how prior referendums in New Brunswick and Canada have divided voters along linguistic lines. He provides data illustrating this in the recent New Brunswick case dealing with video lottery terminals, an issue not thought to divide voters along linguistic lines that, nevertheless, did see "the largest gaps between Anglophone and Francophone ridings." This analysis is particularly salient given that contemporary New Brunswick seems to have reached a successful, but hard-won, political accommodation between the two principal linguistic communities.[5] Belkhodja's analysis speaks to the New Brunswick commission's recommendation that referendums not be used for any issues that might undermine or diminish minority community rights.

One of the key questions that political elites have been concerned with is how to engage more young Canadians in the political process. In Chapter 12,

Paul Howe provides a broad overview of the competing explanations for the decline in youth participation in Canadian politics, making use of new data collected through a public opinion survey of New Brunswickers. After surveying the trends in voter participation in recent decades and canvassing the social and institutional factors that are often used to explain the decline in youth participation, Howe turns his attention to possible ways of reversing this trend.

Howe examines a host of potential reforms that should be of interest to policy makers and all those generally concerned with this decline in political participation. He pays particular attention to the issue of low levels of civic literacy, as these seem directly related to low levels of civic engagement. He suggests that a more systematic approach to civics education in our schools would "enhance young peoples' knowledge and understanding of the political system, giving them a firmer grounding that would enable them to grasp the meaning and relevance of real-world politics as it unfolds." He describes an appropriate civics program as one that encourages students to follow political events in the media and impresses upon them the significance and relevance of politics and government to their lives, thereby encouraging them to become active and to continue their engagement with politics once they are finished with their studies.

The final chapter, by historian Gail Campbell, reminds us that the current round of interest in democratic reform is not unprecedented. Campbell's detailed assessment of democratic reform in New Brunswick illustrates how the province has never been a laggard in adapting its democratic and electoral practices to meet the evolving norms and expectations of its citizens. Indeed, New Brunswick was at the forefront of such important reforms as the adoption of the secret ballot and standardized voter registration.

By reviewing how our democratic institutions and practices have been reformed many times before, Campbell reminds us that we should not think of existing structures as necessarily bound in long tradition and therefore untouchable. The New Brunswick electoral system is itself only several decades old, as it was adopted to replace an earlier multimember system in which several members were chosen to represent each of the province's counties. Thus, when opponents of reform talk of the long tradition of single-member representatives representing small communities, we should be skeptical. Campbell's essay brings us back to where this introduction and the current New Brunswick reform initiative started—with a call from Premier Lord for citizens to evaluate their democratic and electoral practices to ensure that they continue to meet their changing democratic values. This is not something new or unprecedented; rather, it is part of a long and noble tradition of periodic democratic renewal.

Notes

1. For a discussion of the impetus for some of these reform initiatives, see Cross (2005).
2. Comments by Premier Bernard Lord on the floor of the New Brunswick Legislature, 19 December 2003.
3. For comprehensive data on gender representation in Canadian legislatures, see Trimble and Arscott (2003).
4. The phrase "boundary drawing revolution" is R. Kenneth Carty's (1985).
5. For more on this, see Cross and Stewart (2001).

References

Carty, R. Kenneth. 1985. "The Electoral Boundary Revolution in Canada." *American Review of Canadian Studies* 15(3): 273–287.

Citizens' Forum on Canada's Future. 1991. *Report to the People and Government of Canada*. Ottawa: Ministry of Supply and Services Canada.

Courtney, John. 2004. *Elections*. Vancouver: UBC Press.

Cross, William. 2005. "The Rush to Electoral reform in the Canadian Provinces: Why Now?" *Representation* 41(2): 75–84.

—. 2004. *Political Parties*. Vancouver: UBC Press.

Cross, William, and Ian Stewart. 2001. "Ethnicity and Accommodation in the New Brunswick Party System. *Journal of Canadian Studies* 36(4): 32–58.

Docherty, David. 2005. *Legislatures*. Vancouver: UBC Press.

Howe, Paul, and David Northrup. 1990. "Strengthening Canadian Democracy: The Views of Canadians." *Policy Matters* 1:5. Montreal: Institute for Research on Public Policy.

Leduc, Larry, and Jon Pammett. 2003. "Explaining the Turnout Decline in Canadian Federal Elections: A New Survey of Non-Voters." Ottawa: Elections Canada.

Milner, Henry,. 1999. *Making Every Vote Count: Reappraising Canada's Electoral System*. Peterborough, ON: Broadview Press.

—, Ed. 2004. *Steps Toward Making Every Vote Count: Electoral System Reform in Canada and its Provinces*. Peterborough, ON: Broadview Press.

Royal Commission on Electoral Reform and Party Financing. 1991. *Reforming Electoral Democracy: Final Report*, 4 volumes. Ottawa: Ministry of Supply and Services Canada.

Savoie, Donald. 1999. *Governing from the Centre: The Concentration of Power in Canadian Politics*. Toronto: University of Toronto Press.

Trimble, Linda, and Jane Arscott. 2003. *Still Counting: Women in Politics Across Canada*. Peterborough, ON: Broadview Press.

White, Graham. 2005. *Cabinets and First Ministers*. Vancouver: UBC Press.

◂┤ CHAPTER TWO ├▸

The New Brunswick Commission on Legislative Democracy

DAVID MCLAUGHLIN

Introduction

WHY A MAJOR examination of the state of democracy in New Brunswick? What was behind creating the Commission on Legislative Democracy, how did it work, and what lessons can be learned from it? These are the main questions this chapter answers.

The commission was unlike any other in the history of New Brunswick's political life, for four reasons. First, its mandate was unparalleled in scope and depth. Virtually everything in contemporary provincial and national political discourse and debate about the state of democracy was placed in its mandate to study. Second, this was not the brainchild of an opposition party newly arrived in power after having campaigned on the need for widespread democratic renewal; rather, it was the product of a second-term government that had just been re-elected by the slimmest of margins in an election whose most dominant political issue had been auto insurance, not proportional representation. Third, the model chosen was of a large, broad-based commission of outside individuals selected for their regional, political, and personal profiles appointed by order-in-council and reporting to the premier. There was no formal link to the legislature or elected officials. Fourth, the commission was given a relatively short time frame in which to complete its work: one year. As will be seen below, these four elements created particular opportunities and challenges for the commission. Each subsequent decision of the commission—time frame, budget, staff, research, consultation, and recommendations—would follow from these initial choices.

Genesis

It began with a political party platform. The June 2003 provincial election reduced Premier Bernard Lord's Progressive Conservative government to a bare majority in the New Brunswick legislature. Despite this near loss, the re-elected premier declared on election night his intention to fulfill the mandate he felt had been given by the voters: "To the people of New Brunswick I say, I hear your message and accept this challenge and I accept this mandate and we will provide good government for the next four years." For this premier, that meant following through on all of his platform commitments. (More ambiguously, he also declared: "But you know, it's not always how big is your majority. It's what you do with it.")

Reaching Higher, Going Further was the title of the party's election platform. Inside was a commitment to "establish a Commission on Legislative Democracy to study the concept of proportional representation, fixed election dates, and other mechanisms to ensure the full range of people's voices are represented in government and legislative debate and decision-making." Importantly, the platform mentioned two other democratic renewal initiatives the government would undertake: establishing an electoral boundaries commission to review riding boundaries and introducing a New Brunswick Referendum Act. Each of these items, and more, would ultimately find their way into the final, formal mandate of the commission.

Democratic renewal was framed within the larger context of creating a more prosperous New Brunswick. Modern, effective institutions and processes—governance, in a word—were considered an essential support to successful economic and social progress. Like a more competitive taxation system to create jobs or an education system focussed on early literacy, democratic renewal was seen as essential to fostering more prosperity for New Brunswickers. In a phrase, strengthening democracy was essential to supporting prosperity.

In this sense, the commission was a natural next step to actions taken during Premier Lord's first mandate to bring decision-making in health care, education, and economic development closer to people and communities. Each of these initiatives—to create locally elected and representative regional health authorities, district education councils, and community economic development councils—flowed from specific platform commitments in the 1999 election. Studying what further steps could be taken to "continue to strengthen our democratic institutions even more by focusing on new ways to consult New Brunswickers and involve people in meaningful decision-making"—as the 2003 platform put it—was consistent with the premier's overall political philosophy and direction.

The first concrete step taken to establish the commission occurred on 13 September 2003, with the appointment by the premier of myself as deputy minister responsible. Although no mandate was yet developed, the premier was signalling his intention to move forward quickly. This was an important development for the future. If he and the government were going to be in a position to act upon any or all of the recommendations over the course of their second mandate, the commission needed to be up and running relatively quickly in order to report before the mid-point of the mandate. That would then leave just over two years to implement the commission's report.

The formal mandate and terms of reference were developed over a series of meetings that fall between the deputy minister and the premier. The platform had set out the core elements the commission would study: proportional representation, referendums, a process for drawing electoral boundaries, the number of MLAs, and fixed election dates. Beyond this, it became clear that there was both a need and an opportunity to consider a fuller range of democratic challenges facing the province, including declining voter turnout; youth disengagement; the appointments process for government agencies, boards, and commissions; and the electoral process itself. A mandate that was broad and deep rapidly found favour with the premier, who was prepared to ask fundamental questions about the nature and efficacy of democracy in the province.

Accordingly, on 19 December 2003, Premier Lord announced the actual formation of the Commission on Legislative Democracy. Nine commissioners were chosen (one resigned after four months for personal reasons) with two co-chairs, Lorne McGuigan of Rothesay and Lise Ouellette of Shippagan. The remaining commissioners were Brent Taylor (Doaktown), Lynne Castonguay (Moncton), Gerald Allain (Edmundston), Christine Augustine (Eel Ground Reserve), Albert Doucet (Beresford), and Connie Erb (Saint John). The commission was well balanced with four anglophones and four francophones, four women and four men. All regions of the province were represented. Three of the commissioners were former elected MLAs from the Progressive Conservative, Liberal, and Confederation of Regions parties. Commissioners were appointed to represent themselves and their own views, rather than any particular group, organization, or political party.

The commission's formal mandate was deliberately structured to give the commission strategic guidance and internal coherence. Given the often abstract, yet personal nature of democracy and how people view it, this was essential to ensure a commission of this size and scope could function effectively within a short timeframe and arrive at effective recommendations. It included a mission statement ("to create a more citizen-centered democracy") aimed at providing an overarching focus to the commission's work. As well, specific terms of reference reflecting each of the items it was to "examine and make recommendations" on (e.g., "recommend a fixed election date best suited for New Brunswick") required the commission to consider not just whether to adopt the concept but to provide an actual date, which brought an additional rigour to the commission's deliberations. The commission was given a charge to "seek the views of New Brunswickers" on each aspect of its mandate; this was to be a consultation commission. Finally, it was entitled to conduct independent research and hold whatever types of meetings it deemed necessary to fulfill its mandate.

In this manner, the structure and process of the commission's work revealed themselves. Clearly, its mandate determined its structure. A broad-based study of democratic issues required a broad-based commission composed of a range of representatives. Given the "political" (as distinct from "partisan") nature of the topics, at least some of the commissioners were expected to have experience with the political process. Because representation is at the heart of any democratic process, the commission required representation from all parts of the province, the two official linguistic communities, the major political parties, and both genders. The mandate's wording ensured that the commission would be a consultative commission, but its recommendations would be based not just on what it heard, but also on what it learnt through research.

In all of this, Premier Lord was personally and politically central to the commission's existence. Preparation of the election platform had been his responsibility. He appointed the deputy minister for the commission, who had previously been his deputy minister of policy planning, deputy minister of intergovernmental affairs, secretary of the policy and priorities committee, and chief of staff—all senior positions reporting solely and directly to the premier. Finally, as was noted, Lord developed the commission's mandate directly with his deputy minister, appointed and phoned personally each of the commissioners to invite them to serve, and formally received the final report of the commission and tabled it himself in the legislature.

Here, an important caveat is required. Premier Lord imbued the commission with his personal political will, but once it was launched, he took no direct or indirect actions to influence its outcome. He met with the commissioners only once, for an hour at their first meeting, to answer any questions they might have on the mandate or process. He informed them that it was their job to conduct themselves as they saw fit. He did not give them any indication of what he was expecting or wanted from the commission, telling them he would read their final report with interest once it was completed. Indeed, he never once interfered or otherwise tried to influence the commission's work and recommendations, save for one important area: during debate on the commission's estimates in the legislature, he indicated that, in his view, any change to the province's electoral system would require approval by the voters through a referendum. This did have an impact upon the commissioners' final thinking.

Mandate

The commission's mandate was broad, deep, and expansive.[1] It was divided into three main areas: electoral reform, legislative reform, and democratic reform. This typology was designed to provide an encompassing framework to gather each of the specific terms of reference under which the commission would "examine and make recommendations." Electoral reform encompassed changing the electoral system to a "model of proportional representation best suited to New Brunswick"; steps to implement a new PR system; fixed election dates; a process for drawing new electoral boundaries, including recommending the number of MLAs; and boosting voter turnout and participation particularly amongst young New Brunswickers. Legislative reform encompassed enhancing the role of MLAs and the legislature to make both more relevant and accountable, as well as changing the process for making appointments to agencies, boards, and commissions. Under democratic reform, the commission would recommend a New Brunswick Referendum Act and measures to enhance citizen participation in government and legislative decision-making.

Goals were also set for the commission by which it was to formulate its conclusions. Together, its recommendations were to bring about the following:

- Fairer, more equitable and effective representation in the Legislative Assembly;

- Greater public involvement in decisions affecting people and their communities;

- More open, responsive, and accountable democratic institutions and practices;

- Higher civic engagement and participation of New Brunswickers.

Four aspects of the mandate and terms of reference played an especially important role in steering the commission towards a successful conclusion. First, although the menu on this "democratic buffet" appeared staggering, it reflected how the premier viewed the integrated nature of the issues. You could not, for example, examine the role of MLAs without thinking about the electoral system that got them there in the first place. Placing all of the issues on one table allowed the commission—indeed, required it—to consider how each of these items worked together, if at all. That is why the focus of "citizen-centred democracy," as set out in the commission's mission statement, helped provide the additional cohesion as almost a default perspective for the debate that occurred on the importance of one democratic reform over another. Although each item could be and was considered singly, recommendations in one area had to fit with recommendations in another.

Second, although the commission was independent and could recommend whatever it wished, the terms of reference helped to keep it focused and to prevent internal tensions. For example, regardless of whether the commissioners thought PR was good or bad, they still had to recommend a model "best suited" for the province. They could offer commentary on whether adopting the model was the right thing or not, but they could not escape the responsibility of doing the necessary heavy lifting to arrive at a model, hopefully one based on consensus.

Third, the commission was given just one year—to 31 December 2004—to complete its charge. This short time frame meant it could not debate issues ad nauseum while postponing specific recommendations on the main issues. As noted above, the premier deliberately set a tight time frame to give himself the flexibility to act on some or all of the recommendations during this mandate. A commission that studied for more than a year would jeopardize this prospect plus be open to political charges of waste and inefficiency. Ultimately, the commission completed its work on time and under budget.

Fourth, this was no "pie-in-the-sky" exercise. The deliberate wording of the terms of reference, together with the model of commission selected, required it to exercise judgement and realism in arriving at final conclusions and recommendations. Explicit in the wording of the PR terms of reference, for example, was the requirement to recommend a model of PR that resulted not just in "fairer representation" and "greater equality of votes," but also "an effective legislature and government." This meant considering trade-offs between different electoral models to arrive at a model of PR that would, in the final analysis, be workable. The commission was not there to simply initiate a public debate (although this was always welcomed); it was expected to provide an answer to any such debate, in the form of solid analysis and recommendations.

These rigorous guidelines were influenced by an assessment of what other provinces were doing. By the fall of 2003, a royal commission in PEI was in the midst of its one-person study of electoral reform and PR; BC was about to embark upon a citizens' assembly to recommend electoral reform; and the new Liberal government in Quebec was making noises about introducing a bill on PR during its first mandate. The Law Commission of Canada would soon complete a major report on electoral reform. The soon-to-be-installed Paul Martin government in Ottawa had coined the phrase "democratic deficit" to highlight the need for reform of the role of MPs and the House of Commons, although Martin had not stated interest at that time in embarking upon consideration of electoral reform.

These initiatives reinforced the premier's view that democratic renewal could not be considered on a piecemeal basis; it had to be examined comprehensively from both an institutional and a procedural basis. And, most importantly, it had to be contemplated from the perspective of the citizen. If disengagement and disillusionment were rising, then democratic renewal had to be framed as much as possible from the point of view of the citizen looking outward, rather than that of institutions looking inward. In the process, New Brunswick could lead the rest of Canada in democratic renewal.

Reaction

Reaction to the commission's existence was muted publicly and sharp politically. Although noted in the media, democratic reform was not an issue that had been gaining any real salience over time. Unlike health care, for example, it was not a top-of-mind concern in New Brunswick. There were not, and still are not, any dedicated advocacy groups calling for reforms.

Political reaction divided along partisan lines and was sharply focused by the Official Opposition on the executive nature of the commission, its direct reporting to the premier, and the appointment of a deputy minister who had been a close advisor to the premier throughout the first mandate. The opposition was not formally consulted in the creation of the commission or in the development of its terms of reference. They cited the lack of legislative involvement as a flaw in its makeup. Accordingly, they would not consider themselves bound in any way by its recommendations; indeed, they would not commit to participating in its process. Ensuring that the commission conducted itself in an absolutely non-partisan manner, and was as open and transparent in its procedures as possible, took on an added importance as a result.

Challenges

Several obvious challenges presented themselves rather quickly. The first was time. Getting the work done, to a high-quality standard, while meeting the one-year deadline preoccupied all. Everything became a deadline—research, writing, meetings, consultations, translation, and so forth. Internally, the commission would have to set deadlines to focus its own learning and deliberations. Rather than finalize decisions or recommendations too early, commissioners agreed to setting "directions" on key items from the mid-point onward, to allow for more detailed research to be conducted. This approach also gave the commissioners time to become comfortable with what might become ultimate recommendations and to produce a consultation document for public reaction called *Options*.

The second challenge was participation and engagement. The Commission on Legislative Democracy was a study commission with a consultation mandate. To enable consultation, the commission had to create a range of mechanisms and opportunities allowing people to give their views, rather than a one-size-fits-all approach. Preceding this had to be knowledge. In general, the public had very little knowledge or understanding of the commission or the issues it was studying. Democratic disquiet in New Brunswick (as the commission's report ultimately described it) did not automatically translate into a consensus on either the problem or solutions. Electoral engineering remains a very abstract and distant concern for the vast majority of citizens. Raising awareness of the commission and its issues was an ongoing preoccupation, and a challenge that was never fully overcome.

The third challenge was credibility and legitimacy. This is a challenge facing any government consultation process, but one that is magnified when dealing with issues of democracy. The commission had to take steps to ensure its process was more open and transparent than any other, offer full participation to all political parties and elected officials, travel widely in the province, and meet with everyone who was interested. The commission could not make people speak to it, but it could open every door possible to help them do so.

More than that, the commission knew that the quality of the final report and recommendations would be the most determining factor in its ultimate success. Ensuring a strong research and analytical base was essential to meeting this goal. Recommendations would be based not just on what the commission heard, but also on what it learned, examined, and considered.

Structure and Process

The commission's structure and process reflected the key ingredients in its formation: a broad and deep mandate, a short time frame, a need to research and examine issues in-depth, an obligation to consult New Brunswickers, and a blank sheet as to how it was to proceed. To undertake its work, the commission received a budget that totalled approximately $1.2 million over one and a half fiscal years. By comparison, this was less than the total expenditure of the Premier's Health Quality Council in New Brunswick, which examined the structure and service delivery of the health care system. It was also less than had been allocated to the Royal Commission on the Future of Newfoundland and Labrador, a study commission examining that province's place in Confederation.

The commission had a full-time staff of five: a deputy minister, two policy advisors, a communications/consultation director, and an administrative assistant. A director of research, Dr. Bill Cross, then director of the Centre for Canadian Studies at Mount Allison University, was also engaged. The office had full bilingual capacity. The policy advisors were both lawyers with practical political experience in the PC and Liberal parties.

Three distinct phases characterized the commission's work: research (January–April) consultation (May–June and September–October), and deliberation (November–December). In practical terms, there was overlap amongst all three phases throughout the process. Learning never really ended, and research results were presented in the fall.

The research phase began with the engagement of Dr. Cross, who directed the academic research component of the commission's work. Few original writings existed on democratic reform in the province, requiring the commission to initiate its own academic research plan. A wealth of writings and publications exists on democratic reform in Canada and around the world. What was missing, however, was an understanding of how such reforms would affect New Brunswick and how New Brunswick perspectives should be integrated into consideration of these reforms. To fill that gap, respected academics from New Brunswick and across Canada were commissioned to prepare original research papers from a New Brunswick perspective (now published in this volume) on the specific areas of the mandate. The aim was to ensure the commission had access to informed academic research with up-to-date data, to stimulate debate and discussion on the subject areas by commissioners and others, and—most importantly—to ensure the commission had a strong research focus to its work. To bring together the fruits of this research and give commissioners direct access to the academics so they could pose their own questions, two academic research conferences and four expert roundtables on specific areas of the mandate were held over the course of 2004. Beyond the academics, various experts and interested parties were also invited to each event to ensure the learning was widely disseminated and discussed. These events and the academic research program were crucial to the commission's ultimate success.

The consultation phase was equally broad and comprehensive. It consisted of three basic parts: traditional public hearings and invited community leaders roundtables around the province; targeted forums aimed at specific segments of society—youth, women, francophones—in partnership with established provincial organizations; and an e-democracy component involving on-line questionnaires and information.

Fourteen public hearings were held—in the spring and fall—and eleven roundtables with community leaders were organized. Three major consultation documents were published to assist citizens in learning about the commission and its mandate, the issues under consideration, and, significantly, the specific options for reform being considered by the commission. Two comprehensive questionnaires were developed and made available on-line as well as in paper form to solicit input. Unfortunately, few "ordinary" New Brunswickers participated in the public hearings, but the events with community leaders were generally well attended. The lack of organized participation by the political parties and MLAs was a source of concern. Individual members did, however, participate.

The deliberation phase began internally with commissioners in late June (following the first round of public hearings) and in November and December (following the second round of public hearings). The first part led to the publication of *Options: A Progress Report to New Brunswickers*, which set out the main reforms being considered by the commission. Copies of *Options* were distributed widely in newspapers to households. It was designed to stimulate more precise input and feedback, based on reactions to specific reform proposals. In part, it was also designed to ensure that there would be few surprises in the final report, that the directions being considered had been as thoroughly aired as possible, and that New Brunswickers had the opportunity to provide specific feedback on specific reforms, rather than purely abstract notions of democratic renewal.

The research, consultation, and deliberation phases were really components of an ongoing phase: learning. Setting out the issues for New Brunswickers' consideration meant learning what the issues were to begin with. The commission therefore engaged in a lengthy and deep examination of all aspects of its mandate to ensure it understood fully how electoral systems work, the "ins and outs" of mixed-member proportional representation, constitutional prerogatives surrounding fixed election dates, and so forth. Background presentations on issues and concepts provided by staff and the director of research were essential for both commissioners and staff. As part of its commitment to openness and transparency, all of the commission's agendas and presentations were placed on the Web site, as were synopses of the public hearings, roundtables, forums, and events.

Final Report and Recommendations

The commission formally released its Final Report and Recommendations to Premier Lord on 19 January 2005. He tabled it in the Legislative Assembly that same day. The report contains 89 specific recommendations in a document that is 227 pages long. The recommendations were wrapped around three core themes: Making Your Vote Count, Making the System Work, and Making Your Voice Heard. This reflected the citizen-centred mission of the commission.

To make votes count for New Brunswickers, the commission proposed adopting a new regional PR electoral system called New Brunswick Mixed Member Proportional. Two-thirds of MLAs would be elected as now under the current first-past-the-post system, and one-third would be elected from party lists in four regions. It also recommended that a province-wide referendum be held no later than the next election to allow all New Brunswickers the chance to have their say on such a change.

The commission recommended that in the future all elections be held on the third Monday in October, every four years. It proposed a new Representation and Electoral Boundaries Act, under which boundaries would be redrawn after every decennial census. It also called for the creation of a new independent elections commission called Elections New Brunswick, which would have an expanded education mandate and would combine the current positions of chief electoral officer and superintendent of political financing.

To make the system work better for New Brunswickers, the commission recommended a rebalancing of authority away from the executive branch to the legislature, with significant new measures to make MLAs more independent and free from party discipline, relevant, effective, and accountable. It recommended a new, independent, and merit-based process to appoint New Brunswickers to agencies, boards, and commissions, as well as significant new rules governing the financing and conduct of political party nomination and leadership campaigns, and new party policy foundations to make political parties stronger.

To make the voices of New Brunswickers heard, particularly those of the youth, it recommended creating a mandatory K–12 civics education program and promoting political awareness and participation in the schools through mock elections and other means. To increase the number of women elected to the legislature, the commission recommended providing specific financial incentives to parties to nominate more women.

Finally, it proposed a New Brunswick Referendum Act for holding binding, province-wide referendums on an exceptional basis, and a range of measures to increase the involvement of citizens in participatory democracy and decision-making.

The commission's report went further than simply writing recommendations. It also designed and recommended an actual draft Referendum Act, a draft Representation and Boundaries Act, a fixed election date amendment, and amendments to the Elections Act and Political Process Financing Act governing limits and disclosures for financial contributions to nomination and leadership contests, along with new organizational rules. It also proposed a legislative calendar, standing rules amendments, a mandate for Elections New Brunswick, and so forth. To buttress its recommendations on PR, it set out three separate simulations that modelled election results based on the proposed NB MMP system.

Premier Lord accepted the report without offering an immediate declaration of intent as to what he would do with it. The opposition, while formally critical of the process, allowed that some elements of the report were useful and worthwhile. As this is an executive branch report, it is up to the government to determine its ultimate disposition. The report is designed to allow the government to select one or more items and proceed with their implementation individually, although the commissioners expressed their preference formally in the report to "consider our report as a whole package."

Lessons Learned

As described in Chapter 1, five provinces (including New Brunswick) and the federal government are engaged in democratic renewal. New Brunswick was unique in that it chose a broad-based study commission with an expansive, integrated mandate as its preferred process. Now other jurisdictions are contemplating further initiatives in this area. The federal government is going beyond parliamentary reform to consider what is the best process for electoral reform. Ontario has established a citizens' assembly to recommend some form of electoral system change. Quebec has tabled initiatives to bring an MMP electoral system into effect as well as change some of the rules of the National Assembly to link MNAs more closely with citizens. Incrementally, one new initiative appears to be piling on top of the other to achieve a deeper examination of democratic renewal and results.

THE NEW BRUNSWICK COMMISSION ON LEGISLATIVE DEMOCRACY

So what lessons can be learned from the New Brunswick Commission on Legislative Democracy? There are several.

First, democratic renewal cannot be a piecemeal exercise if it is to be effective. The broad-based disengagement and disillusionment Canadians are experiencing requires a broad-based consideration of the essentials of our democracy—its Westminster institutions and practices. The expansive mandate of the commission was the right one for New Brunswick. You cannot parse democratic reform; it must be viewed from an integrationist perspective. Changes in the electoral system will have consequences for the effective role of the legislature and MLAs. Boosting voter turnout requires both long- and short-term measures with virtually everything—type of electoral system, partisanship in the legislature, the education system, accessibility of the electoral process—playing a role. Examining this range of items together allows specific priorities to be drawn and realistic trade-offs to be made.

Second, democratic values provide a common ground for contemplating democratic renewal. Most citizens are not familiar with the ins and outs of electoral systems or other democratic institutions and practices. But they know what they like and what matters to them. Typically, they express this in terms like "fairness," "equality," and so forth. These are democratic values that shape their perspectives on what is wrong with the current system and what changes they are willing to contemplate.

Third, real citizen engagement in democratic renewal is not guaranteed. Put another way, "if you build it, they will not necessarily come." Of 100 things that matter to people on a daily basis, democratic reform appears to be number 101. This is due, in part, to what was stated above, but also finds general expression in citizen cynicism and disengagement, as measured by low voter turnout and declining trust and confidence in our governance institutions. Traditional processes, such as a study commission, are effective in treating the issues in a substantive and measured manner. They are, by definition, one step removed from the daily democratic "hurly-burly" of dealing with citizens. They may be less effective, however, in engaging average citizens. The largest single turnout for a public hearing of the commission was in the Miramichi, where a local hospital issue had galvanized the community. This was legitimate democratic expression, but it was not democratic engagement for renewal. Increasingly, citizens are questioning why they should bother to participate in a consultation exercise if they have no guarantees it will lead to results. New deliberative democracy exercises, such as citizens' assemblies, offer new ways to engage citizens much more directly in debate and decision-making (albeit one step removed).

Fourth, democratic renewal is really about a shift in power sharing and legitimacy. Those at the apex will have to confront this uncomfortable reality in the form of institutional and procedural change, but the questioning of legitimacy and outcomes is well underway among citizens. They are, essentially, seeking to recapture some of their lost authority, which they see as having become too diffuse and distant from their everyday realities. Any form of fundamental democratic renewal will have to confront this basic political algorithm.

Fifth, the political class (parties, politicians, media) are still the real decision makers when it comes to democratic renewal and must be implicated in any process. They determine both the substance and pace of reform by determining what issues are up for discussion and when and how they will be discussed. Why? Their immediate interests are the ones most at stake. Despite their self-interest, implicating them in the process on a non-partisan basis, to the greatest extent possible, is necessary to help bring about any real reform. But one should not overestimate their knowledge about democratic institutions and processes or their willingness to reform them. Their perspective remains an insiders' perspective, as members of a club viewing change through a very particular personal and political prism. It is to be expected, therefore, that they will often be skeptical about the benefits of reform. But they still bring an important reality check to the process.

Sixth, democratic renewal must move away from abstract notions and get to specific recommendations if it is to occur. Everyone knows the vocabulary of democracy, but the terms can mean different things to different people. Values provide common ground, as noted above, but people want specifics to know exactly what they mean. Since governments and parties are known to have their own interests, specifics allow voters to decide for themselves what might be best.

Seventh, democratic reform requires implementation mechanisms and processes. Governments and legislatures are habitually ill equipped with internal implementation levers of this magnitude. Few have ongoing, centralized reform secretariats. However fundamental, responsibility for these issues is fragmented across governmental institutions. Changing the standing rules of the legislature, for example, is solely the responsibility of members, with their own traditions and conventions. Political bargaining ("consensus") amongst parties is obligatory. For public servants, as well, "political" (and what is the legislature if not political?) is often equated with "partisan." They shy away from readily offering solutions to what is viewed, in a somewhat false distinction, as the province of politicians.

Eighth, leadership and political will by elected politicians in general and premiers and prime ministers in particular are vital to effect reform. New Brunswick's traditional political culture and party-based democracy put a premium on political leadership if transformational democratic change is to occur. This has been the pattern in the past with equal opportunity, bilingualism, health care reform, and local governance restructuring. A commission can set the stage, but only a premier can walk out on it.

Conclusion

The Commission on Legislative Democracy will end up on the shelf, or in the statute books. Commissioners called it "a once-in-a-generation opportunity to renew their democracy on behalf of citizens and communities." It may yet prove a milestone in democratic renewal in New Brunswick. Its comprehensive nature, original research, and forceful recommendations make it a unique and potentially lasting contribution to New Brunswick's democratic life.

As of fall 2006, the ultimate outcome remains in doubt, but the prognosis is not good.

On 20 June 2006, Premier Bernard Lord released a formal response to the commission's report called "Improving the Way Government Works." It accepted in full the commission's recommendations with a few exceptions and refinements. "This response," said Lord, "sets out some of the most significant democratic reforms ever undertaken in New Brunswick." This included establishing fixed election dates; holding a binding, province-wide referendum on proportional representation on 12 May 2008; creating Elections New Brunswick by combining the offices of the chief electoral officer and the superintendent of political process financing; introducing new, lower political donation limits; introducing a New Brunswick Referendum Act; and establishing a more open and independent process for appointments to government agencies, boards, and commissions. The government had already followed through on the commission's recommendations for an independent electoral boundaries commission and process.

Lord's PC government, however, was narrowly defeated in the provincial election of 18 September 2006, losing to Shawn Graham's Liberals. The new premier did not campaign on democratic renewal. As opposition leader he was critical of the Commission on Legislative Democracy, the process, and its staff, although he has publicly supported fixed election dates in the past and voted for the new electoral boundaries law. As democratic reform was not an issue in the election campaign and public reaction to the report was muted, he may well feel free to ignore the report and the response to it by the previous government.

This would be unfortunate. The issues studied by the commission remain valid. Although the legislature remains balanced for the second time in a row, it is worth noting that Graham won three more seats than the opposition Tories but actually came second in the popular vote—a manifestation of the first-past-the-post electoral system.

New Brunswick has been a national leader in democratic reform in the past—from political process financing to boundaries adjustment. It should continue to be a leader. Paradoxically, the impetus for change heard from citizens and confirmed by the commission now resides with the very institutions and processes that the commission recommended changing: government and the legislature. Without a champion for democratic reform within those very institutions, the roadmap for renewal set out by the commission could well remain on the shelf.

Note

1. The commission's mandate and all of its publications can be found at www.gnb.ca (keyword: democracy).

⇥ CHAPTER THREE ⇤

Electoral Systems and Evaluations of Democracy

ANDRÉ BLAIS AND PETER LOEWEN

Introduction

Elections are a substitute for less fair or more violent forms of decision making. Democracy is based on the assumption that it is both fairer and less costly to let the party or parties with more votes govern, rather than the groups with more military might, the right lineage, or just more money.

Democracy, however, is not without its challenges. Central to the notion of making decisions through the ballot box is the assumption that participants in a democracy will abide by democratic outcomes. The hope is that even those who lose an election will consent to being governed by their "enemies," presumably because they accept the process through which the governors were chosen. Voters' consent is also crucial in a democracy. Citizens must believe that democracy is working properly.

This chapter addresses the fundamental question of the influence of electoral systems on individuals' assessment of democracy. As more and more jurisdictions, in Canada and abroad, consider electoral reform, this becomes an increasingly important question. As discussed in Chapter 1, this importance is only increased by the tendency of reform proponents to assert that electoral reform can help cure democratic malaise. This chapter tests that proposition. Our demonstration takes four parts. First, we outline why it matters whether people evaluate the democratic process positively or negatively, and we present complementary aspects (and measures) of that assessment. Second, we discuss why and how we would expect various factors, including electoral systems, to affect people's evaluation of the democratic process. Third, we present and discuss our results. Finally, we conclude.

Why Citizens' Views Matter

For democracy to be perceived as a good substitute for other decision-making processes, a number of conditions must be fulfilled. First, and perhaps most crucial, citizens must feel that the elections in which they participate (or choose to not participate) are conducted fairly and justly. If citizens feel that elections are rigged in some fashion, that some groups or parties have an undue advantage, that the system is biased against them or their views, then they are more likely to cease participating in elections, or, worse, seek other methods for the selection or removal of their political leaders.

Second, democracy relies on a certain level of trust among citizens that politicians can affect change, that who is elected matters, and that politicians are responsive to the demands of citizens. If citizens lack this basic level of trust in the actions of their elected representatives, then they are less likely to participate in the electoral process.

We should note that citizens need not evaluate the democratic process in black or white terms, as a complete success or a complete failure. They may well appreciate certain aspects of the process while being critical of other dimensions. And they may express degrees of satisfaction or dissatisfaction. While democracies—especially long-established ones—face a low risk of collapse, they still depend to a good extent on the consent of citizens at large. The absence of such consent is likely to jeopardize the quality of representation.

In this chapter, we consider three dimensions of respondents' assessments of the democratic process: their evaluation of the fairness of the most recent election, their evaluation of the responsiveness of elected representatives, and, finally, their overall satisfaction with the way democracy works in their country.

To obtain a cross-national sample of respondents, we utilize the Comparative Study of Electoral Systems (CSES). This survey includes election studies in 32 countries between 1996 and 2001. These election studies consist of a series of interviews of between 1,000 and 2,500 individual voters in each country, most often immediately after an election. They present the obvious advantage of a wide range of countries and a very wide range of party supporters, and thus enable us to examine the impact of country-level and party-level factors, as well as individual-level factors.

To simplify our analysis, we consider only legislative elections, and among those only elections in which a presidential election did not occur concurrently. By limiting our analysis to legislative elections we can unambiguously identify those voters who chose winners, those who chose losers, and those who chose not to vote at all. As a result of this paring, we consider 20 elections in 19 countries: Australia, Belgium, Canada, Czech Republic, Denmark, Germany, Great Britain, Iceland, Japan, Mexico, Netherlands, New Zealand, Norway, Poland, Portugal, Slovenia, Spain, Sweden, and Switzerland. Spain is the only country in our sample with two election studies.

Overall satisfaction with democracy was measured by a standard question: "On the whole, are you satisfied, fairly satisfied, not very satisfied, or not at all satisfied with the way democracy works in (country)?" Evaluation of fairness was tapped by the following question: "In some countries, people believe their elections are conducted fairly. In other countries, people believe that their elections are conducted unfairly. Thinking of the last election in (country), where would you place it on this scale of one to five, where ONE means that the last election was conducted fairly and FIVE means that the election was conducted unfairly?" That question was not asked in Australia and Belgium, and so the number of cases is slightly reduced with respect to that dimension.

Three questions were designed to determine the degree of responsiveness. The first has to do with the capacity of elected representatives to understand the concerns of ordinary voters: "Some people say that members of Parliament know what ordinary people think. Others say that members of Parliament don't know much about what ordinary people think. Using the (one to five) scale, where would you place yourself?" The second concerns the willingness of parties to respond to voters' concerns: "Some people say that political parties in (country) care what ordinary people think. Others say that political parties in (country) don't care what ordinary people think. Using the (one to five) scale, where would you place yourself?" The third question ascertains the system's perceived responsiveness: "Some people say it makes a difference who is in power. Others say that it does not make a difference who is in power. Using the (one to five) scale, where would you place yourself?"

The responses to these three questions were combined and then averaged to form a responsiveness index. The following analysis thus utilizes three dependent variables: "satisfaction," "fairness," and "responsiveness," which constitute three dimensions of voters' overall assessment of how electoral democracy works in their country. Each of these three dimensions is measured on a scale where −1 represents the most negative evaluation and +1 represents the most positive evaluation. The correlations between the three variables are modestly strong, ranging between .24 (fairness and responsiveness) and .29 (satisfaction and fairness).

What Affects Evaluations of Democracy?

Our main objective is to determine whether citizens' assessments of electoral democracy depend on the kind of electoral system that is used in their country. The basic argument advanced in favour of proportional representation (PR) is that it is a fairer system. If indeed people believe that fairness is a crucial dimension of democratic representation, we would expect evaluations of the democratic process to be more positive in PR systems than in other countries.

The question is thus whether assessments of democracy vary across electoral systems. Two principal challenges confront the researcher who wishes to know how electoral systems affect evaluations of democracy. First, we need a good measure to distinguish between different electoral systems. Second, we need to consider and control for the other factors that are likely to also affect citizens' evaluations of their satisfaction with democracy. We first justify our measure of systemic differences—namely, the disproportionality index—and then turn to identifying other factors likely to affect satisfaction.

The literature distinguishes four basic types of electoral systems (Blais and Massicotte 2002), each with its own logic. In plurality systems, the candidates with the most votes win. In majority systems, candidates are required to obtain a majority of the votes (more than 50%) to be elected. In systems of proportional representation, the number of seats a party wins is proportional to

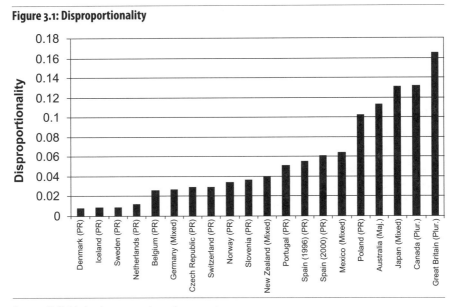

Figure 3.1: Disproportionality

Source: Official election returns in each country

its votes. And, finally, there are mixed systems, as in Germany, where plurality constituency races are combined with proportional representation in the allotment of extra seats.

There are, however, many varieties of PR systems, and PR systems vary much in the degree of proportionality (between vote and seat shares) they produce, depending on the size of the districts, the electoral formula, and the presence or absence of thresholds and/or upper tiers. We thus propose to distinguish electoral systems on the basis of the degree of disproportionality between vote shares and seat shares that is observed at a given election. To that effect, we use the disproportionality index proposed by Gallagher (1991), which tells us how disproportional the percentage of seats a party won is to the percentage of votes it obtained. The more a system is biased—that is, the more it rewards those parties that received the most votes—the more disproportional it is. The scores of our countries are graphed in Figure 3.1. It can be seen that Denmark, Iceland, Sweden and the Netherlands are the most proportional systems, while, Britain, Canada, Japan, Australia, and Poland are the most disproportional.[1]

Table 3.1: Distributions of voters by country

	% voting for losing parties	% voting for winning parties
Norway (PR)	72.59	27.41
Spain (1996) (PR)	66.70	33.30
Canada (Plur.)	64.86	35.14
Denmark (PR)	64.05	35.95
Sweden (PR)	61.62	38.38
Japan (Mixed)	58.97	41.03
New Zealand (Mixed)	54.27	45.73
Portugal (PR)	52.55	47.45
Great Britain (Plur.)	51.78	48.22
Czech Republic (PR)	49.91	50.09
Spain (2000) (PR)	49.46	50.54
Germany (Mixed)	49.10	50.90
Australia (Maj.)	47.99	52.01
Poland (PR)	47.73	52.27
Slovenia (PR)	43.15	56.85
Mexico (Mixed)	40.98	59.02
Iceland (PR)	37.66	62.34
Netherlands (PR)	36.87	63.13
Belgium (PR)	34.84	65.16
Switzerland (PR)	15.36	84.64

Source: Comparative Study of Electoral Systems (CSES), www.cses.org

How, then, do we expect differences in electoral systems to affect evaluations of democracy? The hypothesis is that citizens feel more negative about electoral democracy in more disproportional systems. The logic underlying this is that losing parties receive more fair treatment in more proportional systems, as their seat share better corresponds to their vote share. While supporters of losing parties may dislike the outcome of the election, they can less easily reason that their party was unfairly treated. Moreover, as Lijphart (1984) observes, the more proportional a system is, the more it moves from the majoritarian ideal of rule by the majority of the population to the proportional response of "as many people as possible." As such, disproportional systems generate a larger number of losers than more proportional systems. This can be seen in Table 3.1, which charts the percentage of individuals who voted for losing and winning parties in the elections studied, with winning parties defined as those who took part in the government formed after the election. As can be seen, proportional representation systems generally have more winners. Furthermore, it is only in systems with some element of proportionality (i.e., mixed and pure PR) that more than 50% of voters chose parties that eventually formed the government.

There is a second reason why proportional systems may generate more satisfaction. Specifically, more proportional systems generally feature a more equal balance between men and women within national legislatures. Such systems are likely to be seen as more representative of the total population, and thus as more responsive and fair.

Finally, there is a contrary reason why more proportional systems may generate lower evaluations of democracy. Specifically, the most proportional systems are less likely to be comprised, in whole or part, of locally elected representatives responsible to a clearly defined geographic area. As such, respondents may evaluate such a system as less responsive.

We are also interested in a direct consequence of electoral systems that may affect citizens' judgments of democracy, and that is whether the government that is formed after the election is a single-party government or a coalition government. PR systems usually lead to coalition governments, and disproportional systems, most especially first past the post, generally produce single-party majority governments (Blais and Carty 1987). We expect the presence of coalition governments, everything else being equal, to lower peoples' evaluation of democracy. Specifically, coalition governments are much more likely to involve messy negotiation. This, in turn, is likely to lead to frustration with the short-term operation of democracy. Moreover, this is likely to lead to policy outcomes that represent a compromise between the positions of the coalition parties. Such a compromise is likely to disappoint the supporters of each respective party, and thus reduce satisfaction with democracy.

We also expect citizens' evaluations to be affected by characteristics of the country they live in, the type of party they vote for, and the kind of persons they are.

We use three measures to capture the type of country a respondent lives in. The first two regard its democratic history, while the third measures its level of economic development. Our first hypotheses concern the length of the democratic experience in a country and its current degree of democracy. To this end, we distinguish three types of countries. First, those that were clearly democratic at the time of the examined election and that had a long, established experience with democratic elections. We regard these as "established democracies." Second, those countries that were clearly democratic at the time of the election, but whose experience with democracy is comparatively recent, are considered "non-established democracies." Finally, those countries whose current level of democracy is more dubious are considered "non-democracies."

To determine the level of a democracy in a country, we turn to Freedom House scores. Following a long- and well-established procedure, we consider those countries that received the "best" scores of 1 or 2 on political rights to be democratic. Any score worse than this leads to a country being considered a non-democracy. Of the 19 countries considered, 13 qualify as established democracies, meaning they have had significantly high scores (1 or 2) on political rights ratings over the previous 20 years: Australia, Belgium, Canada, Denmark, Germany, Iceland, Japan, Netherlands, New Zealand, Norway, Britain, Sweden, and Switzerland. Six countries are considered non-established democracies: Spain, Slovenia, Portugal, Poland, Hungary, and the Czech Republic. These six countries are coded as 1 on our "non-established" democracy variable. We have only one country, Mexico, which is considered non-democratic.

Our hypothesis is that individuals in established democracies are more likely to be satisfied than those in non-democracies. It should be the case that in countries where basic political rights are strongly respected even losers are willing to recognize that elections are conducted fairly, that politicians care about voters, and that elections matter. The proposition may appear tautological, though it must be kept in mind that judgments are subjective calls and that expectations may be higher in more democratic countries and that these higher expectations may sometimes feed disappointment.

We also make a distinction between established and non-established democracies. Among other things, democracy involves messy compromises between different segments of the population. It may take time for citizens to appreciate that such messiness remains valuable. It may also take time for losers to understand that there are many viewpoints in society and that it is unfortunately impossible to satisfy every one of them, that it is impossible for everyone to win every time. Thus the hypothesis: citizens' evaluations are more negative in non-established than in established democracies. The opposite pattern could also occur. It could be that those who have experienced how bad things can be when certain basic political rights are not respected are more appreciative of the benefits of democracy and are more prone to accept its shortcomings.

The final hypothesis concerning the type of country a respondent lives in regards the level of economic development in each country. The observation has been especially made by Lipset (1959) that a substantial level of economic development is required for a functioning democracy. As such, we hypothesize that individuals feel more positive about electoral democracy in more economically developed countries. We take as our indicator the United Nations Human Development Index. Country scores are graphed in Figure 3.2. We do note, however, that the importance of the economy in evaluating democracy has been seriously questioned, specifically in Eastern Europe (Evans and Whitefield 1995).

Figure 3.2: Human development scores

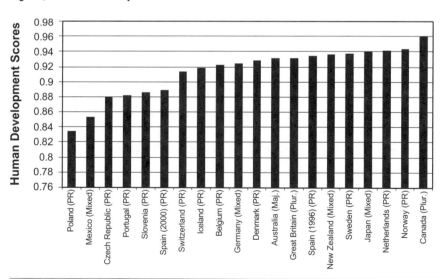

Source: United Nations Human Development Index country data

Every election produces winners and losers. Thus, we can divide respondents based on whether they voted for the elections' eventual winning party (or parties) or if they voted for the losing party (or parties). Winning parties are those that took up positions in the government following the election. We hypothesize that those who vote for winning parties are more likely to feel satisfied with democracy than those who voted for a losing party. Moreover, we feel that those who do not vote are less likely to be satisfied with democracy than those who vote. To test these hypotheses we create a variable that measures whether an individual voted for a winning party and another to measure whether a voter chose a losing party. Accordingly, those who did not vote score 0 on both of these variables.

Finally, we distinguish between different types of respondents, focusing on education and ideological orientation. We expect the better educated to provide more positive evaluations of electoral democracy. Education makes people more tolerant of opposing viewpoints and more open-minded (Hyman and Wright 1979). Moreover, tolerance is related to support for democratic values (Gibson 2002). Finally, those with more education are more likely to have been exposed to the dominant norm that one should lose gracefully in a democracy (McClosky and Zaller 1984). Education is coded from 0 to 7, from no schooling at all to a completed university education.

It is easier to be satisfied in a democracy when one does not hold strong views about what government should and should not do. If governments are eager to find compromises that are bound to displease those who favour substantial changes to the status quo, we should find individuals who hold "radical" views to be particularly critical of electoral democracy. Everything else being equal, therefore, citizens who are on the extreme right and those who are on the extreme left of the political spectrum should provide more negative assessments of representative democracy.

The CSES survey included the following question: "In politics people sometimes talk of left and right. Where would you place yourself on a scale from 0 to 10 where 0 means the left and 10 means the right?" Those who placed themselves at 0, 1, or 2 on the scale are construed to be on the extreme left, and those who placed themselves at 8, 9, or 10 are considered to be on the extreme right. All others constitute the reference group. The left/right question was not asked in Japan, and so the following multivariate analyses do not include Japanese respondents.

Results and Discussion

Figures 3.3, 3.4, and 3.5 report mean evaluation of fairness and responsiveness as well as overall degree of satisfaction, on the -1 to +1 scale. Figure 3.3 shows that most citizens in the countries examined here thought that the last election had been conducted fairly. In fact, 76% of the respondents gave a favourable evaluation on this criterion,[2] so that the mean score is positive in all countries. That being said, evaluations are particularly positive in the Scandinavian countries, which all have systems of proportional representation, and much more ambivalent in Japan and Mexico, which are mixed systems. Note that Canada scores relatively low on this dimension.

Figure 3.3: Evaluation of fairness

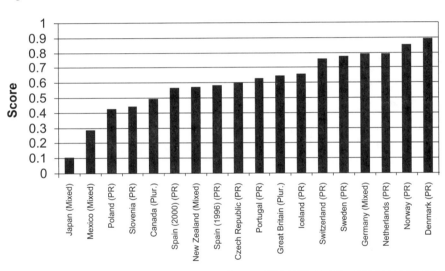

Source: Comparative Study of Electoral Systems (CSES), www.cses.org

Figure 3.4 indicates that assessments of responsiveness are muted. All in all, 54% of the scores on the responsiveness index are positive. Iceland, Denmark, and Norway, all of which use proportional representation, get the most positive evaluations, while Japan, Portugal, and Canada, representing mixed, proportional, and plurality systems, respectively, come at the bottom. Taken separately, the three questions used to determine evaluations of responsiveness indicate that only 15% of respondents felt that who they vote for makes a difference, that 69% believe who is in power makes a difference, and that 29% believe that political parties care what ordinary people think.

Figure 3.4: Evaluation of responsiveness

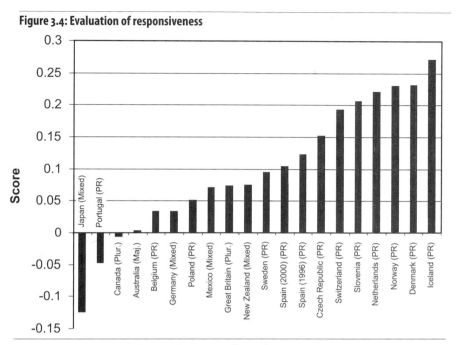

Source: Comparative Study of Electoral Systems (CSES), www.cses.org

Figure 3.5: Evaluation of satisfaction

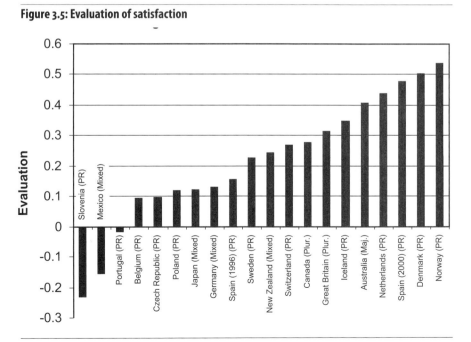

Source: Comparative Study of Electoral Systems (CSES), www.cses.org

Figure 3.6: Disproportionality and fairness

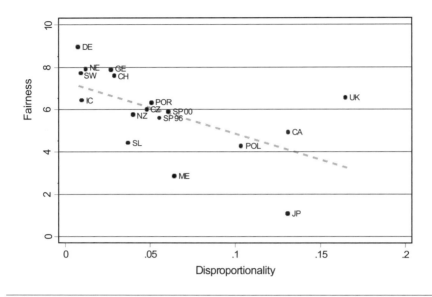

Source: Comparative Study of Electoral Systems (CSES), www.cses.org

Figure 3.7: Disproportionality and responsiveness

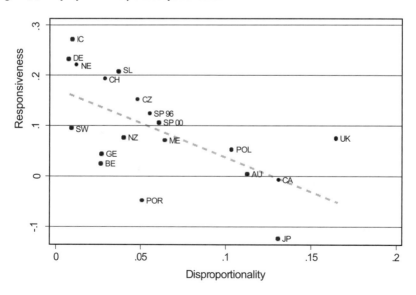

Source: Comparative Study of Electoral Systems (CSES), www.cses.org

ELECTORAL SYSTEMS AND EVALUATIONS OF DEMOCRACY

Figure 3.8: Disproportionality and satisfaction

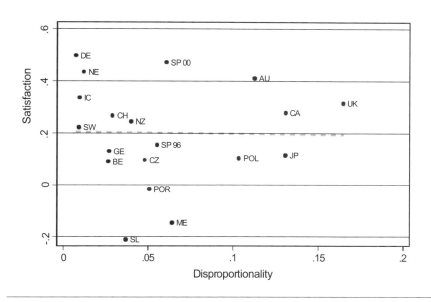

Source: Comparative Study of Electoral Systems (CSES), www.cses.org

Figure 3.5 displays mean overall satisfaction scores. Citizens tend to be relatively satisfied with the way democracy works in their country: 68% of the respondents across the 19 countries said that they are satisfied or fairly satisfied. The highest scores are again found in Norway and Denmark, and the lowest in Slovenia, Mexico, and Portugal. It is interesting to observe that on this issue Canadians appear quite sanguine.

The question is whether cross-country differences are systematically related to characteristics of electoral systems, most importantly, their degree of proportionality or disproportionality. Figures 3.6, 3.7, and 3.8 provide some useful information to that effect. Figures 3.6 and 3.7 show a clear and systematic pattern: assessments of fairness and responsiveness are much more negative (or less positive) in countries where there is a poor fit between seat and vote shares. As can be seen in Figure 3.6, mean scores are typically around .8 in very proportional systems, while they tend to hover around .4 in the least proportional ones. The same pattern emerges with respect to evaluations of responsiveness.

The situation is somewhat different in the case of overall satisfaction with democracy. There is no apparent correlation between the degree of disproportionality and mean satisfaction with democracy. This is illustrated by the fact that while Canadians are somewhat less satisfied than the Danes and the

Table 3.2: Evaluations of the fairness of the most recent election

	Coefficient	Standard error
Non-democracy	-0.52**	0.03
Non-established	-0.19**	0.01
Human Development Score	-0.73**	0.20
Disproportionality	-1.42**	0.09
Coalition	-0.06**	0.01
Education	0.02**	0.00
Left	-0.03**	0.01
Right	0.02*	0.01
Voted for winner	0.15**	0.01
Voted for loser	0.10**	0.01
Constant	1.36**	0.19
N	28144	
Adjusted R2	0.08	

*** Significant at 0.01
* Significant at 0.05

Source: Comparative Study of Electoral Systems (CSES), www.cses.org

Table 3.3: Evaluation of the responsiveness of elected officials

	Coefficient	Standard error
Non-democracy	0.05*	0.02
Non-established	0.06**	0.01
Human Development Score	0.65**	0.16
Disproportionality	-0.65**	0.07
Coalition	0.02*	0.01
Education	0.02**	0.00
Left	0.01*	0.01
Right	0.09**	0.01
Voted for winner	0.13**	0.01
Voted for loser	0.07**	0.01
Constant	-0.65**	0.15
N	32558	
Adjusted R2	0.04	

** Significant at 0.01
* Significant at 0.05

Source: Comparative Study of Electoral Systems (CSES), www.cses.org

Table 3.4: Satisfaction with the functioning of democracy

	Coefficient	Standard error
Non-democracy	-0.52**	0.03
Non-established	-0.18**	0.01
Human Development Score	0.01	0.23
Disproportionality	-0.40**	0.11
Coalition	-0.14**	0.01
Education	0.02**	0.00
Left	-0.13**	0.01
Right	0.07**	0.01
Voted for winner	0.13**	0.01
Voted for loser	0.08**	0.01
Constant	0.25	0.22
N	32319	
Adjusted R2	0.06	

** Significant at 0.01
* Significant at 0.05

Source: Comparative Study of Electoral Systems (CSES), www.cses.org

Norwegians, who have proportional systems, they are slightly more than the Swedes, who also have a proportional system. These initial analyses thus suggest that the degree of disproportionality of the electoral system affects citizens' evaluations of fairness and responsiveness but not necessarily their overall satisfaction with democracy.

These analyses are only suggestive, however. We need to take into account the other factors that may also influence citizens' evaluations. This is what is done in Tables 3.2, 3.3, and 3.4, which present a multivariate model of our three dependent variables.

Our findings confirm many of the hypotheses formulated above. As expected, those in non-democracies are less likely to feel that the election in question was conducted fairly. They also feel less satisfied about the general functioning of democracy in their country. They are, however, slightly more sanguine than those in established democracies about the responsiveness of their electoral officials. Those in non-established democracies give lower evaluations of the fairness of elections than those in established democracies, but these evaluations are more positive than those in non-democracies. They are similarly less satisfied about the general functioning of democracy than those in established democracies, but more content than those in non-democracies.

Finally, contrary to our expectations, those in non-established democracies feel marginally more positive about the responsiveness of their electoral representatives than those in established democracies.

Contrary to our expectations, higher levels of human development do not foster greater satisfaction with the way democracy works. In fact, people from more developed countries are less likely to feel that the election in question was fair, perhaps because they have higher expectations. They do, however, have more positive feelings about the responsiveness of elected officials.

The electoral system performs as expected. Indeed, the more disproportional an electoral system, the lower respondents' evaluations of the fairness of the election, the less satisfied they are,[3] and the more negative their feelings about the responsiveness of their elected officials.

But PR systems often entail the formation of coalition governments, and our findings indicate that the presence of a coalition government may contribute to more negative evaluations. Respondents tend to be less satisfied in general, and with the fairness of the election in particular, in countries with a coalition government. The presence of a coalition seems, however, to have a small positive effect on perceived responsiveness.

Our results also confirm that those who voted for winning parties are more positive on all measures than those who voted for losing parties. The latter are, in turn, more positive than those who did not vote.

Finally, we turn to individual characteristics. Education consistently performs as expected. Indeed, as education increases, so does every indicator. The better schooled simply possess more positive feelings about democracy, regardless of the electoral system in which they vote and/or the country in which they live. The results are more mixed for ideology. As expected, those on the left are less positive about the general functioning of their political system, as well as less positive about the fairness of the last election. However, contrary to our expectations, those on the right are more positive than those in the center for all three measures, and those on the left are marginally more positive in their assessments of the responsiveness of elected officials than those in the center.

To bring these data closer to home, we extend these estimates to New Brunswick, a province that has recently considered movement from a single-member plurality system to a mixed-member system. Table 3.5 shows the predicted impact associated with a change in the electoral system that would substantially reduce the degree of disproportionality in New Brunswick from .2125 (the mean disproportionality index in the last two elections) to .05, the median disproportionality index observed in our sample. Because a change to a more proportional system may also increase the probability of a coalition

Table 3.5 Simulated effects of switching electoral systems on evaluations of democracy

Switch	More proportional, no coalition	More proportional, coalition
Fairness	0.23	0.17
Responsiveness	0.11	0.13
Satisfaction	0.07	-0.08

Source: Comparative Study of Electoral Systems (CSES), www.cses.org

government, the simulations also indicate the predicted impact depending on whether a coalition government would be formed.[4]

These simulations are only suggestive, because many citizens' evaluations of democracy depend on many factors besides the electoral system, and they should thus be interpreted cautiously. Nevertheless, they indicate that evaluations of fairness and responsiveness are likely to become more positive after a change in the electoral system, particularly if the system still produces one-party governments. Things are more ambiguous with respect to overall satisfaction. In this case, the simulations suggest that satisfaction would slightly increase with a one-party government and somewhat decrease with a coalition government.

Conclusion

We have argued that for a democracy to perform optimally citizens must be satisfied with how their electoral system functions in a general sense, they must have a feeling that elections are administered fairly and justly, that elections matter, that politicians care, and that their elected representatives are responsive to their demands.

We have found that assessments of satisfaction and of the fairness of elections are lower in weak and non-established democracies, but that assessments of responsiveness are higher. We have found that education uniformly increases assessments of the fairness of elections and the responsiveness of electoral officials, as well as overall satisfaction. And we have found that those who are more ideological have mixed feelings about the functioning of democracy. We have also found that those who vote for winning parties are more satisfied on all measures than those who vote for losing parties.

Most importantly, we have found two consistent and strong effects related to electoral systems. First, we have demonstrated that disproportionality consistently reduces individuals' assessments of fairness and responsiveness, as well as overall satisfaction. More proportional systems simply produce more satisfied individuals. In sum, holding all other factors constant, an electoral system will generate more positive evaluations the more proportional its results.

Second, we have found that the presence of a coalition government dampens individuals' evaluations of the fairness of elections and their general satisfaction (and marginally increases their evaluations of responsiveness). It should be said, though, that coalitions are not a given in proportional systems. Indeed, Sweden and Norway are both examples of highly proportional systems that have been governed by single-party governments as often as by coalitions.

There is, in conclusion, no single factor that determines individuals' evaluations of democracy. But it is clear that individuals in more proportional systems are more likely to possess the consent that makes democracy an acceptable substitute for war. This finding provides support to those who argue that electoral system reform is an appropriate response to citizen disaffection with their democratic institutions and practices.

Notes

1. In recent elections, New Brunswick has produced disproportionate results. In the 1999 election, the disproportionality score was 0.24, which would make New Brunswick more disproportional than all the elections considered here. In the closely fought 2003 election, the disproportionality score was a smaller 0.07. However, even this score makes the province's current electoral system less proportional than 15 of the elections considered.
2. That is, 75% gave a 1 or a 2 on the questionnaire scale that went from 1 to 5. In our analyses, 1 was transformed to +1, 2 to +.5, 3 to 0, 4 to -.5, and 5 to -1.
3. Note that there is no significant bivariate correlation (see Figure 3.6). But Table 3.4 shows that, after controlling for the other factors, overall satisfaction is indeed lower in more disproportional systems.
4. Given the small size of the province, one-party majority governments would still be possible with the new electoral system, as would one-party minority ones.

References

Blais, André, and Ken Carty. 1987. "The Impact of Electoral Formulae on the Creation of Majority Governments." *Electoral Studies* 5:109–218.

Blais, André, and Louis Massicotte. 2002. "Electoral Systems." In *Comparing Democracies 2: New Challenges in the Study of Elections and Voting,* ed. Lawrence LeDuc, Richard G. Niemi, and Pippa Norris. London: Sage Publications.

Evans, Gregory, and Stephen Whitefield. 1995. "The Politics and Economics of

Democratic Commitment: Support for Democracy in Transition Societies." *British Journal of Political Science* 25:485–514.

Gallagher, Michael. 1991. "Proportionality, Disproportionality, and Electoral Systems." *Electoral Studies* 10:33–51.

Gibson, James L. 2002. "Becoming Tolerant? Short-Term Changes in Russian Political Culture." *British Journal of Political Science* 32:309–334.

Hyman, H.H., and Ch. R. Wright. 1979. *Education's Lasting Influence on Values.* Chicago: University of Chicago Press.

Lijphart, Arend. 1984. *Democracies: Patterns of Majoritarian and Consensus Government in Twenty-One Countries.* New Haven: Yale University Press.

Lipset, S.M. 1959. "Some Social Requisites of Democracy, Economic Development, and Political Legitimacy." *American Political Science Review* 53:69–105.

McClosky, Herbert, and John Zaller. 1984. *American Ethos: Public Attitude Toward Capitalism and Democracy.* Cambridge: Harvard University Press.

⊰ CHAPTER FOUR ⊱

The Effects of Differing Electoral Systems on Party Politics, Government Formation, and Voter Turnout

ALAN SIAROFF

Introduction

WITH ELECTORAL REFORM back on the Canadian agenda, both federally and especially provincially, the alternate systems being considered are not hypothetical: they exist in the real world, and it behooves us to see how they actually work in other democracies. Consequently and specifically, this analysis seeks to outline the effects of different electoral systems on (1) party systems, (2) (dis)proportionality of elections, (3) patterns of government formation, and (4) turnout, while bearing in mind that it is the party system that primarily affects the patterns of government formation, meaning that the electoral system can only be seen as playing an antecedent role here. Nevertheless, the electoral system is argued to affect all of these factors and thus lead to variations therein. Indeed, above and beyond the issue of greater fairness (read: proportionality) that has driven the demand for electoral system change in Canada, the other factors mentioned are all either additional goals of electoral system change (higher turnout) or potential trade-offs of alternate electoral systems (too many parties represented and thus fragmentation and perhaps paralysis; too long a time needed to form governments).[1] Yet both the positive and (arguably) negative effects of electoral system change away from single-member plurality depend crucially on the specific alternate model, as we shall see.

For the sake of simplicity and comparability from a Canadian perspective, this analysis assesses only "Western," advanced, industrial, non-presidential democracies, normally since the first election in the 1970s. The focus is overwhelmingly on national realities, although certain sub-national systems—those of Tasmania, Scotland, and Wales—are also included because of their respective uses of relatively unique electoral systems. Thus 27 cases are included in the overall analysis (with France and New Zealand each being two separate cases due to electoral system change). Specific in-depth analyses are given on systems whose legislative size most approximates that of New Brunswick (and most other small Canadian provinces), since these are the most logical points of comparison.

Electoral Systems and Their Aspects

Electoral systems have four different aspects: (1) the district magnitude, (2) the specific electoral formula(e), (3) the structure of the ballot, and (4) the total number of seats. The fourth point is not always noted, but Lijphart (1994, 12) rightly does so. The first three aspects allow us to classify varying national electoral systems into several key types. How many types are there? This depends in part on what one considers a significant distinction between two electoral systems. For the purposes of this study, I consider crucial the differences that affect (dis)proportionality, and thus I propose six categories—admittedly somewhat more than other classifications. These six categories are as follows: (1) single-member systems (with varying formulae), such as in Canada; (2) single-transferable vote systems (with small district magnitudes), such as in Ireland; (3) list proportional representation systems (which are assumed to have large district magnitudes, and which usually do), such as in the Nordic countries; (4) list proportional representation systems that in fact have generally small district magnitudes, these being Greece and Spain; (5) mixed-member proportional (MMP) systems (which have both local constituency and list seats and which aim for true proportionality through sufficient list seats), these being Germany and now New Zealand; and (6) additional-member systems (which have local constituency seats and some regional "top-up" seats, but which do not aim to produce full overall proportionality), these being Scotland and Wales.[2]

In the Canadian context, electoral system reform is effectively constrained by our desire to preserve "communities of interest." This can be seen in the mandate of the New Brunswick Commission on Legislative Democracy, which was tasked to find a fairer (more proportional) electoral system while preserving "an effective legislature and government, and a continued role for directly elected MLAs representing specific geographic boundaries." Given the strength of the Canadian tradition of local representation, it is unlikely that any Canadian jurisdiction will adopt a system that completely eliminates the principle of elected officials representing geographic communities. This would preclude any system with electoral regions that are too large, and certainly any system with just one at-large region (as in Israel, the Netherlands, and Slovakia). In this context, it is useful to separate out the list PR systems with small districts, as we do.

One could further subdivide most of the above categories based on assembly size, the aforementioned fourth aspect of an electoral system. However, this would lead to an unnecessary increase in the number of categories. Instead, one needs to focus on the key issue here, this being that large district magnitudes are generally necessary to achieve very high proportionality. By the same token, larger parliaments have more potential to be fully proportional than do smaller ones, since smaller ones tend to have smaller districts, a point that is particularly relevant in systems that are formally proportional. In other words, assembly size is central in allowing (or conversely limiting) greater proportionality under PR systems. In this regard, Lijphart's (1994, 100–102) analysis thus first groups PR systems into four categories based on assembly size, and then shows that disproportionality decreases as one moves step-by-step from the smallest category to the largest. In particular, he notes that "the biggest difference is between the smallest assemblies, with up to 81 members, and the next category of assemblies with 100 to 200 members" (102).

Since New Brunswick currently has a legislature of (only) 55 seats (the provincial range in Canada is from 32 seats in PEI to 125 in Quebec), and any change is unlikely to vary greatly from this number, it follows that perfect or near-perfect proportionality is basically an unfeasible goal. Moreover, it is crucial for the purposes of comparison to look at alternative electoral systems where possible under conditions of similarly sized legislatures. Thus, after the overall analysis in each section, I shall outline the specifics of four similarly sized legislatures using three alternatives to the single-member system: the single transferable vote (STV) system used in Malta (currently with 65 seats), which also has made provisions to produce parliamentary majorities for the party with the plurality (earlier, the majority) of the popular vote; the list proportional representation system used in both Iceland (currently with 63 seats) and Luxembourg (currently with 60 seats); and finally the additional member system used in Wales (also with 60 seats). Conversely, although Tasmania is of interest as one of the few STV systems, it is now one with only 25 seats in its House of Assembly.[3] Malta, Iceland, Luxembourg, and Wales are unlikely to be familiar to the reader, not least because they rarely receive much comparative analyses—hence the need to cover each in depth so as to provide the relevant context.

Electoral Systems, Party Systems, and Disproportionality

To repeat, in this section I shall first assess the general patterns of differing electoral systems and then go into depth on the actual party politics in each of Malta, Iceland, Luxembourg, and Wales so as to give the reader a "feel" for politics under alternate electoral systems in small-sized legislatures.[4] I shall assess the effects of each of the aforementioned systems in terms of several criteria, as shown in Table 4.1. Again, this table assesses the cases only since 1970 (or later, depending on when democratization occurred).

First there is the issue of how many parties get elected. For this purpose I shall only consider numerically relevant parties, defined as those that get at least 3% of the seats. Here I measure both the range over time and the median value (normally an integer). Next I assess the extent of disproportionality (and thus its inverse proportionality) using the Loosemore-Hanby index. This is the absolute value of the difference between the vote percentage and the seat percentage for each party (with a theoretical maximum of 100%), summed for all parties and then divided by two—since, for example, if some party is over represented then some other party or parties must be underrepresented. Higher values here indicate greater disproportionality. Much of said disproportionality is likely to accrue to the largest party (in terms of seats). Consequently I measure the average "seat bonus" (seat share less vote share) for the largest party. I also give the average seat share of the largest party to indicate the extent of single-party dominance of the legislature. What is crucial here is whether or not one party tends to win a majority of seats. Where this does not occur there is thus a "hung parliament," and consequently I indicate the frequency (percentage) of hung parliaments, ranging from 0% to 100%. Next and related, I look at every government formed during the period in question, and indicate which (if any) of three types—a single-party government, a two-party coalition, or a multiparty coalition—has been the dominant type. (Here I make no distinction between majority and minority governments.) Finally, for general information I give average turnout values—to be analyzed below.

As Table 4.1 shows, single-member systems are rightly known for having a small number of relevant parties in their legislatures, high disproportionality,

Table 4.1: Electoral systems and party system features

(Pattern of national elections since 1970 or democratization through early 2005, unless otherwise noted)

	Number of parties with 3% or more of the seats		Average disproportionality	Average seat bonus largest party	Average seat % largest party	Frequency of "hung parliaments" (%)	Typical government	Average turnout (%)
	range	median						
Single-member systems								
Australia	3 to 3	3	15.0	9.2	52.1	28.6	Two-party coalition	95.0
Canada	3 to 5	4	15.7	12.7	54.0	30.0	Single party	70.2
France (except 1986–1988)	4 to 6	5	25.0	17.8	46.8	71.4	Multiparty coalition	71.8
New Zealand through 1993	2 to 2	2	18.4	15.5	59.0	0.0	Single party	88.2
United Kingdom	2 to 3	3	18.5	13.3	55.6	11.1	Single party	72.8
Single transferable vote (STV) systems								
Ireland	3 to 6	3	6.4	3.4	47.7	90.0	Two-party coalition	71.5
Malta	2 to 2	2	1.6	1.1	52.1	0.0	Single party	95.5
Tasmania	2 to 3	2.5	5.8	3.1	53.5	20.0	Single party	94.4
List proportional representation (PR) systems								
Austria	3 to 5	4	2.6	0.9	44.7	72.7	Two-party coalition	86.9
Belgium	7 to 10	8	7.1	1.5	22.4	100.0	Multiparty coalition	92.6
Denmark	5 to 10	7	3.2	1.0	34.1	100.0	[No dominant pattern]	87.0
Finland	5 to 8	7	6.5	2.5	27.5	100.0	Multiparty coalition	75.5
Iceland	4 to 6	5	3.8	0.8	37.1	100.0	Two-party coalition	88.7
Israel	5 to 12	7	5.6	2.2	34.1	100.0	Multiparty coalition	77.6
Italy through 1992	4 to 7	5.5	5.0	3.1	38.6	100.0	Multiparty coalition	90.6
Luxembourg	5 to 5	5	7.0	3.6	35.6	100.0	Two-party coalition	88.7

Netherlands	4 to 9	6	2.9	1.1	30.7	100.0	Multiparty coalition	81.4
Norway	4 to 6	5.5	8.2	4.3	40.0	100.0	Single party	80.3
Portugal	3 to 5	4	7.4	5.3	44.1	80.0	Single party	74.4
Sweden	5 to 7	5	2.7	1.1	43.7	100.0	Single party	87.6
Switzerland	5 to 7	6	6.7	2.5	25.8	100.0	Multiparty coalition	48.0
List PR systems with small district magnitudes								
Greece	3 to 5	3	10.8	9.4	55.2	18.2	Single party	79.6
Spain	2 to 5	4	12.8	8.5	49.4	66.7	Single party	73.9
Mixed-member proportional systems								
Germany	3 to 5	4	3.4	1.8	45.9	100.0	Two-party coalition	84.7
New Zealand since 1996	4 to 6	6	6.4	2.3	40.3	100.0	Two-party coalition	81.1
Additional member systems								
Scotland since 1999	4 to 6	5	10.8	9.7	41.1	100.0	Two-party coalition	54.1
Wales since 1999	4 to 4	4	12.5	12.3	48.3	100.0	[No dominant pattern]	42.2

Source: Siaroff 2000a, with updates

with this disproportionality benefiting the largest party in terms of seats, and a tendency to single-party majorities ("manufactured" through such disproportionality). France is somewhat of an outlier here, reflecting the way its majority-plurality two-ballot system facilitates multiple parties. List proportional representation systems are largely the flip side of single-member systems, since list PR systems generally have many legislative parties (sometimes awfully many, as in Belgium, Denmark, Finland, and Israel), low disproportionality, hung parliaments, and coalition governments. That said, some list PR systems (Austria and Portugal) have had few relevant parties, and some even normally have single-party governments—but only where there is one large party (in terms of both votes and seats) combined with negative parliamentarianism (see below). Thus, although one cannot conclude that list PR guarantees political fragmentation, it does make this fairly likely. Of course, these comments are based on "standard" list PR systems; they are less applicable to the list PR systems with (intentionally) small district magnitudes. Theses systems (Greece and Spain) have few parties, the main ones of which usually (Greece) or sometimes (Spain) win single-party majorities; these systems also have fairly high levels of disproportionality—although still less than single-member systems. Basically the same points can be made about the additional-member (AM) systems, except that these have never yet yielded a single-party majority. (Remember that additional member systems do not aim explicitly for overall proportionality.)

This discussion still leaves the single transferable vote (STV) form of PR and the mixed-member proportional (MMP) systems, all of which have some intriguing results. First of all, the three STV systems listed each have a limited number of relevant parties, and the two MMP systems each have only a moderate number of relevant parties. For the STV systems, though, this point largely relates to the small district magnitude that is central to the feasibility of STV. Second, both the STV systems and the MMP systems are on average even more proportional than the list PR systems! (The group averages are 5.3 for the list PR systems, 4.6 for the STV systems, and 4.9 for the AM systems.) One needs to be somewhat careful here: the extremely high proportionality in Malta relates to both its party system and its "bonus seats" (both discussed below). It should also be noted that the MMP systems used in the German *Länder* do not usually produce quite the level of proportionality of the national German system, where the voters nowadays rarely "waste" their votes on parties that fail to clear the 5% hurdle (on the contrasting patterns in the German *Länder*, see Siaroff [2000b, 27]). That said, both the STV form of PR and the MMP systems must be considered proportional, as their names imply. Thus, by having proportionality without an excessive number of parties, both STV and MMP may appear to be ideal, or at least preferable to list PR, for those who do not want too many parties represented. That said, the aforementioned point about the size of legislatures must be repeated: those in New Zealand and especially Germany are quantitatively larger than the New Brunswick legislature, and thus, as noted, one should not hypothesize exactly the same outcomes from the same electoral system.[5] I shall thus begin with Malta as an example of a similar-sized legislature using a non–single member system.

Electoral Systems and Party Systems in Four Small Legislatures

Malta

Malta uses a single transferable vote system in which the country is divided into 13 constituencies, each with five seats. It must be stressed that STV as an electoral system does not guarantee "linearity"; that is, under STV the party that wins the most votes does not necessarily win the most seats, the party that wins the second most votes does not necessarily win the second most seats, and so on. This point proved particularly problematic in the Maltese case. As shall be outlined, a constitutional amendment in 1987 dictated that the party winning the majority of votes be given the necessary amount of seats to have a parliamentary majority if it did not win this outright, thus preventing any more "manufactured minorities." A subsequent constitutional amendment in 1995 changed the threshold here from a majority of votes to a plurality. This change thus ensures that the plurality party will always have a (bare) majority of seats—at least initially. Conversely, no election can ever result in a hung parliament. Such seat bonuses have been awarded twice, in 1987 and 1996.

Table 4.2 gives the results of elections in Malta since 1971. Malta has a two-party system that is marked by intense partisanship and extremely high voting turnout. Only two parties have ever been in power; indeed, only two parties have won seats since its first post-independence election in 1966. The first of these is the Maltese Labour Party (MLP). The MLP adheres to a socialist domestic policy, advocating universal education and health care, and resisting privatization. It also has supported a neutralist foreign policy in which Malta is conceived as a link between the Arab countries of North Africa and the Middle East and the countries of Europe. Thus the MLP consistently argued against the membership of Malta in the European Union (which finally occurred in 2004). The other main party is the Nationalist Party (PN), which is in power today. The PN advocates a more right-of-centre policy with regards to the national economy, preferring less government intervention and lower taxes. The party has often run campaigns calling for cleaner government and for guarantees of human rights. The party supported EU membership and favours closer cooperation with NATO. Support for the party comes mainly

Table 4.2: Elections in Malta since 1971

Election	Total seats	Maltese Labour Party		Nationalist Party		Others	
		Vote %	Seats	Vote %	Seats	Vote %	Seats
1971	55	50.8	28	48.1	27	1.1	0
1976	65	51.5	34	48.4	31	0.1	0
1981	65	49.1	34	50.9	31	0.0	0
1987	69*	48.9	34	50.9	35*	0.2	0
1992	65	46.5	31	51.8	34	1.7	0
1996	69*	50.7	35*	47.8	34	1.5	0
1998	65	47.0	30	51.8	35	1.3	0
2003	65	47.5	30	51.8	35	0.7	0

* Includes 4 bonus seats to create a parliamentary majority.

Source: Siaroff 2000a; Parties and Elections in Europe (www.parties_and_elections.de)

from white-collar professionals and religious adherents. There are other parties in Malta that, although not receiving representation in parliament, have received votes, albeit a very small share since 1971. The strongest of these has been the Democratic Alternative (DA), which was founded prior to the 1992 elections mainly as a form of protest against the existing two-party system. In terms of policy, the party is concerned primarily with ecological and environmental issues.

That said, Maltese politics functions overwhelmingly on a single, highly polarized left–right dimension. The elections held on 12 December 1981 stand out, not so much for the campaign, but for the result. The MLP won a majority of seats but at the same time polled a smaller percentage of votes than the PN. The PN accused the MLP of rigging the elections by redrawing electoral districts so it could hold on to its majority. The MLP was also accused of monopolizing state-run TV and radio, forcing the PN to make broadcasts out of Sicily. Foreign policy was a key issue, with the PN calling for full membership of Malta in what was then called the European Community, while the MLP campaign contained an anti-British element.

The problem of the non-linear elections of 1981 (which resulted in the PN boycotting parliament for some time) was addressed by a constitutional amendment made in January of 1987, which was agreed upon by both parties. The amendment dictated that the party winning the majority of votes be given the necessary amount of seats to have a parliamentary majority. It is unclear whether the MLP would have agreed to this amendment if the party had known how the elections of 9 May of the same year would have turned out. The results were virtually the same as those from 1981. The MLP received fewer votes but more initial seats than the PN. Nevertheless, because of the change in the constitution, the PN was granted four additional seats (for having received the majority of votes) so as to ensure a parliamentary majority for the party. The campaign issues included the PN's continued push to move Malta's foreign policy towards closer cooperation with Western Europe. The Nationalist Party victory was the party's first since the elections of 1966.

In the 1996 elections it was the MLP that benefited from the constitutional amendment of 1987. The party, like the PN in 1981 and 1987, received the majority of votes but not initially the majority of seats; therefore, it was given four additional seats to produce a parliamentary majority. In large part these elections were seen as a referendum on the foreign policy of the PN government, which had launched efforts to attain full membership in the EU and maintain current membership in NATO's Partnerships for Peace. The MLP campaigned on reversing both these policies. The MLP also gained support for its campaign promise to abolish the 15% value added tax, which the PN had imposed.

The 1996 Labour government soon found itself in a minority position, though, as the former leader and prime minister Dom Mintoff broke ranks in 1997 over the economic austerity measures of the government. Thus, in the summer of 1998, Prime Minister Sant decided to call early elections. These featured the ongoing themes of Maltese politics—membership of the EU or not, and the NP's plans to reintroduce a value added tax. The two main parties essentially changed vote shares from 1996, and this time the NP won the decisive majority of seats. In 2003, the results would almost exactly repeat those of 1998.

Iceland

Iceland uses a party list system of proportional representation, but did not fully adopt this until 1959, much later than elsewhere in Nordic Europe. For some time thereafter, most members were elected in eight multimember constituencies (ranging in size from 5 to 19 seats) using the D'Hondt method, with the remaining seats being national "top-up" seats for parties winning at least one constituency seat. The current system, in use since 1995, has cut the number of multimember constituencies down to six, with each having 10 or 11 members. This allows for greater proportionality in each district, and thus overall. Moreover, there still remain national "top-up" seats, now nine, in addition to the 54 seats allocated at the district level. The threshold for these "top-up" seats is 5% nationally.

As Table 4.1 shows, Iceland has varied between four and six parties of relevant size since the 1970s. Until 1999, its party system involved four traditional core parties—in ideological terms, conservatives, liberal agrarians, social democrats, and communists—to which were added both "new politics" parties (such as the Women's Alliance) and splinter parties. These splinter parties do not last long, but they serve to fragment the party system while they exist. The various parties and their performance can be seen in Table 4.3.

The role of personalities is a very important one in Icelandic politics. Politics are also very localized. For these reasons parties do not take up a very firm position on the classic left–right spectrum. The most evident cleavage dividing political parties in Iceland is a urban versus rural one. Attitudes towards Iceland's NATO membership and the maintenance of US military forces in Iceland are other issues that have produced sharp divisions amongst the various political parties.

The strongest party in Iceland is the Independence Party, a pragmatic conservative party. Founded in 1929 by the union of smaller conservative and liberal groups, the Independence Party has traditionally been the most powerful party in Icelandic politics, having participated in almost all the country's post-war governments. Indeed, in every post-war election, the Independence Party has received the plurality of both votes and seats—but never has it received the majority of either. These pluralities arise from its broad combination of rural and urban strengths. The party is supported most strongly by the nation's fisherman and commercial interests, but it also enjoys pronounced support from upper income professionals and those with a university education—thus it also dominates the densely populated urban areas. In terms of policy, the party adopts a pro-NATO position, stands for limited state intervention, and espouses a liberal economic policy.

The Independence Party has a tradition of strong individualism and, as a result, has been difficult to manage at times and has suffered from splits and defections. Some members have left to create new parties, most notably in 1983 when a popular ex-minister left to form the short-lived populist Citizens' Party. The main effect of the Citizens' Party splinter in the subsequent elections of 1987 was to produce an all-time poor result for the Independence Party, which won only 27.2% of the vote but still managed to remain the largest party. The next elections held in 1991 saw the Independence Party return to its pre-1987 levels with respect to percentage of votes; indeed, it won more seats than in all previous post–World War II elections. This can be attributed in large part to the complete collapse of the Citizens' Party, which retained none of its seats. The 1991 campaign was not centred much on policies; instead, personalities, local issues, and the general record of the previous governments were the major areas of debate and conflict. This helped the Independence Party as well because it did not participate in the coalition governments from September 1988 until the 1991 elections.

Iceland's second strongest party traditionally was the Progressive Party, which was founded in 1916 to represent largely agrarian interests. It therefore does much better in rural areas than urban ones. The party began as a relatively conservative party but in the mid-1960s began to move to a slightly left-of-centre position on economic policy. The party is against privatization and deregulation largely because these policies would hurt farmers. The party is a qualified supporter of NATO while advocating the withdrawal of United States forces from the country.

The Social Democratic Party (SDP) was founded in 1916. While the party was initially in favour of classic social democratic policies such as state ownership of large enterprises and substantial increases in spending for social welfare, in the latter post–World War II period the party occupied a more centrist position with respect to socio-economic policy. With regards to NATO, the party was second only to the Independence Party in terms of the degree of its support for Icelandic membership. Compared to other political parties in

Table 4.3: Elections in Iceland since 1971

Election		1971	1974	1978	1979	1983
Total seats		60	60	60	59	60
Independence Party (Conservatives)	Vote %	36.2	42.7	32.7	35.4	38.7
	Seats	22	25	20	21	23
Progressive Party (Agrarians)	Vote %	25.3	24.9	16.9	24.9	18.5
	Seats	17	17	12	17	14
People's Alliance (Communist / far left)	Vote %	17.1	18.3	22.9	19.7	17.3
	Seats	10	11	14	11	10
Social Democratic Party	Vote %	10.5	9.1	22.0	17.5	11.7
	Seats	6	5	14	10	6
Union of Liberals and Leftists	Vote %	8.9	4.6	3.3		
	Seats	5	2	0		
Social Democratic Alliance (Social Democratic Party splinter)	Vote %					7.3
	Seats					4
Women's Alliance	Vote %					5.5
	Seats					3
Others	Vote %	2.0	0.4	2.2	2.5	1.0
	Seats	0	0	0	0	0

Election		1987	1991	1995	1999	2003
Total Seats		63	63	63	63	63
Independence Party (Conservatives)	Vote %	27.2	38.6	37.1	40.7	33.7
	Seats	18	26	25	26	22

Citizens' Party (Independence Party splinter)	Vote % Seats	10.9 7				
Progressive Party (Agrarians)	Vote % Seats	18.9 13	18.9 13	23.2 15	18.5 12	17.7 12
People's Alliance (Communist / Green)	Vote % Seats	13.4 8	14.4 9	14.3 9	(into United Left)	
Left-Green Alliance	Vote % Seats				9.1 6	8.8 5
Social Democratic Party	Vote % Seats	15.9 10	15.5 10	11.4 7	(into United Left)	
Social Democratic Alliance (Social Democratic Party splinter)	Vote % Seats	0.2 0				
People's Movement (Social Democratic Party splinter)	Vote % Seats			7.2 4		
Women's Alliance	Vote % Seats	10.1 7	8.3 5	4.9 3	(into United Left)	
United Left / Social Alliance	Vote % Seats				26.8 17	31.0 20
Liberal Party	Vote % Seats				4.2 2	7.4 4
Others	Vote % Seats	3.4 0	4.3 0	1.9 0	0.7 0	1.4 0

Source: Siaroff 2000a; Parties and Elections in Europe (www.parties_and_elections.de)

Iceland, the Social Democrats had the least firm association with any one particular interest group. The SDP has suffered from defections as well. One such defection resulted in the creation of the more neutralist Union of Liberals and Leftists (ULL) in the 1970s. Another resulted in the creation of the populist and more clearly splinter Social Democratic Alliance in 1983, which contested two elections but only managed to win seats in the first. Most recently, in 1995 a splinter group of the Social Democrats formed the Awakening of the Nation (or People's Movement [PM]).

The only truly classic left-of-centre party in Iceland was the People's Alliance. This party first appeared in 1956 as an electoral coalition of the former Socialist Party, which had contested the first three post-war elections, and the more hardline members of the Social Democratic Party, who had grown disenchanted with their party's shift to the centre. The party initially advocated radical socialist reforms but gradually softened their rhetoric over time. However, the People's Alliance remained committed to a neutral foreign policy and maintained its call for Iceland to withdraw from NATO. The party did well in urban areas and was supported most heavily by public sector employees and intellectuals.

Besides these four traditional parties, the only other party of some relevance and durability has been the Women's Alliance. Founded in 1983, the party was the political manifestation of Iceland's modern feminist movement. The party had a very informal party structure and preferred to be called a "movement" rather than a political party. The Women's Alliance strove for more recognition for women in Iceland and also emphasized environmental issues (rather than, say, foreign policy ones). The Women's Alliance was not explicitly opposed to NATO.

That said, a significant realignment in Icelandic politics occurred prior to the 1999 elections. Specifically, the three most left-of-centre parties—the People's Alliance, the Social Democrats, and the Women's Alliance—formed what is called the Unified Left, under the leadership of a woman from the People's Alliance. The United Left has called for a redistribution of the growing economic wealth and higher welfare spending. However, consequently yet another splinter group arose in 1999, this time from the People's Alliance. Called the Left-Green Alliance, this group opposed the formation of the Unified Left. For its part, the incumbent centre-right government of conservatives and Progressives stressed the strong domestic economy, with its high growth, low unemployment, and falling inflation.

The elections themselves produced little change across the left–right divide. Certainly the Unified Left was disappointed with its 17 seats, but adding in the 6 won by the Left-Green Alliance yielded the same 23 leftist deputies as in

1995. The relative victor was clearly the Independence Party, which was back above 40% of the vote for the first time since 1974. The Independence Party would drop back again in 2003, though. The 2003 elections would also see a modest increase in support for the United Left, now called the Social Alliance. Consequently the gap between the two largest political formations in Iceland is now the smallest it has been in the period since 1970. Yet any change of government still rests with the Progressive Party, which holds the balance of power in the parliament.

Luxembourg

Luxembourg uses a list PR system, with seats allocated by the Hagenbach-Bischoff method. Voters may vote for a party list or a specific candidate on the list. The country is divided into four multimember constituencies, with 23, 21, 9, and 7 seats respectively. Given that two of the constituencies are of modest size, and that there are no national "top-up" seats, Luxembourg has relatively high disproportionality for a list PR system. Likewise, overall linearity is not guaranteed. Voting is compulsory, under sanction of a fine.

Table 4.4 gives the results of all elections in Luxembourg since 1974. Luxembourg is clearly a moderate (rather than extreme) multiparty system with a balance amongst the parties in terms of size. That said, in Luxembourg there is a high importance placed on individual candidates. In terms of the political parties themselves, the centrist—and pivotal—Christian Social People's Party has traditionally been Luxembourg's strongest party. It has participated in nearly every government since its founding in 1914. Since 1945 the party has won the plurality of votes in all but three elections and has never failed to win the plurality of seats. The 1974 election was the most recent example of such non-linearity (see Table 4.4). The Christian Socials have also provided all but one of the country's post–World War II prime ministers. The party is pro-monarchy, supports the social market economy, is in favour of subsidies for small business and farmers, and is strongly supportive of the EU and NATO. The party's main sources of support are farmers and Catholics.

The second largest party next to the Christian Socials has usually been the Socialist Workers' Party of Luxembourg. The party was founded in 1902 and is a moderately left-of-centre party. The party is pro-EU and pro-NATO and supports the concept of a mixed economy so long as the social security net is protected and maintained. The party enjoys a fairly broad base of support but is particularly strong amongst the urban lower/middle classes and trade union members. In 1971 more conservative members spilt from the party and created the Social Democratic Party, which was itself dissolved in 1983 after competing in only two elections.

Table 4.4: Elections in Luxembourg since 1974

Election		1974	1979	1984	1989	1994	1999	2004
Total seats		59	59	64	60	60	60	60
Christian Social Party	Vote %	27.6	34.5	34.9	31.7	30.3	30.4	36.1
	Seats	18	24	25	22	21	19	24
Socialist Workers' Party	Vote %	29.2	24.3	33.6	27.2	25.4	22.6	23.4
	Seats	17	14	21	18	17	13	14
Democratic Party	Vote %	22.2	21.3	18.7	16.2	19.3	24.0	16.1
	Seats	14	15	14	11	12	15	10
Communist Party / The Left (from 1999)	Vvote %	10.5	5.8	5.0	5.1	1.8	1.7	1.9
	Seats	5	2	2	1	0	1	0
Social Democratic Party	Vote %	9.2	6.0					
	Seats	5	2					
Enrolés de force	Vote %		4.5					
	Seats		1					
Independent Socialists	Vote %		2.2	2.5				
	Seats		1	0				
Greens	Vote %			5.2	8.9	9.9	8.5	11.6
	Seats			2	4	5	5	7
Action Committee for Democracy and Pensions Justice	Vote %				7.3	9.0	9.4	10.0
	Seats				4	5	7	5
Others	Vote %	1.3	1.4	0.1	3.6	4.3	3.4	0.9
	Seats	0	0	0	0	0	0	0

Source: Siaroff 2000a: Parties and Elections in Europe (www.parties and elections.de)

The Democratic Party, the last of Luxembourg's three main parties, was founded in 1945. The party occupies a liberal centrist position on most issues. The party supports the concepts of economic liberalism and free enterprise but is nevertheless committed to maintaining social welfare. The Democratic Party is pro-EU and pro-NATO and is mildly anti-clerical. The party is mainly supported by the upper middle class and professionals.

The Communist Party of Luxembourg was founded in 1921. The party began as an orthodox communist party and called for the total nationalization of the economy. The Communist Party of Luxembourg was pro-Soviet while the Soviet Union still existed; indeed, it was one of the most pro-Soviet Western European Communist parties. From the 1999 elections the party has simply been called "the Left." Prior to 1979 the party enjoyed fairly high levels of popular support from intellectuals and some of the country's urban and industrialized workers, totalling around 10% of the vote (Luxembourg being traditionally very industrial). However, having won only a single seat in the last three elections, the party has now clearly been marginalized. In that sense, it does show how parties can effectively disappear under list PR, at least where there is a certain effective threshold.

The Green Alternative was formed in 1983 and advocates a mixture of green and leftist policies. Some of the party's campaigns centred on calling for a 35-hour workweek and developing a more ecologically friendly agricultural sector. In 1986 the Green List–Ecological Initiative was formed by a prominent ex-member of the Green Alternative who had been forced out of the party. The two parties nevertheless competed together in the 1989 and 1994 elections so as to maximize their combined seats. In 1995 the two parties reunited and are now simply known as the Green Party.

Although party splinters have been much less relevant than in Iceland, Luxembourg has had some notable single-issue parties. One such party in the 1970s was the Enrôlés de force, representing those Luxembourgers who were forcibly enrolled into the German Wehrmacht in World War II. A much more durable single-issue party has been the Action Committee for Democracy and Pension Justice. This was formed in 1989 as the Five-Sixths Action Committee, but adopted its current name prior to the 1994 elections. The party argues for the introduction of an across-the-board pension plan worth five-sixths of a person's final salary.

Wales

Devolution under the Blair Labour government has given Wales an assembly, as in Northern Ireland, as opposed to the parliament established in Scotland. The nomenclature is important, as the Welsh legislature has less power than that of Scotland—although there is already pressure to increase its power. For the elections to its National Assembly, Wales is divided into five regional electoral districts. Two-thirds of the seats in the National Assembly (40 out of the 60) are constituency seats elected by single-member plurality, with eight such seats in each region. The remaining 20 seats are elected via a separate regional ballot, and are assigned to "top up" the results in each region so as to make the regional results as proportional as possible. Each of the five regions thus has four, and only four, "top-up" seats. Once these four seats are awarded, that is the end of the process even if not every party has been fully equalized in terms of seats to votes. (In other words, there is no possibility of expanding the legislature as in the MMP systems of Germany or New Zealand.) It is also important to stress that the calculation is done within each region, rather than for Wales overall (which would be more proportional). Although there is no legal threshold to receive "top-up" seats, the effective threshold in a region is 7% to 8%.

The three main British parties—Conservatives, Liberal Democrats, and Labour—contest the elections to the Welsh National Assembly. Labour has traditionally been the strongest party in Wales, often winning mining constituencies with huge majorities. The Green Party also competes in Wales. Yet the main indigenous party is the Welsh National Party, Plaid Cymru. Founded in 1925, it did not win its first seat in the United Kingdom House of Commons until a by-election in July 1966. It won its first seat in a British general election in February 1974. Plaid Cymru has always stressed self-government for Wales rather than outright independence. Its support has traditionally been limited to rural Wales, especially the Welsh-speaking northwest. Non-Welsh speakers—even those with nationalistic tendencies—have been somewhat suspicious of it. There is consequently a clear ethnic/linguistic cleavage in Wales in addition to its overall left-right ideological divide.

Table 4.5 gives the results for the two elections held so far for the National Assembly of Wales. In the first (1999) elections the Labour Party started from the position of the traditional dominant party in Wales, and hoped for an absolute majority. However, the imposition of the party leader (and prospective "first secretary," or premier) by the party leadership in London, overriding a more popular but also more independent local personality, proved to be a liability. Labour thus failed to win the overall majority that seemed within its grasp in the months leading up to the vote. In contrast, Plaid Cymru was able to make a major breakthrough (compared with United Kingdom elections), winning constituencies in the mining areas of the South Wales valleys. The party stressed that it should no longer be seen just as a party for Welsh speakers, and referred to itself with the bilingual label "Plaid Cymru–The Party of

Table 4.5: Elections in Wales since 1999

Total seats = 60 (40 constituency seats and 20 regional "top-up" seats)

1999 Elections	Vote % (constituencies)	Vote % (regional lists)	Constituency seats	Regional top-up seats	Total seats
Labour Party	37.6	35.4	27	1	28
Plaid Cymru – The Party of Wales	28.4	30.6	9	8	17
Conservative Party	15.8	16.5	1	8	9
Liberal Democrats	13.4	12.5	3	3	6
Green Party	0.1	2.5	0	0	0
Independents and others	4.7	2.5	0	0	0

2003 Elections	Vote % (constituencies)	Vote % (regional lists)	Constituency seats	Regional top-up seats	Total seats
Labour Party	40.0	36.6	30	0	30
Plaid Cymru – The Party of Wales	21.2	19.7	5	7	12
Conservative Party	19.9	19.2	1	10	11
Liberal Democrats	14.1	12.7	3	3	6
Green Party	0.0	3.5	0	0	0
Independents and others	4.8	8.3	1	0	1

Source: Parties and Elections in Europe (www.parties_and_elections.de); National websites

Wales." Plaid Cymru was still unsuccessful in urban areas, though. Moreover, its support decreased in the 2003 elections in both the constituency and regional list ballots.

Wales is thus a moderate multiparty system with, however, a dominant party in the Labour Party, which has always won a comfortable majority of the 40 constituency seats ("manufactured" from a minority of the constituency votes). In turn, this majority of constituency seats has meant that the Labour Party has been overrepresented (even if shy of a majority) overall, due to the limited number and regional allocation of the "top-up" seats. In sum, what a local political scientist in Wales wrote after the first Welsh elections is still true today, namely that the additional member system "can only be described as 'roughly' proportional. It is better in terms of proportionality than the single member plurality system but it is not fully proportional" (Broughton 1999, 219).

Electoral Systems and Government Formation

In this part of the analysis I shall assess the relationship between the different categories of electoral systems and both the speed of government formation after an election and the durability of governments. Yet before discussing the relationship between electoral systems and government formation, it should be noted that there are two contrasting processes of government selection in parliamentary democracies, as is shown in Table 4.6: in some parliamentary systems there is a formal vote by the parliament on a would-be government/prime minister, which/who must then win this *vote of investiture*. Such a procedure is called *positive parliamentarianism*, since there must be a positive endorsement of a new, or continuing, government (even if the voters apparently did so).

In contrast, under *negative parliamentarianism* there is no vote of investiture. A prime minister and government are simply appointed by the head of state, and they are assumed to be acceptable ("negative" confirmation) unless or until there is a successful motion of non-confidence moved by the opposition. Crucially, in situations where no party wins a majority, positive parliamentarianism is likely to lead to a majority coalition (so that it will have the votes to be invested), whereas negative parliamentarianism is likely to lead to a minority government of the largest party. Related and moreover, it is also generally the case that it takes longer to form a government under positive parliamentarianism (Bergman 1993, 287–289). Indeed, the slowest country in this regard, the Netherlands, does effectively have positive parliamentarianism (see Table 4.6). Broadly speaking, positive parliamentarianism is the more common version globally, although the cases examined in this analysis are more balanced, with negative parliamentarianism being used in Britain, Canada, and the other former British colonies (but not Scotland and Wales), as well as Austria, France, Portugal (effectively), and most of the Nordic countries.[6] Despite all the discussion of electoral system reform in Canada (especially at the provincial level), this author is not aware of any discussion on changing from negative to positive parliamentarianism.

There is also a second contextual factor regarding government formation that may be of interest: the extent to which the incumbent (outgoing) government is favoured in the government formation process. At one extreme, the convention in, for example, Luxembourg and the Netherlands is for the incumbent government to resign right after an election regardless of the outcome; consequently the government formation process always starts from scratch, or at least from the election results. At the other extreme, the British convention is that a government does not have to resign after an election but rather is free to continue governing and to wait and "meet parliament," even if it has lost its majority (such as the federal Liberal Party under Paul Martin in 2004, or the Ontario PCs under Frank Miller in 1985) or even if it is no longer the single biggest party in parliament (such as the federal Liberals under Mackenzie King in 1925). This convention obviously favours the incumbent government, which in turn keeps the formation period somewhat shorter. Only if some other party won an absolute majority would an incumbent party in Canada be expected to resign right after an election.

Having established these contextual factors, there are certain relationships between electoral systems and the time it takes to form a government after an election, as are shown in Table 4.6 (this table also repeats for comparison the typical type of government from Table 4.1). All of the single-member systems have on average quick or even very quick formation times (less than 20 days on average). Of course, all of these are also systems using negative parliamentarianism. Quick formation times are also found in the additional member systems of Scotland and Wales, and even the STV systems—although here Ireland (using positive parliamentarianism) averages a little above 20 days.

One might expect that the list PR systems, with their tendency to more fragmented parliaments, would take the longest to form governments. This is certainly true in terms of the group average (46 days), but in fact there are huge variations within this category. Some list PR systems have quick or modest formation times, especially the three Scandinavian countries. However, these are all systems of negative parliamentarianism, with Norway and Sweden also having a general pattern of single-party government. On the other hand, it is also the case that the six countries with the longest formation periods (above 40 days on average)—in descending order, the Netherlands, Belgium, Austria, Switzerland, Finland, and Portugal—are all list PR systems. Thus list PR must

Table 4.6: Electoral systems and government formation

(Pattern of national elections since 1970 or democratization through early 2005, unless otherwise noted)

	Type of parliamentarianism	Number of days to form a post-election government			Typical government
		Minimum	Maximum	Average	
Single-member systems					
Australia	Negative	5	25	12.8	Two-party coalition
Canada	Negative	9	43	19.9	Single party
France (except 1986–1988)	Negative	1	32	14.1	Multiparty coalition
New Zealand through 1993	Negative	4	42	16.1	Single party
United Kingdom	Negative	1	8	3.2	Single party
Single transferable vote (STV) systems					
Ireland	Positive	14	48	22.6	Two-party coalition
Malta	Negative	2	7	4.4	Single party
Tasmania	Negative	10	47	17.7	Single party
List proportional representation (PR) systems					
Austria	Negative	1	124	55.6	Two-party coalition
Belgium	Positive	33	146	69.7	Multiparty coalition
Denmark	Negative	1	35	12.2	[No dominant pattern]
Finland	Negative until 2000, Positive since then	23	74	46.1	Multiparty coalition
Iceland	Negative	10	74	39.8	Two-party coalition
Israel	Positive	20	65	39.8	Multiparty coalition

Italy through 1992	Positive	45	89	60.5	Multiparty coalition
Luxembourg	Effectively positive	23	60	36.0	Two-party coalition
Netherlands	Effectively positive	54	208	101.4	Multiparty coalition
Norway	Negative	8	39	27.4	Single party
Portugal	Effectively negative	11	96	40.5	Single party
Sweden	Effectively negative	9	45	21.7	Single party
Switzerland	Positive	38	60	50.3	Multiparty coalition
List PR systems with small district magnitudes					
Greece	Positive	15	37	22.4	Single party
Spain	Positive	19	63	36.9	Single party
Mixed-member proportional systems					
Germany	Positive	24	47	34.6	Two-party coalition
New Zealand since 1996	Negative	12	59	29.7	Two-party coalition
Additional member systems					
Scotland since 1999	Positive	13	13	13.0	Two-party coalition
Wales since 1999	Positive	6	6	6.0	[No dominant pattern]

Source: Siaroff 2000a, with updates

be seen as a facilitating factor in, but not a guarantee of, long formation times. Interestingly, neither Iceland (narrowly) nor Luxembourg is on this list, so long formation times may not be such a concern for smaller legislatures. Iceland and Luxembourg, although not quick, can be argued to have modest formation times—as do the list PR systems with small district magnitudes, and the MMP systems.

Electoral Systems and Government Formation in Four Small Legislatures

Malta
As noted, all Maltese governments have been single-party majorities. Malta also uses negative parliamentarianism. Consequently, its governments have all been formed very quickly.

Iceland
Although it has always been the plurality party in terms of election results, the Independence Party cannot be considered a strong party in terms of cabinet formation, in the sense of it always being in government if it so wished. In fact, a wide range of coalitions have occurred in Iceland, one of which even included the Independence Party and the People's Alliance together. In 1999, though, a clearer left–right polarization (at least in terms of party strategy) led to the first ever re-election of a centre-right government, that of the Independence Party and the Progressive Party. Also, David Oddsson of the Independence Party served a record four straight terms as prime minister, although in September 2004 (as agreed) he handed over the prime ministership to the leader of the Progressive Party (and previous foreign minister), Halldor Asgrimsson. This promise had been crucial to maintaining the coalition with the Progressive Party after the 2003 elections, in which (as noted earlier) the Independence Party lost seats while the Progressive Party held its own (see Table 4.3).

Luxembourg
Despite the relative balance of the parties, the larger size of the Christian Socials, combined with their centrist position, has meant—as noted above—that the party has provided all but one of the country's post–World War II prime ministers. More generally, governments have always involved a coalition of two of the main three parties, normally either Christian Socials and Socialist Workers or Christian Socials and Democrats. Generally, this choice of coalition partner has reflected simply which party won the second largest number of seats. Thus the 1999 elections led to the replacement of the Socialist Workers' Party by the

Democratic Party as the junior partner in government, and the 2004 elections saw a reverse switch. It must be stressed that the various smaller (and often single-issue) parties in Luxembourg have never been in government, nor have they ever been in a position to leverage their way into government by holding the balance of power.

Wales

Although in 1999 British Prime Minister Blair favoured a Labour–Liberal Democrat coalition in Wales to parallel the one that developed in Scotland, the Labour first secretary (or premier) of Wales, Alun Michael, initially chose to form a minority administration. This pleased Plaid Cymru, which sensed that it would have greater influence in a minority situation. In February 2000 Michael lost a vote of non-confidence 31–27, and was succeeded as first secretary by Rhodri Morgan, who distanced himself from Blair more than had Michael. Yet only a few months later, in October 2000, Morgan did in fact agree to a formal coalition with the Liberal Democrats (Broughton and Storer 2004, 268–269). With the 2003 elections giving Labour 30 of the 60 seats, First Secretary Morgan then announced the ending of the coalition. Although technically Labour did not receive a majority of seats in 2003, it did achieve an "effective majority" inasmuch as the non-voting presiding officer (speaker) of the assembly continued to be a member of Plaid Cymru. Additionally, the deputy presiding officer, the independent socialist John Marek, rarely votes (Broughton and Storer 2004, 273). Thus one presumes that this single-party Labour government will last a full term. Unlike Scotland with its continued two-party coalitions, then, there has been no dominant pattern of Welsh governments.

Electoral Systems and Voter Turnout

What, then, of the relationship between electoral systems and voter turnout? If we simply average the data in Table 4.1, the following turnout means result: 79.6% for single-member systems, 87.1% for STV systems, 81.5% for list PR systems, 76.8% for list PR systems with small districts, 82.9% for MMP systems, and 48.2% for additional member systems. However, as Table 4.1 shows, these means disguise some enormous ranges within most of these categories. It is thus better to consider broader, multivariate analyses of voter turnout. To this end, the following two contextual factors must be stressed: First, although there is general scholarly agreement on the factors facilitating voter turnout, there is some disagreement on the extent of specific factors; that is, scholars have come up with differing values for the precise effects of these factors. Second, such variation may well be related to the fact that scholars are using different data sets—even if all limit their analysis to electoral democracies. For example, three recent scholarly works on cross-national voter turnout are those of Blais and Dobrzynska (1998), which looks at 91 countries globally between 1972 and 1995; Franklin (2002), which looks at 25 advanced industrial countries and also a slightly broader sample of 31 countries, including some developing ones—in both cases from 1960 through 1985; and Siaroff and Merer (2002), which looks at 38 countries in Europe from 1990 through 2001. It is thus not surprising that there is some variation in their findings.

Cutting to the chase, though, the central question here is the effects of proportional representation on voter turnout as compared to plurality and majority systems. For this purpose, it is normal to group STV, list PR, list PR with small districts, and MMP all together as differing variants of proportional representation. Most scholars would thus argue that there is an increase in turnout due to proportional representation when holding all other factors constant, but that this increase is a (very) modest one. Specifically, Blais and Dobrzynska (1998, 251) conclude that, "everything else being equal, turnout is 3 points higher in PR than in non-PR systems." This value is clearly lower than that of Blais and Carty (1990, 179), who found that turnout was 7 percentage points higher in a PR system than a plurality system, and 5 percentage points higher than a majority system; that said, their values are still not large ones. PR is seen to increase turnout due to being fairer, and by making elections more competitive. On the other hand, PR lessens turnout since it lessens the chances of a (decisive) single-party majority (Blais and Dobrzynska 1998, 251), in part due to increased political fragmentation. To emphasize, decisive elections—where one party wins a majority—do have higher turnouts than non-decisive elections, all other things being equal (Blais and Dobrzynska 1998, 250). In summary, then, one could argue that the effects of PR are "two steps forward, one step back," but certainly not a giant leap forward.

Of course, all PR systems do not have the same mechanics, nor do they all translate votes into seats for the same number and size of parties. Thus what may be more crucial here is the (dis)proportionality of elections, which varies even within the same electoral system. Blais and Dobrzynska (1998, 248) find that a list PR system with perfect proportionality produces 6% higher turnout than a non-PR system. However, this increase is ever less as disproportionality increases within a PR system. For his part, Franklin (2002, 158) looks at all his sample countries regardless of electoral system and argues that, all other things being equal, turnout decreases by about half a percent for every 1% increase in disproportionality. Since, as Table 4.1 shows, it is not uncommon for countries with single-member systems to have disproportionality scores well above 10%, this suppresses turnout by 5% or more compared to a proportional representation system (broadly defined) with its much lower disproportionality. Looking at the overall data in Table 4.1, the bivariate correlation between average disproportionality and average turnout is -0.314; likewise, the bivariate correlation between the average seat bonus for the largest party and average turnout is -0.387. Thus disproportionality, and especially the largest party component of this, do relate negatively to turnout.

In summary, shifting from a plurality to a PR system and/or lessening the disproportionality of one's elections will increase turnout, but presumably only by a single digit figure. Why, then, is there such variation in turnout as shown in Table 4.1? This is because many other factors affect turnout. Let us stress five broad categories of these.

First of all, there is compulsory voting. Blais and Dobrzynska (1998, 246) find that compulsory voting increases turnout by 11%, all other things being equal. Siaroff and Merer (2002, 921ff.) focus just on strictly enforced compulsory voting as found in Belgium, Cyprus, and Luxembourg, distinguishing this from the weakly enforced compulsory voting of, for example, Greece and Italy. They thus find that strictly enforced compulsory voting boosts turnout by no less than 15%. The reader should note that Australia (and Tasmania) also have strictly enforced compulsory voting.

Secondly, there are ways in which elections can be more "user-friendly." Specifically, Franklin (2002, 158) finds that, all other things being equal, allowing postal voting and having elections on weekends or Sundays each increases turnout by about 6%. However, Siaroff and Merer (2002, 922) did not find the same positive effects for weekend or Sunday voting in their pan-European study.

Thirdly, there are a broad range of factors that reflect the importance or "salience" (Franklin 2002) of the elections. Are the parliamentary elections the only major opportunity for voters to express themselves? Likewise, are the parliamentary elections definitive in terms of allocating national power? Conversely, are there relevant (elected) presidents, relevant (elected) regional governments, bicameralism, and so forth in a country? Although scholars differ on how they measure and code alternate political actors, there is a clear consensus that the more power is diffused in a country the less crucial any one election is and thus the lower the turnout is for any given election. The situation of Malta—far and away the country with the highest turnout *not* using compulsory voting—is clearly relevant here. Malta concentrates all of its political power in a unicameral legislature, without any upper house, relevant president, or regional governments at all (Siaroff and Merer 2002, 924). The exact same point can be made for New Zealand. In contrast, Scotland and even more Wales are electing only regional parliaments with relatively little power in the comparative scheme of things.

Fourthly, political polarization—the ideological gap between the main parties—and/or political mobilization are argued to lead to higher turnout. In a more polarized society, it matters more in a policy sense which party is in power. Regarding political mobilization, Siaroff and Merer (2002, 920–924) use national party membership as a share of the electorate as a proxy for this and find the results to be robust, concluding that, all other things being equal, a difference of 10% in total party membership as a share of the electorate produces a difference of almost 6% in turnout. Malta again should be stressed here as a country with both strong political polarization and apparently the highest level of party membership in the industrialized world.

Fifthly, demographic factors matter. Turnout is higher in wealthier countries (not too crucial a variation for this analysis) and also in smaller countries (by population) and countries with a higher population density—the latter two factors of course often going together. Smaller populations produce greater senses of both community and efficacy. Blais and Dobrzynska (1998, 244) stress that the relationship between turnout and population is logarithmic, with the key difference being between smaller countries and everywhere else. The very high turnouts in Iceland, Luxembourg, and Malta—the three focus cases in this analysis that are sovereign countries—should be seen (in part) in this light.

Finally, even allowing for all these and other factors, scholars have found that Switzerland's low turnout is idiosyncratic enough that a Swiss dummy variable remains extremely robust in a multivariate analysis (Blais and Dobrzynska 1998, 250; Siaroff and Merer 2002, 924-926). Alternatively, one can simply exclude Switzerland (and the United States) from such comparative analysis, or at least from a specific model (Franklin 2002, 158-161). In brief, both the longstanding (for many decades) nature of Switzerland's four-party coalition government and its constant use of national referenda make voting there particularly moot. For information, if we thus remove Switzerland from Table 4.1, the average turnout for (pure) list PR systems increases from 81.5% to 84.3%.

Conclusion

Electoral systems do produce fundamental differences in party systems and also to some extent in government formation time (less so) and government stability (more so). The single-member system used in Canada and elsewhere is rightly associated with few relevant parties, quick government formations, and stable single-party governments. However, these features do come at the expense of high disproportionality and the tendency to "manufacture" majorities for the winning party. Most any alternate electoral system will produce greater proportionality. Given this point, two key issues arise. First, how much more proportionality? To achieve high proportionality—that is, as high as occurs practically—one would have to adopt standard list PR, MMP, or STV. To achieve better but not necessarily high proportionality, one can adopt (that is, one should settle for) either a list PR system with small district magnitudes or an additional member system. That said, even if more proportional, most of these alternate systems can still produce a non-linear result across the parties. To minimize the possibility of a non-linear result, one needs a reasonably proportional system combined with a sufficient number of compensatory seats allocated at the national level.

The second resulting set of questions is as follows: how many more relevant parties, how much slower government formations, and how much more unstable governments is one willing to accept as a likely trade-off for higher proportionality? The good news here is that these trade-offs are not likely to be as sharp in small legislatures such as that of New Brunswick and the four cases of focus in this analysis. That is, under a moderately or truly proportional electoral system one is likely to have a moderate rather than an extreme multiparty system, and two-party coalition governments that may well be stable (or at least more stable than multiparty coalitions). The chances of avoiding the most extreme trade-offs can be maximized by some combination of small district magnitudes, high electoral thresholds for large districts, limited numbers of compensatory seats, and/or making such compensatory seats regional rather than national. Lastly, as a cautionary note, any change to a more proportional system may well increase electoral turnout, but only modestly, and thus one cannot recommend electoral system change in and of itself as a cure for low or declining turnout.

Notes

1. The issue of electoral systems and government stability is dealt with in Chapter 5 by André Blais, Peter Loewen, and Maxime Ricard, and the issue of electoral systems and democratic satisfaction by André Blais and Peter Loewen in Chapter 3.
2. There are of course even more electoral systems in use, but I am intentionally avoiding here the semi-compensatory mixed system now in use in Italy, the single non-transferable vote system formerly used in Japan, and the parallel system now in use in Japan—since in each case there has been only one advanced industrial nation employing it.
3. Indeed, in 1998 this was reduced from 35 seats (with each of its five districts being

reduced from seven to five members) in a joint effort of the two big parties, Labor and Liberal, to reduce the seats and thus weaken the power of the third party, the Greens (Kellow 2003, 141).
4. This contextual information is taken from Siaroff (2000a), with relevant updates.
5. Moreover, I have not touched on the complex phenomena of "overhang seats" (in German, *Überhangmandate*) and, in the German *Länder*, "compensatory seats" (in German, *Ausgleichsmandate*).
6. As can be seen, Portugal and Sweden are both listed as "effectively negative" parliamentarianism in Table 4.6. Formally, both appear to involve positive parliamentarianism, in that there is an actual vote of investiture. Yet in each case the proposed government does not actually have to "win" the vote in the relative sense of having more votes in favour than against. Instead it merely has to ensure that there is not an absolute majority of votes (of the eligible deputies) against it. In other words, both formal abstentions and absences count on the government side. Thus for example in Sweden in 1981 a government was invested with 102 votes in favour, 174 votes against, 62 abstentions, and 11 absences (of the 349 deputies). See Bergman 1993, 297. Consequently, then, both Portugal and Sweden should be considered to *effectively* have negative parliamentarianism. In contrast, Luxembourg and the Netherlands do not formally require a vote of investiture but each invariably undertakes such a vote, so they *effectively* have positive parliamentarianism.

References

Bergman, Torbjörn. 1993. "Constitutional Design and Government Formation: The Expected Consequences of Negative Parliamentarianism." *Scandinavian Political Studies* 16:285–304.

Blais, André, and R.K. Carty. 1990. "Does Proportional Representation Foster Voter Turnout?" *European Journal of Political Research* 18:167–181.

Blais, André, and Agnieszka Dobrzynska. 1998. "Turnout in Electoral Democracies." *European Journal of Political Research* 33:239–261.

Broughton, David. 1999. "The First Welsh Assembly Election, 1999." *Representation: The Journal of Representative Democracy* 36(3):212–223.

Broughton, David, and Alan Storer. 2004. "The Welsh Assembly Election of 2003: The Triumph of 'Welfarism'." *Representation: The Journal of Representative Democracy* 40(4):266–279.

Franklin, Mark. 2002. "The Dynamics of Electoral Participation." In *Comparing Democracies 2: New Challenges in the Study of Elections and Voting*, ed. Lawrence LeDuc, Richard G. Niemi, and Pippa Norris, 148–168. London: Sage.

Kellow, Aynsley. 2003. "Tasmania." In *Australian Politics and Government: The Commonwealth, the States and the Territories*, ed. Jeremy Moon and Campbell

Sharman, 131–153. Cambridge: Cambridge University Press.

Lijphart, Arend. 1994. *Electoral Systems and Party Systems: A Study of Twenty-Seven Democracies, 1945–1990*. Oxford: Oxford University Press.

Siaroff, Alan. 2000a. *Comparative European Party Systems: An Analysis of Parliamentary Elections since 1945*. New York and London: Garland Publishing.

—. 2000b. "British AMS Versus German 'Personalised PR': Not So Different." *Representation: The Journal of Representative Democracy* 37(1):19–28.

Siaroff, Alan, and John W.A. Merer. 2002. "Parliamentary Election Turnout in Europe since 1990." *Political Studies* 50:916–927.

CHAPTER FIVE

The Government Life Cycle

ANDRÉ BLAIS, PETER LOEWEN, AND MAXIME RICARD

Introduction

THE MEDIA COMMONLY speak of the "death" of a government. Political scientists often refer to the "life cycle" of a government. We believe these are fitting analogies because every government in some sense is "born" and in the same sense "dies." While every life cycle is unique, there are some commonalities. Accordingly, in this chapter we identify four stages of the government life cycle and highlight how these stages differ between countries. We then identify which types of government are likely to live longer and which are likely to die sooner, as demonstrated through an analysis of some 36 democratic countries.

Opponents of PR often point to Italy and argue that PR would result in instability, frequent elections, and chaos. We ascertain the validity of that claim. We examine how electoral systems, together with other institutional rules, affect how governments are formed and defeated. Electoral systems have a proximate effect on the number of parties that run in elections and enter the legislature (Cox 1997). But it is equally important to look at the more distant consequences of electoral systems on the life cycle of governments. This analysis adds to the discussion in the previous two chapters considering the relationship between electoral systems and voter satisfaction, party systems, proportionality, voter turnout, and government formation.

The Four Stages

Most governments pass through four stages. In the first stage, a government is "born" and recognized. In the second stage (which not every government will experience), a government loses a legislative vote, which may or may not represent a major challenge. Third, governments face confidence votes. Fourth, the results of a confidence vote may result in an election.

Stage One: The Birth of Governments

Two factors must be considered with respect to the creation of a government. The first concerns the role of the head of state and *formateurs* or *informateurs* in the formation of the government. The second consideration is whether a formal investiture vote is required.

As has been noted elsewhere (Blais and Carty 1987), coalition governments are more common in systems of proportional representation. In such systems, where a single party rarely wins a majority of seats, parties often have to negotiate a coalition government that can win the support of the majority of the legislature. To ease this process, some countries afford a formal role to the head of state, who helps steer the negotiations.

Table 5.1 indicates which countries assign a formal role to their head of state. In some countries, such as France and Finland, the head of state is a directly elected president, whereas in others, such as the Netherlands and Spain, the head of state is a monarch. More often than direct involvement by the head of state, however, is the appointment of a *formateur* or *informateur*. This person, appointed by the head of state, is responsible for steering negotiations between coalition members. In the Dutch case, for example, the Queen designates a tentative *formateur*, usually the leader of the largest party and the putative prime minister. Should this candidate receive the support of the majority of parliament, she is designated *formateur* and begins negotiation on the formation of a government. Should she fail, the Queen then designates an *informateur* who then leads bargaining among the parties on who should be the *formateur*.

Other states, by contrast, simply leave it to the party (or parties) that emerged from the election in positions of strength to compete for the support of the legislature in a more "free-wheeling" manner (Laver and Schofield 1990, 63). The Canadian experience is largely the latter, as the party with the most seats following an election is presumed to be the party of government, on its own if it has a majority of the seats in parliament, or with the support of other parties if it is in a minority position. The prospect of electoral reform in Canada need not change this custom.

Table 5.1: Summary of conventions by country

Country	Does the head of state play an active role in formation?	Is a formal investiture vote needed?	Must government resign if it loses confidence vote?
Austria	N	N	Y
Belgium	N	Y	Y
Britain	N	N	N
Denmark	N	N	Y
Finland	Y	N	N[a]
France	Y	N	Y[b]
Germany	N	N	Y[c]
Greece	N	Y	Y
Iceland	N	N	Y
Ireland	N	Y	Y
Israel	Y	Y	Y
Italy	Y	Y	Y
Luxembourg	N	N	Y
Malta	N	N	Y
Netherlands	Y	N	Y
New Zealand[e]	N	N	N
Norway	N	N	Y
Portugal	Y	Y	Y
Spain	Y	Y	Y[d]
Sweden	N	Y	Y[b]
Switzerland	N	Y	N
New Brunswick[e]	N	N	N

a) President "may" accept resignation in the event of a non-confidence vote.
b) A majority of the entire legislature (not only those voting) required to pass non-confidence vote.
c) Non-confidence vote must designate new federal chancellor.
d) Motion of non-confidence must specify successor.
e) Both New Zealand and New Brunswick have been added to Laver and Schofield's original table.

Source: Laver and Schofield 1990, 64

Second, and more consequential, is a formal vote of investiture. As discussed in Chapter 4, in some countries, to ensure the support of the majority of the legislature, a government must survive an investiture vote *before* it can begin the work of governing. Typically, this vote of investiture resembles a confidence vote, in which a proposed government is accepted or rejected by a majority of the legislature. This is in contrast to other systems, such as Canada, where a government can begin governing without having to endure a formal investiture vote, as long as it has the consent of the majority in the legislature and the recognition of the head of state. Importantly, as the second column of Table

5.1 shows, there is not a clear association between investiture votes and any particular electoral system. Put differently, a jurisdiction that did not previously rely on investiture votes need not adopt them when moving to a new electoral system. This was the case with New Zealand, which in 1996 moved from a plurality system to a mixed-member proportional system, but did not adopt investiture votes. However, there is no hard and fast rule barring a jurisdiction from adopting confidence votes in the course of electoral reform.

What are the relative merits and demerits of investiture votes? An investiture vote requires that a putative prime minister be able to command the support of the majority of the house before she begins governing. This may potentially delay the governing process, as the government is more likely to be forced to strike formal bargains with potential partners, rather than beginning a process of governing in which deals are made on a vote-by-vote basis. Accordingly, government formation may involve more uncertainty and occur under more rounds in a system requiring an investiture vote. Indeed, it may even precipitate more elections. These are obvious drawbacks. There exist, however, distinct benefits. Specifically, a possible government that is forced to clarify support prior to governing is more likely to strike formal agreements, and these may prolong government length. Furthermore, the need for investiture votes may force parties to identify possible coalition partners prior to an election. From a normative perspective, voters may be better served when they have a clearer picture of likely governments prior to casting a ballot. Third, the need for an investiture vote can more quickly identify unworkable governing coalitions by registering a lack of support before cabinet offices are assumed, rather than after. Finally, a government that passes an investiture vote is likely to possess more legitimacy than one governing vote by vote. We have, then, good reasons both for and against investiture votes. However, we side with investiture votes, feeling they both prolong government length and increase legitimacy.

Stage Two: Legislative Defeats

Legislative defeats constitute important events in the life of a government. They may signal that the life of the government is coming to an end. Yet, contrary to conventional wisdom, legislative losses do not by themselves defeat governments. As Laver and Schofield observe, the loss of legislative bills is no doubt a serious matter for governments, but it is not "automatically fatal." A defeat on a bill is often followed immediately by a confidence vote, or by the resignation of a government in anticipation of defeat in a confidence vote. But it does sometimes occur that a government survives a confidence vote after losing a major legislative vote (Laver and Schofield 1990, 65). Moreover, there are instances in which a legislative defeat does not lead to a confidence motion, as in Britain where the government can lose any vote, except those explicitly conducted under a three-line whip, without the introduction of a confidence motion.

We may thus distinguish two possibilities. In some countries, a confidence vote necessarily follows a legislative defeat, which the government may or may not win. In other countries, a legislative defeat does not always lead to a confidence vote. The last option provides for more stability, assuming that governments typically lose confidence votes after legislative defeats. The Canadian experience is that legislative defeats are immediately followed by confidence votes, and that the government loses these confidence votes. Our next section sheds some light on the pertinent factors in understanding what types of governments are more likely to survive or prevent legislative defeats.

Stage Three: Confidence Votes

Aside from constitutionally mandated investiture votes, confidence votes have two sources: from the government or from the legislature. Governments generally invoke a confidence measure for two reasons. First, they wish to demonstrate that they have the confidence of the legislature. Second, they are forced to call a confidence vote because they have incurred a legislative defeat. Opposition parties can invoke confidence measures to test the government. Various countries impose certain restrictions on opposition confidence motions. For example, in Germany the opposition must present a "constructive" motion of non-confidence, meaning that the motion must designate a new federal chancellor. The requirement is much the same in Spain. This requirement obviously increases the difficulty of passing a non-confidence motion, as opposition parties must agree not only on the need to replace the government, but also on its replacement. In other countries, namely France and Sweden, opposition confidence motions must receive a majority of the whole legislature, rather than a majority of those voting. Such measures increase the difficulty of passing non-confidence motions, and thus tend to foster governmental stability. The Canadian practice is among the least restrictive. In Canadian legislatures, opposition parties proposing non-confidence motions need only a majority of voting legislators, and they have no obligation to identify a successor government.

We do not have the data to test whether confidence motions are more frequent under some rules than others. However, it is clear that, holding all else constant, the stricter the rules surrounding non-confidence motions, the less likely governments are to fall. Moreover, even in systems where confidence motions are easily proposed, such as Canada, they are infrequent.

Stage Four: Does Loss of Confidence Lead to an Election?

If opposition parties can overcome the barriers outlined above and defeat a government on a motion of confidence, then all systems must face the final question of whether or not an election must be called.

As noted in Table 5.1, not all governments must resign after losing a confidence vote. Indeed, in Finland the president need not even accept the resignation of the government, precluding the question of whether there is an election or the formation of a new government. In other systems, notably Ireland and Iceland, it is the convention (though it is not constitutionally mandated) that the defeat of a government leads to an election. This is generally the case in Austria, Luxembourg, and Sweden, though these countries have experienced exceptions to this rule. At the other end of the spectrum, it is quite normal in countries such as Belgium, the Netherlands, and Israel to experience as many as three governments between elections—governments, it should be noted, with sometimes very different party compositions (Laver and Schofield 1990, 220).

The Canadian context provides examples of government defeats that have led to elections, such as when John Hamm's Conservative opposition defeated the Nova Scotia Liberals in 1999, causing an election. Contrary examples also exist, as in Ontario in 1985 when the Conservative minority government of Frank Miller lost a vote of confidence, and was then replaced immediately by David Peterson's Liberals, who had struck an agreement with the New Democrats for their support for a period of two years in exchange for the passing of certain policies.

Which system is likely to lead to more stability: that in which an election automatically follows a loss of confidence, or that in which a new government can be formed without an election? It depends very much on the strength of the opposition parties.

We may distinguish three scenarios. In the first, suppose opposition parties feel that their popularity is on the upswing, but they do not have enough seats in the current legislature to form a government should the incumbent fall. In this case, they are more likely to force a non-confidence motion if they know an election will follow. In the second scenario, suppose an opposition party is on the upswing but that it also has the potential to form a governing coalition within the current legislature. In this case, it does not matter much whether an election will immediately follow or not. In the final case, suppose opposition parties are not on the upswing. In this case, they are unlikely to force a confidence motion regardless of its outcome. Accordingly, it is only in the first scenario, when opposition parties are relatively weak in the legislature but strong in the polls, that it makes a difference whether an election necessarily follows after a loss of confidence, and in those circumstances a system that does *not* require an election after a loss of confidence seems more stable than one that does.

The functioning of legislatures varies, often greatly, from country to country. Indeed, even when two countries operate under highly similar constitutions, tradition and precedent can result in very different practical realities. However, we can understand the differences in legislative systems by examining what happens at each stage of a government's life. Because of the strong influence of precedence and tradition in determining practices, often countries that change their electoral system will retain a legislative system with similar rules at each stage of the government life cycle. But it is possible to design institutions and rules that make it easier or more difficult for a government to survive.

Government Duration

We have established that governments pass through many critical junctures, and that the rules at each juncture exercise some influence over whether the government will pass through intact or fall. However, we have not yet demonstrated whether governments last longer under some electoral systems than others. Thus, we now examine specifically whether governments last longer in plurality systems than in PR systems. We then examine whether elections occur more frequently in PR systems than in plurality systems.

We utilize a dataset compiled by Ricard (2004), which examines government duration in 36 countries that have been continuously regarded as democratic (that is, the country got a score of 1 or 2 on political rights from Freedom House, a lower score denoting more political rights) since 1972 (the date at which Freedom House began its rankings) or, if later, from the point of democratization.[1] The analysis ends on 30 June 2004. Ricard compares countries with single-member plurality systems with those using PR, including mixed corrective systems, such as the German system. Countries with majority systems or mixed non-corrective systems are excluded, as are countries with presidential systems.

Among the countries examined, 12 are considered plurality and 23 proportional. New Zealand, which switched from plurality to proportional in 1996, is counted among plurality systems before that date and proportional systems afterwards. In addition to a variety of electoral systems, an examination of our countries suggests that we also have a good cross-section of cultures and religions, levels of wealth, and geographic location. Accordingly, this analysis should help us uncover broad, generalizable patterns and conclusions about government duration.

A government is defined as coming to an end with a change in the composition of the parties present in a cabinet, a change in the first minister (i.e., prime minister), or a general election. Importantly, the first two types of governmental change can happen without an election. In the first case, a government can witness wholesale change when one cabinet is replaced by another composed of entirely different parties. This was the case, for example, in Denmark in 1993 when a minority coalition of Conservatives and Liberals lost the confidence of the legislature and was replaced by a majority coalition of Social Democrats, Radical Liberals, Centre Democrats, and the Christian People's Party. Denmark experienced a similar change in 1982 when a single-party Social Democratic minority government was replaced by a minority coalition of Conservatives, Centre Democrats, Radical Liberals, and the Christian People's Party. But change in government through changes in party can also be caused by less dramatic changes, as in the case of the exit of one coalition partner and the entrance of another. For example, Israel registered five changes in government between 11 June 1990 and 21 January 1992, but the prime minister never changed, the five major parties in the coalition persisted, and only in the last incarnation was the government in a minority. In sum, a change in government can signal a large change or a marginal change.

In the second case, a change in government could be recorded following the replacement of a party's leader, such as when Brian Mulroney resigned as prime minister of Canada in 1993 and was replaced by Kim Campbell, a fellow member of the Progressive Conservative Party.

The analysis considers 379 governments. Ricard presents three analyses, considering first simple differences in the length of governments under first-past-the-post plurality systems and proportional representation systems. He then introduces controls for the maximum length of a government's term, the size of the population, and the level of democracy in the country, as judged by Freedom House. Finally, he considers different cabinet types, whether majority or minority and coalition or single-party. In the second and third cases he performs ordinary least squares multivariate analysis, regressing the observed length of government on a number of independent or causal variables. This allows him to sort out the individual influence of the competing variables.

We should expect plurality systems to produce longer governments than proportional systems. After all, plurality systems are more likely to produce one-party government. When the government is composed of one party rather than two or more it is likely to last longer for at least three reasons. First, it does not have to engage in legislative bargaining between governing parties, as there is only one. Second, because there is only one "leader" in the government, rather than a prime minister and the leaders of the other governing parties,

Table 5.2: Average length of government by system

Electoral system	Mean length (days)	Number of cases	Standard deviation
Proportional representation	672.4	270	515.7
Plurality	1115.4	109	636.9
Total	799.9	379	587.7

authority is more clearly defined, and thus decisions are made more easily, and enforcement of those decisions is both easier and more efficient. Finally, in a government composed of several parties it is easier for one or more parties to defect and form a new government with opposition parties. When only one party is in government, recalcitrant members of the governing party who may threaten defection to another party for the purpose of forming a new government will face more substantial coordination challenges. Plurality systems are also more likely to produce longer governments because they are more likely to experience single-party majority governments, which are inherently more stable than minority configurations. After all, majority governments do not have to bid for support from outside of their party to pass each legislative proposal.

We also expect the maximum length of a government's term to increase the length of governments on average. The logic supporting this is simple. Governments, especially those with stable configurations, will last longer in systems where mandated elections are less frequent, as they will be able to govern longer before being forced to call an election. We also expect the average life of governments to be shorter in larger countries. Larger populations mean larger legislatures, and larger legislatures mean larger cabinets and more members to appease. In other words, they mean more bargaining. This is likely to lead to more scenarios in which a government will be defeated. Furthermore, single-party majority governments are more likely to occur in smaller legislatures.

The duration of a government also depends on the type of cabinet. Ricard considers four types of cabinets, listed from the longest expected life-span to the shortest: single-party majority cabinets, coalition majority cabinets, single-party minority cabinets, and coalition minority cabinets. As outlined above, the need to constantly bargain that accompanies minority and coalition governments should reduce their average duration.

Table 5.2 shows the simple difference between the average length of governments in plurality and proportional systems. Clearly, electoral system matters: governments typically last 37 months in plurality systems and 22 months in PR systems, a difference of 15 months.

Table 5.3 Determinants of government duration

	Column 1 Exogenous factors	SE	Column 2 Exogenous and endogenous factors	SE
Electoral system	219.0*	(124.2)	-72.3	(134.4)
Mandate (log)	576.6	(442.0)	577.1	(421.5)
Population (log)	-77.8***	(28.1)	-81.8***	(26.3)
Strength of democracy	185.3***	(66.3)	222.7***	(66.5)
Majority coalition			-359.2***	(97.2)
Single-party minority			-362.0***	(108.8)
Minority coalition			-637.6***	(120.7)
Constant	-109.7	(636.5)	230.12	(599.0)
N	379		379	
Adj R2	0.1808		0.2571	

* $p > .90$
** $p > .95$
*** $p > .99$

Dependent variable:
Duration of government in days.
Independent variables:
i) Electoral system: 1 plurality, 0 proportional
ii) Mandate: logged length of maximum number of years allowed between elections.
iii) Population: log of population at start of cabinet
iv) Strength of Democracy: 1 if a country scored the highest rank of 1 on Freedom House rankings of political freedom, 0 if they scored 2.
v) Majority Coalition: 1 coalition with majority of seats, 0 otherwise
vi) Minority Coalition: 1 coalition with minority of seats, 0 otherwise
vii) Single-Party Minority: 1 minority of seats and no coalition, 0 otherwise.

However, we must consider that this result may be caused by factors other than those measured. Countries with plurality systems may tend to be smaller, to have longer mandates, or to be more democratic (that is, to have a score of 1 rather than 2 on the Freedom House rating). To this end, Ricard proceeds to a multivariate analysis that allows him to ascertain the specific effect of the electoral system, controlling for these other factors.

Column 1 of Table 5.3 shows the results of this analysis. They confirm that governments last longer in more democratic and smaller countries. Indeed, moving one Freedom House ranking extends the expected length of a government by nearly six months. The length of the mandate also appears to have an influence, though it does not quite reach statistical significance. But more importantly, the results indicate that when these exogenous factors are controlled for, governments last only seven months (not 15) less in PR than in plurality systems.

The final stage of the analysis consists in specifying why governments are shorter in PR systems. The basic hypothesis is that they are shorter lasting because PR is less likely to produce single-party governments that are in full control of the legislature. That hypothesis is confirmed in the second column of Table 5.3, in which dummy variables corresponding to the presence of a majority coalition, a minority coalition, or a single-party minority government (rather than a single-party majority, the reference category) are introduced.

The results confirm the hypothesis. They indicate that majority coalitions and single-party minority governments typically last a full year less than single-party majorities. As for minority coalitions, which are quite infrequent, they last some 21 months less. And, importantly, when we take into account the type of cabinet that is formed, there is no difference left between PR and plurality systems, which means that the longer duration of governments in the latter is entirely accounted for by the types of cabinet that are found in the two systems. It is only because single-party majority governments are less frequent that governments have shorter lives in PR systems.

In short, Ricard's data show that governments have slightly shorter lives under PR than under plurality rule. The overall difference, everything else equal, is seven months. The data also show that this difference is entirely due to the lesser frequency of single-party majority governments in PR systems. For those considering electoral reform this is extremely important. Indeed, a frequent criticism or caricature of proportional systems is that they are highly unstable, with governments changing at a much faster pace than in plurality systems. However, when we take a closer look at the different systems, we find that it is not proportionality as such that causes shorter life cycles. Instead, it is the tendency of coalition governments to more frequently result in these systems. In sum, while there is a small difference between PR and plurality systems in terms of duration, it is only because one-party majority governments are less frequent in PR systems.

Does the relatively larger frequency of changes in government in PR systems mean that they hold more elections, more frequently? Surprisingly, this is not clearly the case. Because changes in government can occur through changes in leadership, or in the composition of the cabinet, shorter government life cycles do not necessarily indicate more frequent elections. To test for this possibility, we determined the average number of elections per year in plurality and proportional representation systems. We considered all of Ricard's 36 countries, and divided the number of elections by the number of years

Table 5.4: Causes of changes in government

	Proportional	Plurality
Change of parties	33.0 %	11.0%
	(89)	(12)
Change of prime minister	11.1%	16.5%
	(30)	(18)
Election	55.9%	72.5%
	(151)	(79)

Percentages report the share of termination types within each system type. Bracketed numbers indicate the number of terminations.

between their first and most recent election. Measured this way, the average number of elections per year is .33 in plurality systems and .37 in proportional representation systems. In other words, in both systems elections are held on average about every three years. Thus, while governments are more likely to change in PR systems, elections do not occur much more frequently.

Table 5.4 specifies the sources of government change in proportional and plurality systems. In both systems, the most frequent scenario is the one under which the termination of a government entails an election (though this is measurably more common in plurality systems). But in PR systems, one-third of the governments that come to an end are replaced by another government with a different party composition, sometimes a completely new set of parties, but often only marginally changed. By comparison, in plurality systems only about one in ten governments comes to an end through a change in the party composition of government. Finally, we should note that changes of prime minister terminating government are marginally more common in plurality systems.

Conclusion

Four sets of questions help us distinguish the differences in government life cycles between countries. First, does the formation of a government involve the participation of the head of state, and does it entail a formal vote of investiture? Second, what is the consequence if a government faces a legislative defeat? Third, what is the nature of a confidence vote? Fourth, if a government loses a confidence motion is an election necessary, or can another party or group of parties form a new government?

The international experience shows that there exists a wide variety of practices on each of these issues. There are many different ways in which a government can be created, there are many ways in which it can be defeated, and there are many ways in which it can be maintained, brought to an end, and replaced by another government. And it is possible to design rules that facilitate or hinder government stability. Thus, those designing a new electoral system face a basic choice between a system in which governments live longer or a system in which new governments are born more frequently. Our analysis suggests that fundamental to this choice—more fundamental than the mix of conventions and rules chosen over the four stages of a government life cycle—are the types of governments to which a system is likely to give birth.

Note

1. The countries included are Austria, Bahamas, Barbados, Belgium, Belize, Botswana, Bulgaria, Canada, Czech Republic, Denmark, Dominica, Finland, Germany, Greece, Grenada, Guyana, Hungary, Iceland, Israel, Italy, Jamaica, Luxembourg, Mauritius, Netherlands, New Zealand, Norway, Poland, Portugal, Slovakia, Slovenia, South Africa, Spain, St. Lucia, St. Vincent and the Grenadines, Sweden, and the United Kingdom.

References

Blais, André, and Ken Carty. 1987. "The Impact of Electoral Systems on the Creation of Majority Governments." *Electoral Studies* 5:109–218.

Cox, Gary W. 1997. *Making Votes Count: Strategic Coordination in the World's Electoral Systems*. Cambridge: Cambridge University Press.

Laver, Michael, and Kenneth A. Shepsle. 1996. *Making and Breaking Governments: Cabinets and Legislatures in Parliamentary Elections*. Cambridge: Cambridge University Press.

Laver, Michael, and Norman Schofield. 1990. *Multiparty Government: The Politics of Coalition in Europe*. Oxford: Oxford University Press.

Pintor, Rafael Lopez, and Maria Gratschew. 2002. *Voter Turnout since 1945*. Stockholm: International IDEA.

Ricard, Maxime. 2004. "Est-ce que les systèmes proportionnels produisent des gouvernements dont la durée est plus courte que les systèmes pluralitaires?" Master's thesis, Université de Montréal.

Warwick, Paul. 1994. *Government Survival in Parliamentary Democracies*. Cambridge: Cambridge University Press.

⊰ CHAPTER SIX ⊱

Electoral Systems and Representational Issues

JOANNA EVERITT AND SONIA PITRE

Introduction

WHAT IS REPRESENTATION? When are we represented? Who are our representatives? The answers to these questions differ from one political system to another as they are strongly influenced by factors such as political culture and the design of political institutions. One of the political institutions that has the greatest effect on issues of representation is the electoral system. Not only do electoral systems determine how voter preferences are translated into seats in legislative assemblies, but they also reflect a society's representational priorities.

Recently several criticisms have been levelled at the representational deficiencies of the single-member plurality (SMP) electoral system employed in Canada and its provinces and territories. As discussed in earlier chapters, several provinces and the federal government have begun to examine their electoral systems and to consider the possibilities of making changes to it. In response to these discussions this chapter explores the question of representation, focusing in particular on the under-representation of women and various minority groups in the province of New Brunswick. It outlines the impact that different electoral designs have on representation and concludes that in order to enhance the election of under-represented groups in New Brunswick, changes to the electoral system must also include legal requirements for parties to include such groups on their party lists.

What Is Meant by Representation?

Two theoretical approaches dominate the literature on political representation, *descriptive* and *substantive* representation. Descriptive representation focuses on the *being* rather than the *acting*. It refers to the "visible" characteristics of the representative such as age, ethnicity, or gender. It may also include the idea of shared or common experiences (e.g., economic status, geographic location, or even sexual orientation). The advantage of having a representative who shares our descriptive traits or common experiences stems from an old belief that "'being one of us' is assumed to promote loyalty to 'our' interests" (Mansbridge 1999, 629).

The SMP electoral system used in Canada for much of its history has tended to give priority to the representation of territorial interests. Under this system, members of the legislative assemblies are selected to represent particular geographic regions or constituencies. Implicit in this form of electoral system is the idea that citizens who live in proximity to one another have shared concerns and that it is important that these concerns be represented. In some cases, identities based on language, ethnicity, or economics map nicely on to these geographic communities of interest. This is particularly the case in New Brunswick, where the francophone and anglophone communities are mostly found in distinct regions of the province. It is also the case in societies that have discrete urban and rural communities.

Yet descriptive representation goes beyond just territorial representation. It is also referred to as mirror or microcosmic representation; representative assemblies are expected to correspond or resemble the different social groups in numbers similar to their proportion in the electorate. Ideally, assemblies should have exact samples of women, youths, Acadians, aboriginal people, working-class people, gays and lesbians, and so on. The assumption is that the more an assembly replicates the nation the better it will be in producing policies, decisions, compromises, and actions that reflect the nation's interests (Burnheim 1985; Phillips 1995).

However, as only one candidate can be elected in each riding there is little opportunity in an SMP system for the representation of those identities that are less tied to geography. The challenge in a growing, diversifying, and complex society is that it is becoming more and more difficult, even impossible, for an elected representative to reflect or mirror his or her riding. Furthermore, as each party can only nominate one candidate, there is a great incentive for parties to select the "best" or most winnable candidate in a riding. As past successful candidates have tended to be white, middle-class, professional men, parties tend to view those with similar characteristics as their best choices.

Even if central parties want to broaden the range of candidates running under their banner, it is difficult to do so, as local riding associations control the nomination process at both the national and provincial levels.

Throughout its history, the New Brunswick electoral system has given priority to territorial interests and has paid little attention to non-territorial interests other than language and at times religion. As a result, its legislative assembly has been and remains dominated by white, middle-class, well-educated men. Women, aboriginal people, non-Acadian minorities, and the poor have seldom been selected by political parties to run as candidates in winnable ridings and have been notable in their absence from the corridors of power.

It is easier for non-territorial interests such as gender, ethnicity, religion, physical ability, and class to be represented in proportional representation (PR) systems or in quasi-proportional systems such as mixed-member proportional (MMP) systems, as the lists of representatives can be designed to take into account interests that are more evenly distributed throughout the population. Women, for example, tend to hold more seats in legislative assemblies in countries with PR systems than they do in countries with SMP systems (Rule 1994). Similar results are found for other under-represented groups, although there are certain aspects of the system that affect ethnic or visible minorities differently from women. It is for this reason that groups who have traditionally been excluded from political institutions frequently look to changes in the electoral system as a means of ameliorating their under-representation in decision-making bodies.

The second theoretical approach to representation is substantive representation, based on the activity, the "substance," or the content of the acting *for* others. Mansbridge (1999) explains that the substantive representation of a group's interests and perspectives should be, in theory at least, the ultimate goal: "Getting the relevant facts, insights, and perspectives into the deliberation should be what counts, not how many people advance the facts, insights, and perspectives" (635).

Critics of the descriptive approach claim that too much emphasis is put on *who* the representative is rather than on *what* he or she does once he or she gets elected. They argue that a greater microcosmic or mirror representation does not guaranty that the concerns, interests, and needs of citizens would be more efficiently represented, especially in terms of action or policy (Phillips 1995; Squires 1996). According to Tremblay (1999, 24), descriptive traits are at best indicators, not determinants of political action. For example, while it might be desirable for women or minorities to have representatives who look like them in the assembly, it is not by resemblance or similarity of traits that the different groups in society will achieve a better political representation of their concerns, interests, or needs (Pennock 1979; Phillips 1995; Tremblay 1999; Tremblay and Pelltier 2000).

However, one of the critiques of substantive representation is that it does not address in a satisfying manner the matter of the political exclusion or political under-representation as experienced by some groups, such as women and linguistic or ethnic minorities (Phillips 1995, 5). For these groups, descriptive representation becomes a matter of justice and tolerance (Squires 1996, 75), as well as symbolism (Mansbridge 1999). A second critique is that the substantive approach serves as an excellent way of maintaining the status quo (Tremblay 1999). Pretending that the elected representative "represents" as soon as he or she claims that he/she shares the opinions and the concerns of the represented is a convenient way of legitimizing the maintenance of the present political class. In fact, it perpetuates the myth of the universal citizen (Tremblay 1999, 26), often represented by white, middle-aged, upper-middle-class, professional males who allege to represent a very heterogeneous population. This allows men to claim to represent women, anglophones to represent francophones, and white MLAs to represent any and all ethnic community as long as they act for the people they insist they represent. As a result, groups or categories of people have been excluded from the political process without the recognition of any illegitimate practices.

Many have argued that descriptive representation often leads to substantive representation, as having more women in a legislative body may make it more responsive to women's concerns and having more francophones may make it more responsive to the concerns of major minority groups. In this sense it is important to "elect women for the sake of electing women," the same being true for linguistic or ethnic minorities (Thomas 1991). Others, however, have argued that the *who* that are represented and the *what* that is being represented are equally important. For this reason those concerned with questions of representation should not only seek to get more women or other traditionally excluded groups elected, but also hope to elect more of those women or minorities who are willing to defend their interests, as heterogeneous as they may be.

Gender Case Study

Gender provides a useful example of the impact of New Brunswick's electoral system on inadequate political representation in the Legislative Assembly. Despite the fact that legal barriers to women's political participation at the provincial level were removed 70 years ago and important social advances have been made over the last 30 years, women still seem to be facing a glass ceiling. In New Brunswick, women have never held more than 20% of the seats in the

Table 6.1: Seats held by women and other groups in recent New Brunswick elections

Election year	Women	Francophones	Aboriginals
1987	7/58 (12.1%)	17 (29.3%)	0
1991	10/58 (17.6%)	18 (31%)	0
1995	9/55 (16.4%)	17 (30.9%)	0
1999	10/55 (18.2%)	20 (36.3%)	0
2003	7/55 (12.7%)	18 (32.7%)	1 (1.8%)
2006	7/55 (12.7%)	16 (29.1%)	1 (1.8%)

Legislative Assembly. Worst yet, time does not seem to remedy the situation. At the current rate, New Brunswick will achieve equal gender representation in its Legislative Assembly around 2077—and that is assuming a steady increase at every election. Unfortunately, as lessons from recent elections have taught us, there is no guarantee that the representation of women will increase from election to election.

In 1991 women won 17.6% (10/58) of the seats in the New Brunswick Legislative Assembly. As Table 6.1 shows, despite a small increase in this proportion in 1999, the proportion of women elected in 2003 (12.7% or 7/55) dropped to the same levels as in 1987 (12.1% or 7/58). In the federal New Brunswick ridings and at municipal levels in the province, the situation is just as disturbing. In Ottawa, none of the MPs from New Brunswick are women, and in city halls across the province women account for only 23% of city councillors and 12% of mayors, proportions that have hardly increased since 1992 (when 20% of councillors and 12% of mayors were women).

The experience of other groups, such as aboriginal peoples or religious or ethnic minorities, is of even greater concern. New Brunswick's first aboriginal MLA was elected in 2003 (see Table 6.1) and there is little record of more than a handful of religious or ethnic minorities or individuals with physical disabilities ever being elected. On the other hand, the SMP electoral system has been much more successful at representing the territorially based Acadian population. Over the past several elections the number of seats held by Acadian MLAs has been roughly proportionate to the third of the New Brunswick population that claims Acadian heritage.

Why Are These Groups Under-Represented?

While there are several explanations for this under-representation of women and other groups, studies show that certainly in the case of women, the explanation has little to do with the electorate. When the popularity of the political party is taken into consideration, female candidates do not lose votes (Hunter and Denton 1984). This means that women are just as competitive as their male counterparts. According to Tremblay and Pelletier (1995) and Groeneman (1983) female candidates may even benefit from a favourable perception by the electorate. This may be attributed to the fact that women in politics are perceived as more compassionate and considerate, less corrupt than men in politics (Brown, Heighberger, and Shocket 1993; Squires 1996, 75) and are associated with change and modernity (Young 2000).

The true barriers to the political representation of women and other traditionally excluded groups lie in institutions such as the electoral system and the political parties that are involved in the candidate recruitment and selection process. The recruitment of candidates consists of identifying within the greater population, or among party members, people who wish to or could be convinced to run for office (Norris and Lovenduski 1995). However, certain hurdles linked to socialization, situation, or structural barriers have the effect of "keeping women out of certain informal networks from which political élites emerge and are recruited (*eligible pool*)" (Tremblay and Pelltier 1995, 13).

These hurdles are often linked to the private/public dichotomy. This refers to the distinction between the private sphere revolving around domestic or reproductive activities and the public sphere dominated by business or political affairs. Because of their childbearing capacities, women have traditionally been confined to the private sphere whereas men are located in the public sphere. Through gender-role socialization, men and women learn very quickly to recognize that politics is a man's activity, organized according to the male values and norms of competition and confrontation rather than collaboration and consensus building (Shedova 1998). In order to be accepted into politics, many women feel they must adopt a "male style," something that may not be appealing to them.

Even if women do not believe that politics is a man's world, there are still other constraints to consider. As long as women remain in charge of most of the domestic responsibilities, even if they also work outside the home they will be less available to run for office (Bashevkin, 1993; Sapiro 1983; Welch 1981). The sexual division of labour in the workforce means that women remain concentrated in the health sector, childcare, food preparation, clerical work, and house cleaning (Amott and Matthaei 1996). As political elites are mostly recruited from professions such as medicine, law, business, finance, and journalism, most women are at a political disadvantage despite their recent advances in these fields (Maillé 2002; Norris and Lovenduski 1989). To this day, there are still very few parliamentarians who come from the traditional female employment sectors. Women's absence from the traditionally male and prestigious professions also limits their access to the informal networks and financial re-

Table 6.2: Cross-national gender representation by electoral system

World ranking	Country	Proportion of seats (%)	Type of system
1	Rwanda	48.8	List PR
2	Sweden	45.3	List PR
3	Denmark	38.0	List PR
4	Finland	37.5	List PR
5	Netherlands	36.7	List PR
6	Norway	36.4	List PR
7	Cuba	36.0	ABM
7	Spain	36.0	List PR
8	Belgium	35.3	List PR
9	Costa Rica	35.1	List PR
10	Argentina	34.0	SMM
11	Austria	33.9	List PR
12	South Africa	32.8	MMP
13	Germany	32.2	MMP
14	Iceland	30.2	List PR
17	New Zealand	28.3	MMP
24	Australia	25.3	AV
25	Switzerland	25.0	List PR
33	Canada	21.1	SMP
39	Luxembourg	20.0	List PR
43	Portugal	19.1	List PR
48	United Kingdom	17.9	SMP
56	Israel	15.0	List PR
58	United States	14.3	SMP
59	Greece	14.0	List PR
60	Ireland	13.3	STV
66	France	12.2	SMM
70	Italy	11.5	Mixed
96	Japan	7.1	MMP

Situation as of 31 July 2004.
List PR = Proportional representation; MMP = Mixed-member proportional; AV = Alternative vote; SMP = Single-member plurality; SMM = Single-member majority; ABM = Absolute majority.

Source: Inter-Parliamentary Union, www.ipu.org/wmn-e/classif.htm

sources that often serve to build a political career (see Andrew 1984, 1991; Bashevkin 1993; Brodie 1985; Darcy, Welch, and Clark 1987, 1994; Gingras, Maillé, and Tardy 1989; Kirkpatrick 1974; Maillé 1990; Randall 1987; Sapiro 1982, 1983; Welch 1981).

While these social, structural, and situational barriers limit many women from seeing themselves as potential political candidates, institutions such as the electoral system and political parties also play a significant role in limiting the opportunities for the political activity of women and other traditionally excluded groups. For example, many studies have shown that, *ceteris paribus*, systems based on proportional representation manage to elect a greater number of women than the single-member plurality system used in countries like Canada, Great Britain, and the Australian House of Representatives (see Table 6.2) (Rule 1987, 1994, 2001; Matland and Studlar 1996; Young 1994). According to Shvedova (1998), countries using PR elect three to four times more women than other countries of a similar political culture. Electoral institutions establish the rules of the game and in doing so can create critical structural barriers or opportunities for the representation of women and other under-represented groups.

One of the explanations for the increased likelihood that women will be elected under a PR system than under an SMP system is *district magnitude*. Political parties that have the possibility of presenting more than one candidate or to elect more than one person per riding are less resistant to the idea of nominating a female candidate (see Lovenduski and Norris 1989; Moncrief and Thompson 1992; Studlar and McAllister 1991; Welch and Studlar 1990). When the rules of the electoral game allow only one person per riding to run for office, as they do under SMP systems, parties have greater incentives to run candidates that they feel are more likely to win. In the absence of an incumbent, party elites are likely to nominate candidates that possess characteristics similar to other successful candidates. This tendency to replicate the status quo can limit the chances for women due to old prejudices about women's competitiveness. However, unlike in SMP systems where parties might be able to argue that the single "best" candidate in a riding is a man, it is much harder for a party in a multimember district to argue that all of the "best" candidates are men. Parties are faced with more pressures to "ticket balance" or present equal numbers of male or female candidates in a PR system, as the public will be more aware of those parties that do not make efforts to include women or other significantly under-represented groups on their lists.

Lists also make it easier for central parties to have greater control over the nomination of candidates to the list. Unlike in SMP systems, where the choice of who becomes the nominated candidate is generally left to the individual riding associations, PR systems usually involve more participation by the central party in the vetting and ranking of list candidates. This more centralized decision-making process is likely to result in more variety in the backgrounds of candidates. Lists make it easier to employ affirmative action as parties can choose to increase their representation of women and other groups by including more of these candidates on their lists. However, it must be remembered that parties still play a critical "gatekeeping" role even under a PR system.

Ensuring the adequate representation of women or minorities is dependent upon the attitudes of party elites.

Some authors have argued that parties in multimember PR systems may view the nomination of female candidates as a means to promote a better image to a greater number of electors (Caul 1999; Matland 1995). However, if the real objective of having an increased number of female candidates is to get more of them elected to office, then parties must be ready not only to include the names of women on their lists, but to ensure that they are placed strategically on the ballot (Norris 2004).

According to Montgomery (2003), the will to present equal proportions of men and women on the ballot, often referred to as ticket balancing, depends to some extent on the public or legal pressure put on political parties to do so, something that may vary according to the partisan system. Most PR systems have few restrictions on the design of party lists (Norris 1997). For this reason the electoral system in and of itself cannot explain women's weak political representation. For example, Canada and Australia still manage to elect more women using SMP than Israel or Greece, two countries that use a PR system with a list ballot (MacIvor 2003, 28).

Matland and Studlar (1996) believe that contextual factors such as public attitudes, internal party rules, pressure by women's groups, and government legislation can help to explain where women's names are placed on the ballot. Nordic countries like Sweden, Denmark, and Norway that have more egalitarian political cultures are world leaders in terms of gender representation; women constitute close to 40% of the legislators in their lower houses. On the other hand, those countries with political culture less accepting of the idea of women's political involvement, such as many of the countries in the Middle East, have the lowest levels of women legislators (with an average of 5%) despite having PR systems.

Internal party rules are also important. The use of voluntary quotas or targets to ensure that women and other traditionally excluded groups are included on party lists contributes greatly to the likelihood of more representative legislative assemblies. Norris refers to the practice of including a woman as every second name on a party's list as the "zipper" or "zebra" principle (Norris 2004). This was first employed by the Swedish Social Democratic Party in 1994 and has since been adopted by the Swedish Greens and the Christian Democrats. Other left-wing parties in Europe have been employing less stringent voluntary quotas since the mid-1980s, a factor that helps explain the greater number of women in their legislative assemblies.

However, it is crucial to remember two things: first, voluntary quotas are just that, voluntary; and second, such quotas are not limited to PR electoral systems.

Unless requirements for gender parity are included in a country's electoral laws, parties are not legally bound to meet these quotas and can ignore their internal policy positions or change them with little difficulty. Furthermore, voluntary quotas have been employed successfully in SMP systems resulting in greater gender or minority representation. For example, in the mid-1990s the British Labour Party established a policy whereby in half of the seats held by a retiring Labour MP, or in half of the party's main marginal seats, the candidates would be chosen from an all-female shortlist (Norris 2004). While this policy has since been dropped, it contributed to the significant increase in female representation that occurred during the 1997 election in which Labour defeated the Conservatives. For the initial elections to the Welsh National Assembly, the Scottish Parliament, and the London Assembly, the Labour Party ridings were "twinned" with neighbouring seats so that each pair could nominate one man and one woman. This meant that women had the same opportunities as men to participate in these new assemblies.

In Canada political parties have employed, with limited success, different strategies to enhance the representation of women and other under-represented groups (see Chapter 7). Like elsewhere, it has been the New Democratic Party, a party of the left, that has gone the furthest in adopting voluntary quotas or targets (Erickson 1993). Even with these targets, however, the NDP's limited electoral success has meant that other parties have not felt pressure to enact similar targets. Instead they have established much weaker measures that have had very little effect. For example, in New Brunswick, the Progressive Conservative and Liberal parties have no formal regulations to assist women in competing for riding nominations. As a result, women and other minorities remain seriously under-represented among the candidates for these parties, as shown in Table 6.3.

One reason for the ineffectiveness of voluntary quotas in Canada is that the candidate selection process is run at the riding level. Party members are asked to vote at local nominating conventions for the person they feel is best suited to represent the interests and needs of the constituents, or the person they feel is most likely to win the election. Local nominations represent informal power struggles among party elites. As elites have a tendency to reproduce themselves, that is, to recruit according to their own image (Lovenduski 1986, 210; Niven 1998), and as political elites in Canada have traditionally been white, middle-class, and male, women, ethnic minorities and the poor can face significant challenges in gaining support for their nomination. Women and minorities are often viewed as weaker and less electable candidates. As a result, some argue that parties do not encourage women to run in competitive ridings and in some cases party gatekeepers even provide significant road blocks to their candidacies (Brodie 1985; Erickson 1991; Maillé 1990). Thus, it is the biases

Table 6.3: Proportion of women candidates in New Brunswick by political party

Year	Progressive Conservatives	Liberals	New Democrats
2006	14.5% (8/55)	18.2% (10/55)	31.3% (15/48)
2003	16.4% (9/55)	16.4% (9/55)	27.3% (15/55)
1999	18.2% (10/55)	14.5% (8/55)	50.9% (28/55)
1995	9.0% (5/55)	14.5% (8/55)	34.5% (19/55)
1991	10.3% (6/58)	15.5% (9/58)	39.7% (23/58)

among party selectorates that often prove to be the greatest barriers for under-represented groups.

One way to overcome the barriers established by political parties is for governments to enact legislation that requires party lists to include a certain proportion of women or other under-represented groups, and to apply penalties to those parties that do not meet these mandated expectations. In some cases the requirements could be even more stringent and insist that parties rank women high on their lists. For example, Argentinean electoral laws require that political parties nominate a certain percentage of women and place their names in strategic places on the ballot in order for lists of candidates to be approved. In Belgium the electoral laws require that not more than two-thirds of the candidates on a party's list can be of the same sex. If a party does not meet this requirement, they must leave blank those positions on their list that would have otherwise been held by women. Legislative requirements only work, however, if governments are willing to apply the penalties or if the penalties are severe enough that parties are unwilling to incur them. In 1999 France passed a constitutional amendment requiring that 50% of a party's list be women. Unfortunately, this has had little effect on the composition of the French National Assembly because women were concentrated in unwinnable constituencies, and the major parties decided to pay the relatively low fines and reappoint male incumbents to their party lists.

An even stricter measure to offset obvious representational imbalances is to establish reserved seats for women or members of minority groups. Countries such as Morocco, Bangladesh, Pakistan, India, Uganda, Botswana, Taiwan, Lesotho, and Tanzania have seats in their legislative assemblies to which women are either elected or appointed to offset gender imbalances (Norris 2004). Reserved seats have also been used to enhance the representation of ethnic minorities in New Zealand, Pakistan, India, and Bangladesh. For example, between 1867 and 1996 New Zealand had four seats set aside for Maori representatives. With the transformation to a mixed-member proportional system in 1996 this number was increased to reflect the number of Maori citizens who register as Maori voters rather than general voters. Maori citizens can register on either roll, but not both. Currently 55% of New Zealand Maoris are registered on the Maori roll, and as a result there are seven designated Maori seats.

Canada has also explored the idea of creating reserved seats in recent decades. The idea was raised but rejected in the research for the Lortie Commission on Party Financing and Electoral Reform in the early 1990s. The recommendations of this royal commission entailed the creation of aboriginal electoral districts at the national level. As in the case of New Zealand, aboriginal Canadians would have been expected to register to vote in designated districts, and the number of districts (up to eight) would be determined by the number of registered aboriginal voters. While this recommendation was never adopted, the idea of designated aboriginal seats continues to be considered. For example, in the most recent round of electoral redistribution following the 2001 census, the New Brunswick Federal Boundaries Commission included in their initial recommendations a suggestion that all First Nations voters in the province be registered to vote in the Tobique-Mataquac riding so as to concentrate their voting influence. While this proposal was eventually rejected, it was the first time a boundaries commission has seriously proposed the creation of a non-contiguous riding to represent aboriginal interests. Perhaps the closest Canada came to reserved seats was the proposal to have dual-member seats (one man and one woman) in the new territory of Nunavut (Young 1997). This proposal was hotly debated and subsequently defeated in a territorial referendum. As a result, reserved seats have still not been employed anywhere in Canada.

Clearly, the nature of electoral institutions plays an important role in defining what interests get represented and who ends up representing them in a political system. As is obvious from the above discussion, the single-member plurality electoral system used in Canada and its provinces emphasizes the importance of territorial interests and limits the representation of non-territorial interests. These non-territorial interests, particularly those of women and minorities, are better represented under a proportional representation style system.

Considerations for Electoral Reform in New Brunswick

With the establishment of the Commission on Legislative Democracy, the government of New Brunswick indicated its interest in enhancing representation in its Legislative Assembly. The commission has recommended changing from the single-member plurality system to a mixed-member proportional system. However, for such a change to have the effect of increasing the representation of women and other under-represented groups, there are several considerations that must be kept in mind. These relate to the number of seats in the multimember districts, the electoral thresholds that parties must meet to win a seat, and the use of open or closed lists. All of these factors have varying degrees of influence over the accessibility of the system to women and other under-represented groups. Likewise, real change is only likely to occur with the enactment of legal requirements to ensure that parties work to broaden the range of backgrounds from which candidates on a list are selected.

District magnitude is the first factor to consider in the design of a new electoral system. As noted earlier, the number of seats per district often determines how willing parties are to present a list of candidates that reflect a region's population. As several authors have argued, the larger the number of seats, the greater chance that women will be included and ranked high on a party's list (Lovenduski and Norris 1989; Moncrief and Thompson 1992; Welch and Studlar 1990). If a party feels that it has the chance of winning at least two seats, it is more likely that a woman will be one of the first or second names on the list. As a result, the ideal number of seats is at least one more than the number of viable parties. In the case of New Brunswick this would indicate that districts should include a minimum of four, if not five, seats.

A second consideration in an electoral system that will enhance the representation of women and other groups is the electoral threshold. This is the proportion of the votes that a party must win in order to gain a seat. Thresholds can range from 0% in Denmark and Austria to 10% in Turkey. The lower the threshold, the easier it is for parties to win a seat; as a result, systems with low thresholds often have several minor parties in their legislative assemblies. This has the effect of representing the ideological diversity in a political system and can benefit women's representation by allowing small, woman-friendly parties such as the Greens to get elected to a legislative assembly. On the other hand, it may also have negative implications for the representation of women and other groups, as a greater number of parties reduces the chance that any party will win numerous seats in a district. Without restrictions on the placement of female or minority candidates, parties are likely to assign the top position on their lists to a high-profile incumbent, more often than not a white male. If low thresholds result in an increased number of parties winning only one seat, it is unlikely that many women or minorities will be elected. Thus if enhanced representation is a serious concern, any change should require higher rather than lower electoral thresholds.

A final consideration is the use of *closed* or *open* lists. Closed-list proportional representation systems allow parties to determine the ranking of their candidates. Voters vote simply for a party and have little input into which of the candidates on a party's list get chosen as their representative. Open-list systems often provide voters with two votes, one for the party of their choice and one for the candidates of their choice. Such a system allows voters to modify the parties' lists by reordering a list or by striking names off a list. Because two-vote systems are based on multimember districts and allow parties to put forward lists of candidates that are gender-balanced, they are second only to closed-list PR for the representation of women and minorities.

The impact of these two forms of lists on the representation of women and minorities differs depending upon the political culture of an area. Closed lists are beneficial for women and other under-represented groups *when parties are more concerned than the electorate* with the issue of representation and are willing to ensure that their lists adequately reflect the diversity of backgrounds in the population. This is particularly the case when there are government-legislated incentives or penalties to encourage parties to create more representative lists. Open lists are beneficial for women and other minorities *when the electorate is more concerned than the parties* about representation. Open-list systems allow voters to correct for biases held by the party selectorate, although they are themselves susceptible to voter bias. Although there is little evidence of voter bias when presented with a single-party candidate under an SMP system, such bias may appear when voters are asked to rank male and female candidates on a party list. It is also important to remember that even in open-list systems, parties have considerable control over who gets elected, as they remain responsible for deciding who will be on the list.

A final option for electoral change, receiving serious consideration in New Brunswick and most of the Canadian jurisdictions considering reform, is a mixed-member proportional system, one that involves some representation by SMP with "extra seats" filled by PR. Such a system addresses the need for MLAs who are directly elected to represent specific geographic boundaries, yet also allows for the awarding of additional seats to parties to produce election results that better reflect the popular vote. Such a system has many representational advantages. The primary advantage is that it supports the territorial representational interests that are the basis of an SMP system as well as those linguistic or cultural interests that are geographically based. In the case of New Brunswick, this means that the Acadian population, located for the most part in the north of the province, will continue to hold a third of the seats in the legislative assembly. At the same time, the additional list seats can be designed to enhance the representation of other non-territorial interests. For example, in parts of the province where there are larger concentrations of aboriginal peoples, parties could include an aboriginal candidate on their list if one had not been nominated in a winnable riding.

There are however, two potential problems for the representation of women and minorities with an MMP system. First, corrective seats are more likely to be awarded to smaller parties than the larger parties that have traditionally been successful under the SMP system. As was discussed earlier, parties winning just a single seat are likely to allocate it to a male candidate at the top of their list. Second, it produces two tiers of candidates—those who are directly elected and those who are the party's PR candidates. As women and minorities have traditionally had difficulties being nominated under the SMP system, in order to improve the representation of these groups in the legislative assembly, parties are likely to appoint them through the PR seats. While on the one hand, such steps may provide them with the experience needed to compete successfully in constituency elections, they may also hinder them and their credibility due to perceptions of quotas.

While each of these electoral systems (closed-list PR, open-list PR, and MMP) has the potential to increase the representation of women and minorities in the legislative assemblies of provinces such as New Brunswick, their impact will be limited unless the government takes steps to ensure that parties make more concerted efforts to nominate these candidates and rank them highly on their lists. Past history, particularly in New Brunswick, provides little evidence that parties have made such efforts on their own, and there is little to suggest that simply creating new electoral institutions will change the province's political culture. Under-represented groups will remain under-represented unless laws are put in place to penalize parties whose lists of candidates do not reflect the diversity of the province's population.

If governments are not prepared to go as far as countries such as Belgium or Argentina (i.e., refusing to accept party lists that are not gender balanced), an alternative option is to create financial incentives or financial penalties that encourage parties to meet representational targets. Financial incentives could take the form of additional government funding or higher rates of election reimbursement, as was suggested by the Royal Commission on Party Financing and Electoral Reform in the early 1990s as a way to increase the representation of women in the House of Commons. Parties with higher numbers of women elected to the legislative assembly could be rewarded with higher tax refunds than those that do not meet minimum representational standards. The royal commission recommended that this minimum be set at 20%. As only the New Democratic Party in New Brunswick has managed to surpass this bar (and only because its one elected member was a woman), this form of incentive could potentially have a significant effect on the number of women elected. Similar incentives could be used to enhance the representation of aboriginal people in regions of the province where there are larger aboriginal populations.

Alternatively, parties that do not meet representational targets could be penalized for their failure to do so. They could face penalties or fines as is the case in France. While this option has had little effect in France, it is likely to be more successful in the Canadian political system. Canadian political parties rely more heavily on tax refunds to run their campaigns and maintain their party apparatuses than do parties in France. As a result, fines for failures to meet representational targets would likely have a greater impact on increasing the number of women and other under-represented groups than they might in countries where parties are more independent of government funding.

Conclusion

As this chapter has attempted to demonstrate, the current single-member plurality system used in New Brunswick and the rest of Canada has been very effective in representing territorially based interests, including those of the geographically distinct Acadian population in the province. However, other non-territorially based interests continue to be under-represented to a significant degree because parties can run only one candidate in each constituency. Changing from an SMP system to a complete proportional representation system or even a mixed-member system has the potential to enhance the representation of non-territorial interests, including those of women and various minorities, such as First Nations peoples.

However, institutional reform can only go so far unless there is the belief among the public and political elites that the representation of such interests is important. The situation of women and other under-represented groups will not automatically change unless parties make a concerted effort not only to include these individuals on their party lists, but to rank them highly so as to increase the chance that they will be elected. Unfortunately, there has been only limited concern expressed by political parties in the past about the issue of representation in provinces such as New Brunswick. As a result, it is difficult to imagine that electoral reform in and of itself will reduce the marked under-representation of women and other social groups in legislative assemblies. Thus, to have any effect, proposals for electoral reform must be combined with the development of legal measures such as financial penalties or incentives for parties. Only then will electoral reform truly enhance the representative nature of political institutions.

References

Andrew, Caroline. 1984. "Les femmes et la consommation collective: Les enjeux de l'engagement politique." *Politique* 5:109–122.
—. 1991. "Le pouvoir local: Stratégie de pouvoir ou nouvelle impasse pour les femmes."

In *L'égalité: Les moyens pour y arriver*, 63–75. Quebec City: Les Publications du Québec.

Amott, Teresa, and Julie Matthaei. 1996. *Race, Gender, and Work: A Multicultural Economic History of Women in the United States*. Boston: South End Press.

Bashevkin, Sylvia. 1993. *Toeing the Lines: Women in Party Politics in English Canada*. Toronto: Oxford University Press.

Brodie, Janine. 1985. *Women and Politics in Canada*. Toronto: McGraw-Hill.

Brown, Clyde, Neil Heighberger, and Peter Shocket. 1993. "Gender-Based Differences in Perception of Male and Female City Council Candidates." *Women & Politics* 13(1):1–17.

Burnheim, John. 1985. *Is Democracy Possible?* Cambridge: Cambridge University Press.

Caul, Miki. 1999. "Women's Representation in Parliament: The Role of Political Parties." *Party Politics* 5(1):79–98.

Darcy, Robert, Susan Welch, and Janet Clark. 1987. *Women, Elections, and Representation*. New York: Longman.

—. 1994. *Women and Elections and Representation*. 2nd ed. Lincoln: University of Nebraska Press.

Erickson, Lynda. 1991. "Women and Candidacies for the House of Commons." In *Women in Canadian Politics: Toward Equity in Representation*. Volume 6 of the Research Studies of the Royal Commission on Electoral Reform and Party Financing, ed. Kathy Megyery. Ottawa and Toronto: RCERPF/Dundurn Press, 111–137.

—. 1993. "Making Her Way In: Women, Parties and Candidacies in Canada." In *Gender & Party Politics*, eds. Joni Lovenduski and Pippa Norris. London: Sage, 60–85.

Gingras, Anne-Marie, Chantal Maillé, and Evelyne Tardy. 1989. *Sexe et militantisme*. Montreal: Éditions du CIDIHCA.

Groeneman, Sid. 1983. "Candidate Sex and Delegate Voting in a Pre-Primary Party Endorsement Election." *Women & Politics* 3(1):39–56.

Hunter, Alfred A., and Margaret Denton. 1984. "Do Female Candidates 'Lose Votes'? The Experience of Female Candidates in the 1979 and 1980 Canadian General Elections." *Canadian Review of Sociology and Anthropology* 21:395–406.

Kirkpatrick, Jeane. 1974. *Political Woman*. New York: Basic.

Lovenduski, Joni. 1986. *Women and European Politics: Contemporary Feminism and Public Policy*. Brighton: Wheatsheaf.

Lovenduski, Joni, and Pippa Norris. 1989. "Selecting Women Candidates: Obstacles to Feminisation of the House of Commons." *European Journal of Political Research* 17:533–562.

MacIvor, Heather. 2003. "Women and the Canadian Electoral System." In *Women and Electoral Politics in Canada*, ed. Manon Tremblay and Linda Trimble, 22–36. Don Mills, ON: Oxford University Press.

Maillé, Chantal. 1990. *Vers un nouveau pouvoir: Les femmes en politique au Canada.* Ottawa: Conseil consultatif canadian sur la situation de la femme.

—. 2002. *Cherchez la femme: Trente ans de débats constitutionnels au Québec.* Montreal: Éditions du Remue-ménage.

Mansbridge, Jane. 1999. "Should Blacks Represent Blacks, and Women Represent Women? A Contigent 'Yes'." *Journal of Politics* 61(3):628–657.

Matland, Richard. 1995. "How the Election System Structure Has Helped Women Close the Representation Gap." In *Women in Nordic Politics: Closing the Gap*, eds. Lauri Karvonen and Per Selle. Dartmouth: Aldershot, 281–309.

Matland, Richard E., and Donley T. Studlar. 1996. "The Contagion of Women Candidates in Single-Member District and Proportional Representation Electoral Systems: Canada and Norway." *Journal of Politics* 58:707–733.

Moncrief, Gary, and Joel Thompson. 1992. "Electoral Structure and State Legislative Representation: A Research Note." *Journal of Politics* 54:246–255.

Montgomery, Kathleen A. 2003. "Introduction." In *Women's Access to Political Power in Post-Communist Europe*, eds. Richard E. Matland and Kathleen A. Montgomery. Oxford: Oxford University Press, 1–19.

Niven, David. 1998. "Party Elites and Women Candidates: The Shape of Bias." *Women & Politics* 19(2):57–80.

Norris, Pippa. 1997. "Choosing Electoral Systems: Proportional, Majoritarian, and Mixed Systems." *International Political Science Review* 18(3):297–312.

Norris, Pippa, and Joni Lovenduski. 1989. "Pathways to Parliament." *Talking Politics* 1(3):90–94.

—. 1995. *Political Recruitment: Gender, Race and Class in British Parliament.* Cambridge: Cambridge University Press.

Pennock, J. Roland. 1979. *Democratic Political Theory.* Princeton: Princeton University Press.

Phillips, Anne. 1995. *The Politics of Presence.* Oxford: Claredon Press.

Randall, Vicky. 1987. *Women and Politics.* London: MacMillan.

Rule, Wilma. 1987. "Electoral Systems, Contextual Factors and Women's Opportunity for Election to Parliament in Twenty-Three Democracies." *Western Political Quarterly* 40(3):477–498.

—. 1994. "Women's Underrepresentation and Electoral Systems." *PS: Political Science and Politics* 27(4):689–692.

—. 2001. "Political Rights, Electoral Systems, and the Legislative Representation of Women in Seventy-Three Democracies." In *Handbook of Global Social Policy*, eds. Stuart Nagel and Amy Robb. New York: Marcel Dekker, 73–91.

Sapiro, Virginia. 1982. "Private Costs of Public Commitments or Public Costs of Private Commitments? Family Roles Versus Political Ambitions." *American Journal of Political Science* 26(2):265–279.

—. 1983. *The Political Integration of Women: Roles, Socialization, and Politics.* Urbana: University of Illinois Press.

Shvedova, Nadezhda. 1998. "Obstacles to Women's Participation in Parliament." In *Women in Parliament: Beyond Numbers*, ed. Azza Karam, 19–41. Stockholm: International IDEA.

Squires, Judith. 1996. "Quotas for Women: Fair Representation?" *Parliamentary Affairs* 49(1):71–88.

Studlar, Donley T., and I. McAllister. 1991. "Political Recruitment to the Australian Legislature: Toward an Explanation of Women's Electoral Disadvantages." *Western Political Quarterly* 44:467–485.

Thomas, Sue. 1991. "The impact of women on state legislative policies." *Journal of Politics* 53(4):958–976.

Tremblay, Manon. 1999. *Des femmes au Parlement: Une stratégie féministe?* Montréal: Éditions du Remue-ménage.

Tremblay, Manon, and Réjean Pelletier. 1995. *Que font-elles en politique?* Ste-Foy, QC: Les Presses de l'Université Laval.

—. 2000. "More Women or More Feminists? Descriptive and Substantive Representations of Women at the 1997 Canadian Federal Election." *International Political Science Review* 21(4):361–380.

Welch, Susan. 1981. "Recruitment of Women to Public Office: A Discriminant Analysis." *Western Political Quarterly* 34(1):372–380.

Welch, Susan, and Donley Studlar. 1990. "Multimember Districts and the Representation of Women: Evidence from Britain and the United States." *Journal of Politics* 52:391–412.

Young, Lisa. 1994. *Electoral Systems and Representative Legislatures: Consideration of Alternative Electoral Systems.* Ottawa: Canadian Advisory Council on the Status of Women.

—. 1997. "Gender Equal Legislatures: Evaluating the Proposed Nunavut Electoral System." *Canadian Public Policy* 23(3):306–315.

—. 2000. *Feminists and Party Politics.* Vancouver: UBC Press.

CHAPTER SEVEN

Candidate Nomination in New Brunswick's Political Parties[1]

WILLIAM CROSS AND LISA YOUNG

Introduction

CANDIDATE NOMINATION LIES at the centre of democratic practice in both New Brunswick and Canada. Nomination processes largely determine which individuals and groups have access to elected office and have substantial impact on the effectiveness of participatory opportunities offered to voters. And, in recent years, there is evidence that they have negatively influenced voters' confidence in their electoral system and institutions of democratic governance more generally.

Political parties dominate our electoral competition and in doing so they effectively control access to elected office. An example of this is the fact that there has not been a single independent candidate elected to the New Brunswick legislature in at least the last 12 elections; every MLA since 1960 was elected as a member of a political party. This means that the first hurdle to be cleared in securing election to the legislature is obtaining nomination in one of the province's three principal political parties (Progressive Conservative, Liberal, and New Democratic). A corollary of this is that when voters go to the polls at election time, their choice of a local representative has already been dramatically narrowed. Voters choose from among those candidates nominated by the parties—usually choosing from among three names. In "safe" seats, where one party is almost certain to win, the nomination contest is arguably more important than the election itself.

This chapter examines the present system of candidate nomination in New Brunswick and contrasts it with nomination systems in use in jurisdictions with alternative electoral systems. We focus on countries with mixed-member proportional (MMP) systems. We do so for two reasons: first, because the New Brunswick Commission on Legislative Democracy has recommended an MMP system; and, second, because parties in these systems choose both list and constituency members, permitting an examination of differences in the selection of the two types of candidates.

We begin from the hypothesis that the choice of an electoral system has significant effects on certain aspects of candidate nomination but does not dictate how political parties will choose to select their candidates. Most notably, the electoral system is often thought to influence the ability of traditionally under-represented groups to win access to elected office, the amount of choice voters have in selecting their local representative, and the relationship between local and central party officials in terms of party democracy. The democratic culture within each party is also an important factor, and thus we find differences among parties operating in similar electoral systems while finding some consistency within parties in the selection of both list and constituency members.

In assessing the nomination processes in various jurisdictions, we consider how participatory the processes are, how fair they are, how much choice is provided to voters, the balance of power between central party offices and local party members in selecting candidates, and, finally, the success of traditionally under-represented groups, such as women and First Nations, in winning a nomination. In answering these questions we begin with a description of the current nomination process in New Brunswick and a discussion of its strengths and weaknesses. We then contrast it with the nomination experience in similar parliamentary democracies that use a mixed-member proportional electoral system.

Current nomination practices do not always accord with democratic ideals and conceptions of due process. Accordingly, we enumerate relevant issues for potential regulators to consider as they review the nomination process. We also outline several approaches to the regulation of nomination contests, drawing on experiences from other jurisdictions, and we examine the issues surrounding nomination that must be addressed by regulators and political parties in the event of a change in the electoral system.

Candidate Nomination: Democratic Norms and Electoral Systems

Candidate nomination in New Brunswick is similar to that found in the other nine Canadian provinces and at the federal level. All of these jurisdictions have single-member plurality electoral systems coupled with party-dominated Westminster legislatures. These two traits have a significant impact on their candidate nomination processes. The two most important characteristics of candidate nomination in New Brunswick are that *one* candidate is nominated by each party in each of the province's 55 electoral districts, and that the parties themselves decide how they will select their candidates.[2]

The first of these traits is a direct result of the electoral system. In the SMP system, votes are tabulated separately in each electoral district and the candidate with the most votes is elected. This system dictates that each party run only one candidate in each district in order not to dilute their vote.

The second defining characteristic—that parties themselves determine the rules and processes of candidate nomination—is not dictated by the electoral system. Canadian parties, including those in New Brunswick, employ some of the most decentralized nomination processes found in any democracy (Carty and Cross 2006). This is not, however, a simple result of our electoral system. Other SMP countries (for example, the United States) use candidate nomination processes that are organized under strict state regulations. Conversely, some jurisdictions using proportional representation leave candidate nomination largely to the prerogative of the political parties. In general terms, the Westminster systems with relatively strong legislative parties appear to allow their parties more latitude in choosing candidate nomination processes (Carty, Cross, and Young 2000).

It is important to keep in mind throughout this discussion that some characteristics of candidate nomination will reflect the electoral system in place while others are largely independent of it. This becomes particularly clear when we examine the experience of jurisdictions that have moved from an SMP electoral system to a PR system: in these cases, we find that the method of candidate selection for lists is an adaptation of parties' existing practices.

Participation and the Balance of Power between Local and Central Party Authority

The number of people eligible to participate in selecting a party's candidates is not a function of the electoral system. In all electoral systems, some method of internal party selection of candidates precedes the election of representatives to the legislature. It is this initial winnowing of the field that is of interest to us here. The extent of participation can range from very narrow, with only party leaders selecting candidates, to very broad, as in the US primary system, where any registered voter can participate in the candidate selection process.

Voting in candidate nomination contests in all major Canadian political parties is restricted to party members—those individuals whose names appear on their membership rolls. Typically, this is a very small subset of those eligible to vote in a general election. The best estimates are that between 1% and 2% of Canadians belong to a political party (Cross and Young 2004). The large majority of each party's supporters (and voters) are not members. Membership in a political party normally requires the payment of a small annual fee (around $10) and the signing of a membership form. While these obstacles are not dramatic, they help suppress membership numbers.

Membership in New Brunswick's two principal parties is among the most accessible in the country. The New Brunswick Liberals have traditionally charged no annual membership fee and automatically renew all memberships. The result is that New Brunswick accounts for about 25% of all Liberal party members in Canada (about 140,000 when the national party membership was extraordinarily high, at about 525,000, during the Martin leadership campaign). The New Brunswick PCs have moved in this direction, charging a one-time fee of $5 and then renewing memberships on an automatic basis, free of charge. Nevertheless, both parties require that an individual's name appear on their membership rolls in advance of the nomination election in order for that individual to be able to participate. For example, the 2003 PC rules mandated that "the deadline for adding new Members for the purpose of voting at a nomination convention shall be seventy-two (72) hours prior to the commencement of the nominating convention" (PC Party of NB Constitution, Article 18, 4.1). The result is that only a relatively small portion of general election voters are eligible to participate in the nomination contest. Given the ease with which one becomes a party member in New Brunswick, more important than the barriers to membership are the obstacles to participation in a nominating contest.

Voting in a nomination contest is New Brunswick is not particularly accessible in terms of either venue or duration. In general elections, Elections New Brunswick operates polling places in virtually every neighbourhood in the province. For example, in the southeastern riding of Tantramar there were 26 voting places in the 2003 election (about one for every 300 voters). This allows voters access to a polling place without having to travel a great distance. In the same riding in the same election, each party had only one polling place for its nomination contest. All three parties held their nomination contests in Sackville, requiring voters from other parts of the riding, such as Port Elgin and Dorchester, to travel up to 50 kilometres to the single voting place.

General election voting takes place over a 10-hour period on a single day common to the entire province. In order to ensure all voters have the time to participate, New Brunswick law requires employers to grant their employees three consecutive hours off work during the time the polls are open (10:00 AM to 8:00 PM). Nomination contests occur on different dates chosen largely at the discretion of the local party association. For example, the PC Constitution states, "The Executive of the Registered District Association shall set the date, time and location of the nominating convention in consultation with the Provincial President" (Article 18, 2). Nominating conventions are almost always held on weeknights or on weekends to facilitate the participation of those working standard nine-to-five jobs. Typically, voters will have only a one- or two-hour window within which to cast their nomination ballot.

Participation in a nomination contest is considerably more time consuming than voting in a general election. In a general election, voters need to travel to their local voting place—usually only a short distance from their home— sometimes wait in line for a few minutes, and then cast their ballot. The entire exercise usually takes less than one half hour. In nomination contests, voters need to travel to a single location in their riding, sit through a meeting that typically takes an hour or longer, then line up to vote. All New Brunswick parties use a majority electoral rule, often requiring more than one ballot to be held. In large, contested nomination meetings, balloting routinely takes several hours before a winner is declared.[3]

All of this makes participation in a nomination contest considerably more onerous than voting in a general election. The obstacles to participation surely chill the participation of some New Brunswickers who would otherwise participate in a nomination contest. We do not have comprehensive data on the numbers of New Brunswickers participating in nomination contests. Reports from the parties and in the media suggest that there is substantial variation depending on whether the nomination is contested and whether the party's candidate is likely to win the general election. Many nomination contests are small affairs with 100 or fewer voters choosing the party's candidate. The number occasionally swells to many times this when there is a contested nomination in a riding in which a party is electorally strong. Data from the federal level, with a virtually identical process, suggest that only a very small percentage of the parties' partisans participate in nomination contests. The most recent comprehensive data relating to participation in nomination contests concerns the 1993 federal election. The average attendance at these nomination meetings was 413, and this number is driven up by a few very large meetings. The median attendance was just 201, and one-third of local party associations had fewer than 100 voters participate. There is further evidence that only between one-third and one-half of the parties' members participate in nomination contests (Cross 2002, 2006).

As outlined above, the obstacles to participation in nomination contests include random dates and times, a single voting location in each riding, lengthy nomination meetings and voting procedures, requirement of party membership, and eligibility cut-off dates. None of these are directly related to the New Brunswick electoral system. Rather, they result from the parties having absolute discretion over the selection of their candidates. Elections New Brunswick plays no role in the conduct of these affairs. They are viewed as the private affairs of private organizations (the political parties), and the parties essentially have absolute discretion over how to conduct them. While this is typical of Canadian jurisdictions it is not the case in all Western democracies. The United States, with a similar electoral system, is an example of a country that provides state regulation of nomination contests. The state holds primary elections under rules and practices almost identical to those in place for general elections. These primaries are comparable to Canadian nomination contests in that their purpose is to choose the candidate of each major party for the general election. Using processes that are considerably more accessible than those used by the Canadian parties, US nomination contests have considerably higher turnouts than do Canadian contests. Turnout in US primaries varies dramatically, but is often in the range of 20% to 25% (and occasionally higher), while the available Canadian numbers suggest a participation rate in the very low single digits when measured as a proportion of eligible voters.

Most parties in the major parliamentary systems are similar to their Canadian counterparts in limiting participation in nomination contests to their card-carrying members. Non-member partisans are not normally permitted to participate. The Canadian practice of permitting all members to vote is not universally followed. While it is now the norm in the United Kingdom, much more restrictive practices are followed in some other jurisdictions. For example, in New Zealand party committees select candidates to run in the SMP portion of their elections. While there are some differences between parties, the case of the New Zealand Labour Party is instructive. Local nomination meetings are held at which would-be candidates make presentations and all members present cast a vote for their preferred candidate. To this point, these exercises are similar to Canadian nomination contests. However, the similarities end here. In the New Zealand case, the cumulative votes of the membership count as one vote in the selection of the candidate. This is one of six votes, with the other five cast by three delegates from the party's national headquarters, one local party official, and one member chosen from the floor of the meeting (Salmond 2003). In this case, members participate but their influence is dramatically less than in the Canadian case.

We find that in MMP systems, there is not a dramatic difference between how candidates are chosen in the SMP and list portions of the election. While the details differ in each case, the norms of who gets to participate are not a direct result of the type of electoral system in play. It is commonly thought that list candidates will be chosen by party elites, while the membership will play a more significant role in the selection of local candidates. In fact, even a cursory examination of nomination practices in proportional systems indicates that this is not always the case. In UK elections, the Liberal Democrats select all of the candidates for list (European) and SMP (National) elections through a poll of their local members. In New Zealand, the role of party members is checked by central party officers in both list and SMP selections. However, in the case of the Tory and Labour parties in Scotland and Wales, we do find an important difference between the two types of elections. Both parties provide a vote to each member in the selection of SMP candidates and use party committees comprised of both local and central party authorities in the selection of list candidates. However, as discussed below, the UK central party is not completely absent from the choice of SMP candidates either, as they traditionally vet all would-be nomination candidates before the local association is able to exercise their choice.

Consistent with the above discussion, it is also generally believed that SMP provides more autonomy to the local party branches in the selection of their candidates. While there is modest evidence to support this hypothesis, a more accurate conclusion is that the norms of the party in terms of the balance of authority between local and central party will manifest themselves in the selection of both SMP and list candidates.

In the New Brunswick and Canadian experiences, candidate selection has traditionally been the sole prerogative of the members of local party associations, but that custom is not directly related to the electoral system itself. In other countries that have SMP electoral systems, political parties have adopted different methods of candidate selection. In Britain, the national parties have traditionally produced lists of acceptable candidates and the local associations were allowed to choose among these pre-approved potential candidates. Even in Canada, we have seen sporadic (and at the federal level, increasing) cases in which the central party authorities have essentially usurped the local members' prerogative in selecting their candidates (Cross 2006). In the past five federal elections, Liberal party leaders Chrétien and Martin appointed a number of candidates, often alienating local members and riding association executives, and both Liberal and Conservative party leaders unilaterally renominated all of their incumbent MPs for the 2006 election. There has been less of this in the New Brunswick case. Nonetheless, in the 2003 provincial election, central Liberal authorities did essentially name candidates in some ridings.

The ability of local members to select their own candidate is directly related to the balance of power between the local and central party branch. This balance is a product of factors independent of the electoral system. For example, as mentioned above, in election to the British Parliament, using an SMP electoral system, the tradition has long been for significantly more central control than is the case in Canada or the US, which have similar electoral systems. Countries with mixed electoral systems (electing both constituency members and list members) generally have a similar level of local or central control in their method of selecting candidates for both constituency and list seats. If there is substantial central party involvement in the selection of constituency candidates, we expect to find the same relationship in the selection of list candidates.

This is illustrated in the practices adopted by parties in New Zealand when the country moved from an SMP to an MMP electoral system. According to Miller (1999, 11), for all New Zealand parties, "the ranking process [for the national list] has been placed firmly in the hands of national moderating committees. This allows the parties to determine the selection outcome in a number of important ways." The national party committees appear to be motivated by a variety of factors, including equity concerns, a desire to have different party factions represented in Parliament, and the need to ensure that high-profile candidates win a seat in Parliament. New Zealand's Labour Party, perhaps especially concerned with this kind of balancing, provides a greater role for its central office in the selection of both constituency and list members than does the rival National Party (Salmond 2003). This reflects the democratic norms of the two parties, with National choosing local autonomy and Labour being more concerned with centrally engineering the composition of its list. The electoral system influences the ways in which these norms are manifested in the two types of candidate nomination, but the democratic values of each party prevail in both cases.

Similarly, parties contesting elections for the MMP-elected new legislatures in Scotland and Wales adapted their party's practices for selecting constituency candidates to create a process for selecting list candidates. The general practice of having both central and local party involvement was followed for both the SMP elections and the construction of the lists. Beyond this, however, the parties varied somewhat in how they constructed their lists. In the case of the Labour Party in both Scotland and Wales, final authority for the rank-ordered lists lay with a centrally created electoral board following consultation with constituency representatives. Denver et al. (2004) report that in the first elections "in Scotland there were examples of lists being imposed and candidates highly ranked in defiance of constituency opinion. In Wales, list selections were caught up in [a] leadership battle ... and there was much that smacked of central manipulation to assist [one of the leadership candidates]." The Conservative Party decided that only individuals who had won constituency nominations could win a place on the party's lists. In Scotland the ranking was done by a joint council of regional and central party officials, while in Wales it was decided by party members at regional meetings on the basis of one member, one vote. The very diversity of procedure among Scottish and Welsh parties demonstrates that the electoral system does not dictate nomination procedures; rather, parties develop their own approaches based on their existing practices, ideological predispositions, and circumstantial factors.

Fairness and Candidate Nomination Contests

Those experienced with candidate nomination contests are familiar with complaints about a lack of fairness in the process. These generally revolve around the lack of uniform, predetermined rules. All Canadian parties permit local associations some discretion in determining the details of their nomination process and in interpreting the rules set by the central party. Details such as the timing and location of the meeting might seem inconsequential, but in practice these decisions can determine the contests' outcome. Again using the example of a nomination contest in the Tantramar riding, we can illustrate this point. A nomination contest in this riding might be held in the community of Sackville or alternatively in the town of Port Elgin. Travelling between these two communities takes about half an hour by car. A candidate with a base of support in the university town of Sackville might have little support in Port Elgin. A decision to hold the nomination meeting in Port Elgin means supporters of a Sackville-based candidate have to travel a good distance to the nomination meeting, ensuring a lower turnout of that candidate's supporters. Well-organized candidates will manoeuvre to place their supporters on the local association's executive so that they can influence these decisions. In extreme cases, candidates running against an opponent supported by those controlling the nomination meeting have complained that the voting location was changed at the last moment without their campaign being notified.

Complaints are also commonly heard regarding the mobilization of supporters as party members. On the one hand, candidates who are not favoured by the local party establishment often complain about difficulties in obtaining membership forms to sign up new supporters. On the other hand, long-time party members often resent the influx of new members with no prior connection to the party, who, because of their numbers, may dictate the outcome of the nomination contest. Eligibility for membership in most Canadian parties is more expansive than is eligibility for voting in general elections. The two most important differences are that those who are not Canadian citizens and are not at least 18 years of age are not permitted to vote in general elections, but are allowed to join parties and vote in nomination contests. For example, both the New Brunswick PC and Liberal parties have a minimum age requirement of 14 and no citizenship requirement for membership and participation in nomination contests (the PCs require permanent residence). The New Brunswick Liberals actually have no standardized rules governing membership eligibility; rather, their constitution leaves this decision to the local branches and merely suggests that the age be set at 14 and residency in New Brunswick be required. Some have argued that standard rules should be set governing eligibility for participation in nomination contests in all parties, and that these should be similar to the rules governing participation in general elections. Others argue that more expansive eligibility requirements permit parties to attract younger residents and non-citizens into the political process. In any event, the lack of established, consistent norms governing these processes often fuels discontent.

Many of the "fairness" criticisms of the candidate nomination process concern the broad discretion often provided to local party officials in overseeing these contests. Losing candidates and their supporters often view the decisions of these officials as favouring a different candidate. There is no standard requirement that all members of the local party association executive remain neutral in the nomination contest. As suggested earlier, well-organized candidates often place their supporters on a local executive in order to control the nomination process. This broad discretion may be less likely under a PR system in which lists are constructed at either a regional or provincial level. With fewer small entities (i.e., local associations) being given broad discretion over rules, timing, and process, there is likely to be less variation and less potential for candidates to try to manipulate the process.

One complaint that has surfaced in other provinces is the lack of an appeal mechanism for candidates or potential candidates who believe the rules have not been followed or that the rules established by the local association were prejudicial. Although some parties do have an appeal mechanism (as was the case with the federal Liberal Party prior to the 2004 election), others do not. For instance, the PC Party of Alberta does not have any appeal mechanism in place. As a result, three disputes over PC nominations during the summer of 2004 ended up before the courts. In one of these cases, the court ruled that in the absence of an appeal mechanism, the court had jurisdiction to overturn the nomination contest and order that a new one be held.

Nomination contestants have also often complained about the lack of any regulations governing the raising and spending of money in these contests. In New Brunswick provincial general elections, candidates' and parties' financial affairs are strictly regulated by the Political Processes Financing Act, but the provisions of this act do not extend to nomination contests. The result is that the parties are free to choose whether they wish to regulate the spending of their nomination candidates. The rationale supporting this lack of regulation is that these are private events of private clubs, beyond the reach of public regulation.

This rationale has recently been under fire in other Canadian jurisdictions. The 2003 amendments to the Canada Elections Act, for the first time, brought nominations under the regulatory framework governing campaign financing. Federal party nomination candidates are now limited in the amount they can spend on their nomination campaign (equal to 20% of the general election cap in their riding) and are required to disclose the sources and amounts of their contributions. Contributions to nomination campaigns are subject to the same limits as contributions to candidates during a general election. The regulation of nomination contests in law is not related to the electoral system, but rather reflects whether the activities of political parties are viewed as private events of private clubs, or as a public matter subject to public regulation.

Voter Choice

The question of candidate nomination and voter choice is influenced by the electoral system. Essentially, this is a question of how much choice voters have when choosing their representatives in a general election. In all SMP systems, parties nominate a single candidate and general election voters choose from among those nominated by the parties. Voting behaviour research confirms that in the Canadian case, voters largely consider their vote a choice between parties and party leaders (Blais et al. 2003). After choosing their preferred party, general election voters have absolutely no input into who their elected representative will be—that choice is left to the party's members.

In list PR elections (and in the list portion of MMP contests), general election voters can be offered considerably greater discretion in the choice of representatives. This is determined by whether a jurisdiction uses open or closed lists. Typically, the major parties in all forms of list systems nominate up to as many candidates as there are elected positions to be filled. In a closed list system, the party ranks the candidates and thus essentially determines which of its candidates are elected. For example, if a party nominates a list of 20 candidates and its share of the popular vote dictates that it is entitled to five seats, the first five names on the list, as ranked by the party, are elected. Essentially, in terms of candidate nomination, this is the same level of voter choice found in New Brunswick's SMP elections—voters determine how many elected members each party receives and the party determines who the elected representatives will be.

In open-list systems, the rank order of a party's candidates is determined by voters, not party members or officials. In open systems, voters are asked to choose their preferred party and then to express their preferences for the party's candidates. This means that voters determine the rank order of the list. The result is that voters determine both the number of members elected by each party and the identity of those members. This represents greater choice for voters than either closed lists or SMP elections. As we will see below, there is concern that this increase in voter choice comes at the expense of increased representation for traditionally marginalized groups.

Inclusiveness of the Candidate Pool

One of the persistent concerns related to nomination practices is the sociodemographic inclusiveness of the candidate pool. This concern is rooted in the belief (discussed in greater detail in Chapter 6) that legislatures should, to some extent, reflect the salient demographic characteristics of the societies they govern. When the composition of legislatures is reflective of these salient demographic characteristics, the legitimacy of the legislature and the broader political system may be enhanced.

We most frequently associate these concerns with calls in recent decades by women and ethnic minorities for representation within elected bodies. In fact, however, considerations of inclusiveness are a perennial feature of representative democracy. It is merely the political salience of various characteristics that changes over time.

Single-member electoral systems are designed to foster an inclusive legislature—as long as place of residence is the only politically salient characteristic. By dividing a polity into geographically defined sub-units and empowering each to elect one representative to the legislature, a single-member system ensures that the geographic diversity of the polity is represented. To the extent that ethnic or linguistic groups are geographically concentrated—as opposed to being dispersed evenly across the polity—a single-member system may produce legislatures that are inclusive of those ethnic or linguistic groups. Single-member systems have proven less adept, however, at ensuring inclusion of groups, such as women, that are not territorially concentrated. Moreover, for groups that are somewhat geographically concentrated but nonetheless remain

Table 7.1: Percentage of women candidates and elected MPs, 2004 federal election

	Candidates (%)	Elected (%)
Liberal	24	25
Conservative	12	12
BQ	24	26
NDP	31	26

Source: Carty and Cross 2006

a minority of voters in any district—for instance, aboriginal people in many Canadian localities—single-member systems have in some instances created a barrier to inclusion in the legislative elite.

As a general rule, multimember systems, most notably list PR, are more amenable to parties' efforts to make their candidate pool more socially inclusive. There is a simple reason for this: in a single-member system, the selectorate can choose only one candidate to represent their party; their desire to select the most electable candidate serves as a barrier to any effort to mandate that a certain portion of candidates should have some particular characteristic. When the selectorate is choosing several candidates for a list, it becomes possible both for the selectorate to be more conscious of issues of inclusiveness, and for parties or government to impose some requirements about the inclusiveness of the list. Gallagher (1988, 253) notes that "ticket-balancing is an obviously rational strategy [under PR]: it ensures commitment to the list from all groups or factions within the party, and might broaden the list's appeal in the voters' eyes. An unbalanced ticket will cause internal discontent and ... any gross underrepresentation of some group is likely to be brought to [voters'] attention."

Although it is more difficult for parties to adopt affirmative action plans under single-member electoral systems, some parties have nonetheless done this with a degree of success. In Canada, the NDP has been at the forefront of efforts to increase the number of female, youth, visible minority, aboriginal, and gay and lesbian candidates. In the most recent election, the party required that in all ridings where there was not an incumbent, a candidate search committee identify at least one individual who is a member of one of the targeted groups to run for the nomination before the nomination contest could be held. In Britain, the Labour Party in recent elections has identified targeted seats, in which only women could contest the nomination. For elections in single-member seats in the Scottish Parliament and the Welsh National Assembly, the Labour Party employed a policy of twinning, whereby constituencies were matched in terms of location and winnability, and party selectors had two votes—one for a man and one for a woman. The man with the highest

Table 7.2. Percentage of women candidates and elected MLAs in New Brunswick, 1987–2003

Year	Candidates (%)	Elected (%)
2003	19	13
1999	23	18
1995	20	16
1991	24	17
1987	17	12

vote was allocated one constituency, and the woman with the highest vote the other. The 2003 Welsh assembly elections produced a legislature with women holding half the seats. In France, which employs a single-member majority system, legislation has created financial penalties for political parties that do not achieve gender parity in their candidate pools. Most parties have, however, chosen to suffer the financial penalty rather than find a means of achieving gender parity.

In the Canadian experience, the number of women nominated and subsequently elected has risen slowly since the early 1970s. In recent years, the rate of increase has slowed and almost stopped, stalling at just over the 20% mark. There is some evidence that until the 1990s, one of the factors that limited the inclusiveness of the Canadian Parliament was the unwillingness of party members to elect women as candidates. Female candidates during this period tended to be found disproportionately in unwinnable ridings, acting as sacrificial lambs for their parties. The general pattern was that the proportion of female candidates for each party was substantially larger than the proportion of female MPs for the party; in other words, women were less likely to win their seats. Given research suggesting that voters do not discriminate against female candidates, this pattern suggested that parties were disproportionately nominating women in hopeless ridings.[4]

In recent federal elections, however, this pattern has all but disappeared. As Table 7.1 shows, it is only in the NDP that we find a larger proportion of women candidates than women elected. These figures suggest that parties are no longer systematically discriminating against female candidates in winnable ridings. Table 7.1 also shows that the three centre and left-leaning parties tend to be much more inclined towards nominating women than the right-of-centre Conservative Party.

The situation in New Brunswick suggests that parties in that province may continue to nominate women disproportionately in hopeless ridings. As Table 7.2 shows, in every provincial election since 1987 women have comprised a substantially larger proportion of the candidate pool than they have the legislature. This suggests that the parties' practices surrounding nomination may be contributing to the very low rate of women's representation in the province. At 13% after the 2003 provincial election, this rate is lower than all but one other Canadian province.

Research regarding the election of women suggests that one of the most significant factors limiting the number of women elected is the number of women who seek a nomination. Simply put, women are far less likely than men to contest a party nomination. The reasons for this are complex: women may perceive that they will have difficulty in raising the necessary funds, or may in fact have difficulty raising the funds (although there is little evidence supporting this notion); women may perceive that political parties are less open to female candidacies; they may assess the life of an elected official as being incompatible with family life; women may also simply be less interested in the formal political arena. All of these explanations are necessarily speculative, as it is extraordinarily difficult to study the question of why women do not seek party candidacies.

An additional means of ensuring representation for a group under a single member system is via reserved seats. The classic example of this is in New Zealand, where a set number of single-member seats are set aside for the Maori population. The country is divided into geographically bound Maori constituencies, which are overlaid on the geographic constituencies for the rest of the electorate. Eligible individuals can opt to place their names either on the Maori rolls or the general rolls. The Royal Commission on Electoral Reform and Party Financing in 1991 recommended a similar system for Canada at the national level (Royal Commission 1991).

Under PR systems, most parties make some effort to ensure that their lists are inclusive. Gallagher notes that one of the most frequently balanced factors under PR is location: "parties almost everywhere try to ensure that their ticket covers the whole constituency, for much the same reasons as they pick local candidates in the first place" (1988, 253). Beyond geographic representation, in recent years equitable representation of both genders has increasingly become a concern governing the construction of lists under PR. Parties in many PR systems, including several of the Scandinavian countries, Germany, and Scotland and Wales, have adopted the practice of "zipping" their lists, whereby the names on the list must alternate between women and men. Parties in other countries have adopted similar practices; for instance, the ANC in South Africa requires that every third name on its national lists be a woman's. It should be noted, however, that not all parties operating under list PR choose to adopt such quotas voluntarily. It is largely centre-left parties that adopt such quotas, and their counterparts on the right tend not to follow suit. In New Zealand, even the left-of-centre Labour party did not adopt quotas, opting instead to mandate a process whereby its selection committee pauses for an "equity review" after selecting five names to place on its list. This equity review is intended to ensure that the list represents Maori, women, ethnic groups, and age groups (Salmond 2003).

In many countries with PR electoral systems, including much of Latin America, electoral law requires that a certain percentage of candidates be women; usually this number is 30% or 40%. In some of these countries, including Argentina, the law also specifies the placement of women on the list (to ensure that they are not grouped entirely in the lower spots) and sets out sanctions for parties that do not comply.

Approaches to the Regulation of Nomination Contests

When we survey nomination practices in established democracies, we find tremendous variation among countries in terms of the extent to which nomination contests are regulated. In some jurisdictions, including New Brunswick, political parties are free to organize their nomination contests in whatever manner they see fit. In other jurisdictions, however, nomination contests are so heavily regulated that they have become entirely state-run affairs. To illustrate this variation, we will examine the advantages and disadvantages of a minimalist approach to regulation, as is found in New Brunswick and several other Westminster jurisdictions, and a maximalist approach, as is found in the United States.

In New Brunswick, as in all the other Canadian provinces, the United Kingdom, and New Zealand, there is effectively no state regulation of nomination contests. The only exception to this is the rule that requires the party leader's signature on a candidate's nomination papers. This has the effect of offering the party leader a veto over local associations' selection of candidates. Beyond this, however, political parties are free to set up whatever process they choose for selecting candidates. The process can be democratic or can involve leader appointment; rules can vary from party to party and even from local association to local association.

This minimalist approach is based on an understanding of political parties as private organizations that should be free of state control. In this conception, democracy requires that political parties be beyond the reach of the state to ensure that they are autonomous entities that can offer choices for free elections. It must be noted, however, that this is a conception that predates the era in which political parties have benefited from tax credits and various public subsidies. The strength of the minimalist approach to candidate nomination is that it retains political parties as private entities, and thereby allows variation among the parties in terms of their nomination practices. Under a minimalist regime, one party might decide to impose spending limits and gender quotas while another could allow a free-for-all; voters could choose between these two alternatives. Moreover, the minimalist regime does not impose any administrative burden on political parties with respect to their nominations.

The minimalist approach does, however, have several drawbacks. First and foremost, to the extent that political parties do not implement fair and accessible democratic practices for their nomination contests, public confidence in the democratic process may well be impaired. The spectacle of nomination contests held on short notice, with allegations of membership forms being denied to challengers and legitimate members being disqualified, does little to enhance citizens' confidence in the political parties that govern them. Moreover, as recent Alberta experience has shown, if parties are incapable of constructing and administering a fair process, challengers will appeal to the courts to step in and adjudicate the process. This introduces regulation by stealth. Finally, to the extent that political parties do not construct fair and accessible processes for their nomination contests, the public is potentially robbed of better political representation.

In sharp contrast to the hands-off approach of most Westminster systems is the extensive regulation of the American primary system. In the United States, candidate selection—for Congress and the presidency, as well as state-level office—has become an entirely public process. Party members do not exist, as such. Rather, the selectorate is potentially comprised of all adult citizens. In some states, voting in a primary is restricted to eligible voters who have registered as supporters of the party in question; in other states, any registered voter can simply elect to participate in either the Democratic or Republican primary. For federal office, federal laws govern the financing of primary campaigns. Candidates running for a primary are subject to the same restrictions on the size and source of campaign contributions as are candidates running in a general election. State laws govern the timing of the primary and who can vote in it.

The prime advantage of such a system is that it vastly expands the rate of participation in the nomination contest. Even with voter turnout in the 20% range, a far broader segment of the electorate participates in nomination decisions in the US than in most other democracies. Moreover, political parties have no opportunity to try to "fix" the result of the contest by disqualifying voters or changing the date of the contest. All contestants must abide by the same restrictions with respect to political finance.

Countering these advantages, however, is the effect that primaries have on political parties. If party members are no longer given the opportunity to select candidates and party leaders, there is little incentive to membership in the party. Political parties become empty shells, animated by the campaign organizations and interest groups supporting various candidates contesting the party nomination. In short, primaries almost inevitably weaken party organization.

Between these two extremes of minimalist and maximalist regulation are some intermediate approaches. In Germany, the Party Law requires that parties' internal operations conform to democratic principles, and specifies that parties must select their candidates by secret ballot. The Electoral Law further requires that constituency candidates must be nominated by either a meeting of the membership of the constituency party or by a meeting of delegates elected by the membership of those local party branches that are located in the constituency. In this way, constituency candidates are either elected directly by party members (usually in smaller parties) or elected indirectly by delegates themselves elected by party members. The Electoral Law also specifies that list candidates be selected by meetings of delegates of local party organizations within each *Land* (i.e., province) (Roberts 1988, 97–98).

As mentioned above, the Canadian Parliament in 2003 introduced regulation of financing for federal nomination contests. All individuals running for a party's nomination are required by law to abide by limits on the size and source of financial contributions, limits on the amounts they can spend on their nomination campaign, and requirements that they disclose the names of their contributors and the amount contributed.

Should the New Brunswick legislature choose to introduce some form of regulation or government supervision of nomination contests, a number of approaches are available. It is, for example, possible to construct a regime in which parties could invite Elections New Brunswick to administer nomination contests. The provincial agency would follow the party's established rules governing voter eligibility and administer voting for the nomination contest. The difficulty with such a scenario is that the integrity of the provincial agency could be thrown into question if it found itself administering a nomination contest in which the party was engaging in unsavoury practices such as giving insufficient notice of the nomination meeting. In all likelihood, any regulatory approach that involves the provincial agency in administering the nomination contest would require that the party abide by set rules about notice, access to the membership list for candidates, and the like. A more extensive regulatory regime could involve having Elections New Brunswick administer nomination contests in which any eligible elector could cast a ballot similar to American-style primaries.

Issues Arising from a Switch to MMP

When a jurisdiction switches from SMP to an MMP electoral system, it is necessary to make a series of decisions regarding how nominations for the list seats will be conducted. In jurisdictions that employ the minimalist approach to regulating candidate nomination, these are largely decisions for the political parties to make. In jurisdictions that intervene more fully in the regulation of candidate selection, these are decisions for the legislature.

The first issue that parties or the legislature must address is who is eligible to contest a nomination for a spot on the list. Beyond the legal restrictions of age and citizenship, there is the question of whether individuals who have already won a nomination for a geographic constituency are eligible to run again for a spot on their party's list. In Germany, the usual practice is to restrict list positions to those individuals who have already won a geographic nomination. This ensures that those individuals elected via the list have a geographic basis and are not entirely free of constituency service. This is also the practice employed by the Conservative Party in Wales. Conversely, it is possible to imagine a restriction preventing individuals who have already won a geographic constituency from seeking a spot on their party's list. This would eliminate concerns that unpopular politicians could be elected through a backdoor, with voters given no opportunity to prevent their election.

The second issue to consider is the process for construction of the list. Is it to be constructed by the central party, or are party members to vote on it? Assuming the latter, there are questions about process: should there be a meeting of party members in the region covered by the list, or should voting take place by postal ballot?

The approach taken may depend on the particular design of the electoral system. If the list-based seats are to be elected from a province-wide list, nominations will require either a series of regional meetings or a province-wide vote by party members. If the list is constructed through a series of regional nominating meetings, then the provincial party will have to establish some mechanism for aggregating these lists. Unless the mechanism involved a strict rotation of some sort, this might increase the provincial party's control over the list at the expense of members' influence over its content. If the list is constructed through some type of province-wide mail-in ballot, members may be given final control over the nomination process. While a mail-in ballot or a similar mechanism has the dual advantages of retaining member control and decreasing the barriers to participation inherent in holding a meeting, it has the disadvantage of asking members to evaluate candidates outside their region with whom they may not be familiar. It is not difficult to imagine a scenario in which such an approach produces factions within parties running slates of delegates, or an exacerbation of regional or other divisions within a party.

The third issue raised has to do with reserving spots on the list for various groups. If the list is to cover the entire jurisdiction, should spots on the list be allocated for various regions within the jurisdiction? Are there to be quotas for women or other under-represented groups? If so, are certain spots on the list reserved for these individuals?

Regional lists avoid the difficulty of guaranteeing regional representation. If, however, a province-wide list is used, parties are almost certain to devise some way to guarantee representation from different regions within the province. The risk of alienating voters in some region or fostering inter-regional rivalries within the party are very serious, and it is reasonable to presume that parties would devise their mechanism for selecting their candidates with regional representation in mind. This could take a variety of forms: as noted above, party members in each region could produce a regional list and the provincial party could aggregate these in some way. Alternatively, parties could reserve spots on their provincial lists by region. For instance, the third spot on the list would be reserved for a candidate from region A, the fourth for a candidate from region B, the fifth for a candidate from region C, and so on.

Similar options are available for parties that seek to achieve a certain rate of representation for women or other under-represented groups. While regional representation is most easily achieved using regional lists, representation of women and other under-represented groups may be more easily achieved under a provincial list because of its larger district magnitude. That said, even if a party is constructing a regional list with as few as three names on it, it is possible for the party to establish rules that would enhance representation of women or other groups. For instance, a party could require that each list include the name of at least one woman. It could specify that the woman's name must be in either the first or second position. It could even establish that if the candidate holding the first position is male, the second and third candidates must both be female.

It must be noted that list making becomes very complex when parties are trying to accommodate several characteristics. Requirements that certain spots on lists be reserved for regions, when coupled with requirements that every second name on a list be female, produce complexities. If you add to this a requirement that every third name be aboriginal, the complexity expands markedly. Trying to achieve these kinds of outcomes via a democratic process is highly challenging. A party that sought to achieve regional, gender, and First Nations representation on its list in a systematic fashion would almost certainly have to give some central party body discretion in constructing the list.

Conclusion

This chapter has addressed two sets of issues relating to candidate nomination in New Brunswick. The first has to do with the current practices of political parties for nominating candidates for geographically based constituencies under the province's SMP electoral system. The second has to do with the implications of a shift to an MMP electoral system for both regulators and political parties.

Current practices for candidate nomination in New Brunswick—and other Canadian jurisdictions—are less than ideal in terms of the possibilities for public participation, their perceived fairness, and the inclusiveness of the resulting candidate pool. There is some potential for government regulation of the nomination process, even if it only involves setting basic rules or administering the voting process. Such measures might well enhance public confidence in the electoral process, although it must be noted that they constitute a step in the direction of heavier public regulation of political parties.

A shift to an MMP electoral system would not necessarily have the effect of reducing local party members' control over the nomination process. In the first instance, our examination of the shift from SMP to MMP in other jurisdictions suggests that political parties generally adapt their existing approach to candidate selection for geographic constituencies to the task of nominating list candidates. If this proved the case in New Brunswick, we would expect to see political parties adopt procedures whereby they gave party members significant, if not total, control over the construction of the list. Beyond this, it is possible for government to regulate the process of candidate selection for list seats in such a way as to ensure that political parties conduct their nominations in a democratic fashion.

Notes

1. This chapter was written prior to the September 2006 New Brunswick election.
2. For a good overview of candidate nomination in Canada, see Carty and Erickson (1991) and Cross (2006).
3. For a full discussion of the barriers to participation in nomination contests, see Cross (2004).
4. For a good overview of the status of women in Canadian nomination contests, see Erickson (1991).

References

Blais, André Blais, E. Gidengil, A. Dobryzynska, and R. Nadeau. 2003. "Does the Local Candidate Matter? Candidate Effects in the Canadian Election of 2000." *Canadian Journal of Political Science* 36:657–664.

Carty, R. Kenneth, and William Cross. 2006. "Can Stratarchically Organized Parties Be Democratic? The Canadian Case." *Journal of Elections, Public Opinion and Parties* 16(2):93–114.

Carty, R. Kenneth, William Cross, and Lisa Young. 2000. *Rebuilding Canadian Party Politics.* Vancouver: UBC Press.

Carty, R. Kenneth, and Lynda Erickson. 1991. "Candidate Nomination in Canada's National Political Parties." In *Canadian Political Parties: Leaders, Candidates, and Organization*, ed. Herman Bakvis, 97–190. Toronto: Dundurn Press.

Cross, William. 2002. "Grassroots Participation in Candidate Nominations." In *Citizen Politics: Research and Theory in Canadian Political Behaviour*, ed. Joanna Everitt and Brenda O'Neill, 373–385. Toronto: Oxford University Press.

—. 2004. *Political Parties.* Vancouver: UBC Press.

—. 2006. "Candidate Nomination in Canada's Political Parties." In *The Canadian General Election of 2006*, ed. Jon Pammett and Christopher Dornan, 171–195. Toronto: Dundurn Press.

Cross, William, and Lisa Young. 2004. "The Contours of Political Party Membership in Canada." *Party Politics* 10(4)427–444.

Denver, D., J. Mitchell, J. Bradbury, and L. Pennie. 2004. "Candidates in the Scottish Parliament and Welsh Assembly Elections" (Full Report of Research Activities and Results). Swindon: Economic and Social Research Council.

Erickson, Lynda. 1991. "Women and Candidacies for the House of Commons." In *Canadian Politics: Towards Equity in Representation*, ed. Kathy Megyery, 101–126. Toronto: Dundurn Press.

Gallagher, Michael. 1988. "Conclusion." In *Candidate Selection in Comparative Perspective: The Secret Garden of Politics*, ed. Michael Gallagher and Michael Marsh, 236–277. London: Sage Publications.

Galligan, Yvonne. 2003. "Candidate Selection: More Democratic or More Centrally Controlled?" *How Ireland Voted 2002*, ed. Michael Gallagher, Michael Marsh & Paul Mitchell, 37–55. London: Palgrave.

Miller, Raymond. 1999. "New Zealand and Scotland: Candidate Selection and the Impact of Electoral System Change." Paper presented to the Joint Sessions of Workshops of the European Consortium for Political Research, University of Mannheim, Germany.

Roberts, Geoffrey. 1988. "The German Federal Republic: The Two-Lane Route to Bonn." In *Candidate Selection in Comparative Perspective: The Secret Garden of Politics*, ed. Michael Gallagher and Michael Marsh, 94–118. London: Sage Publications.

Royal Commission on Electoral Reform and Party Financing. 1991. *Reforming Electoral Democracy: Final Report*. 4 volumes. Ottawa: Ministry of Supply and Services Canada.

Salmond, Robert. 2003. "Choosing Candidates: Labour and National in 2002." In *New Zealand Votes: The General Election of 2002*, ed. Jonathan Boston, Stephen Church, Stephen Levine, Elizabeth McLeay, and Nigel Roberts, 192–208. Wellington, New Zealand: Victoria University Press.

CHAPTER EIGHT

Representation in New Brunswick: Capital and Constituency Concerns

DAVID C. DOCHERTY

Introduction

PROVINCIAL LEGISLATORS WEAR two hats. In the capital, they deal with the acceptance, rejection, and fine-tuning of legislation, and they develop public policy. They also keep the government accountable for its actions and for its spending of public monies. This is the legislative and scrutiny function of elected officials.

The second hat is that of the local fix-it person. In the riding MLAs are the link between citizens and the state. They assist with everything from obtaining large economic development funds to bringing greetings on behalf of the province to family and community events. Here MLAs are lobbyists on behalf of broad constituency interests or caseworkers working for individuals who need assistance finding their way through a bureaucracy they do not fully understand.

To properly perform these responsibilities members require a combination of proper resources (financial and human) and sets of rules (both formal and informal) that allow them to fully participate in the capital and to faithfully represent citizens. Concerns about improving the role of legislators are concerns that are focused on providing them with the necessary tools to do their job. Within Westminster parliamentary systems, we understand that there will never be a level playing field between the government/cabinet/bureaucracy and the backbench. But without proper fiscal and human resources, legislators cannot even hope to ask ministers the right questions or suggest ways of producing better public policy. In the riding, improving the ability of members to provide local service also requires resources. These resources include personnel and office space, and better use of information technology.

Formal rules include the ability to speak openly and represent not just local voters, but also others in the province who share common characteristics, be they occupation, language, religion, gender, or policy interests. We also recognize that politics is by its very nature adversarial, and elections are all about winners and losers, in terms of both people and public policies. Yet proper rules can go a long way to minimize the most blatant and destructive aspects of partisan clashes. Rules can safeguard the ability of members to work in a collegial atmosphere and to work within committees, and they can favour consensus and cross-party cooperation.

This analysis begins with the understanding that changes to one institution or aspect of democracy will have an impact on other areas. For example, changes to the electoral system will undoubtedly spur changes to the manner in which members represent their constituents and conduct their business in Fredericton, whether these changes are as sweeping as moving to some form of mixed-member system or as modest as adopting fixed election dates. This chapter concentrates much of its analysis on the possible implications of a move to a mixed-member system that would include both constituency members and list members. Such a move would produce significant changes to both representation in the constituencies and the work world in the capital.

A mixed-member system will produce several challenges to our traditional understanding of representation and confidence. But Canadian legislatures that choose this route would not be sailing in uncharted waters, as New Zealand, Scotland, and Wales have all had experience with a mixed-member system in a parliamentary setting. Where appropriate, this study will draw on the recent experiences in these jurisdictions, though we recognize that electoral systems are not cookie cutters. The outcomes of electoral rules are influenced by the unique culture, policy fields, and geography of each jurisdiction.

Changes in representation may also have consequences at the ballot box. Moves to improve the ability of members to serve their constituents might result in stronger bases of support for constituency members. This is no doubt desirable for incumbent MLAs but might be seen by others as a weakening of opportunities for democratic renewal. Elected officials in jurisdictions that are characterized as having little turnover and a multitude of safe seats may have a different understanding of what constitutes representation than those who are constantly fighting for re-election.

Just as New Brunswickers can look to external jurisdictions for examples of electoral reform, they also can look to other provinces when it comes to legislative reform. Five provinces are examining or have examined electoral reform. But there is also an increased interest in "modernizing" or reforming legislatures. In Ontario, the Democratic Renewal Secretariat is presently including legislative reform in its attempt to modernize political institutions. Both Alberta and Quebec have also examined legislative renewal. The goal behind these reform attempts is to increase the role of private members and committees in a number of important ways to allow for greater ability to scrutinize cabinet activities. At the provincial level, it is an exciting time for advocates of democratic reform.

This chapter is organized in three complementary sections. The first section examines our present understanding of representation in the Canadian provinces. It will compare New Brunswick MLAs to other Canadian sub-national legislators in terms of resources and ability to properly perform their elected duties. The second section examines the potential impact of electoral reform on constituency services and career patterns. In particular, it looks at the relationship between career success inside the legislature and the method through which members arrive in the capital (via a constituency seat or a list seat).

The final section examines the potential consequences of changes to the electoral system on representation, both in the riding and in the capital. This section draws upon the survey of MLAs explained below. In particular, it will make use of members' attitudes towards confidence and party discipline and how these views might be put to the test in an electoral system that encourages minor party government. The chapter concludes with a discussion on the implications of both legislative and electoral reform on representation in New Brunswick.

Data Sources and Comparators

As indicated above, where appropriate, this chapter draws on experiences in other jurisdictions. In terms of constituency support, we will turn to other Canadian assemblies as the natural comparators, as provincial members across the country deal with many of the same fields.

In examining possible consequences of electoral reform on the work world of legislators we rely more heavily on international examples, particularly Scotland, New Zealand, and, to a lesser extent, Wales. In the cases of Scotland and Wales, devolution in the United Kingdom and successful referenda in these jurisdictions in 1997 created new parliaments. The Scottish Parliament enjoys more authority from Westminster than does the National Assembly for Wales, as the former legislature controls more policy fields and has greater fiscal leeway than the Welsh assembly (though both depend on Westminster for funding) (Hazell 2003, 180–5). The New Zealand experience is perhaps more reflective of the choices facing New Brunswick. In 1993 a successful referendum in that nation led the way to a move from a single-member plurality system to a mixed-member system. There have been three MMP elections in New Zealand since 1996. As a result, the New Zealand parliament has experienced both systems (see Boston 2003).

Finally, this study makes extensive use of two sets of surveys of legislators. The first was a cross-Canada survey of provincial legislators conducted by the author in 2002. The survey of provincial legislators was conducted in the summer of 2002 as part of a larger project. The nationwide response rate of approximately 30% is large enough to safely compare the attitudes and views of provincial legislators. The individual (provincial) response rates vary more widely, and are therefore not conducive to generalizations. Therefore, this chapter makes use of regional comparisons and not comparisons of individual provinces. The second survey was designed specifically for this study. In the late spring of 2004 it was sent to all members of the New Brunswick legislature. A follow-up reminder was mailed in July. The response rate was high for surveys of sitting politicians, at just over 50%. The responses are reflective of both official languages and of urban and rural regions of the province.

Work in the Constituency and the Capital

The role of the elected member inside the constituency is one of the least studied areas of political life. This is unfortunate, as the job that members do outside the legislature is a critical part of representation. It is true that most studies do not rank the local candidate high on the list of factors influencing vote choice (see, for example, Blais et al. 2002). But on election day, when citizens choose a government they are also placing an X beside the name of the man or women they think can best represent their interests and those of the riding.

When it comes to contacting government officials or trying to solve problems, it is not parties that voters turn to, but their local member. Provincially, it is the MLA that represents voters' interests in the capital and resolves concerns at the local level.[1] Provincial members in Canada deal with the largest policy fields, in terms of both costs and direct impact on Canadians—namely, health and education. How do members attend to these duties and what resources are available to them to perform this function?

Table 8.1: Constituency resources in Canadian provinces

Province	Constituency office?	Citizens per riding	Budget for staff
British Columbia	Yes	49465	$84,000/annual
Alberta	Yes	35841	$69 035/annual (avg. based on funding formula)
Saskatchewan	Yes	17174	$38,868
Manitoba	Yes	19462	$41,925/annual
Ontario	Yes	110777	$153,350/annual to be used for constituency and Queen's Park staff
Quebec	Yes	57900	$104,000–122,000
New Brunswick	Yes	13269	$25,000/annual
Nova Scotia	Yes	17462	$48,000/annual
Prince Edward Is.	Regional Service Centres available for constituency work	5010	assistance for MLAs provided via caucus
Newfoundland and Labrador	No	10686	One political assistant provided for each member

Source: Legislative websites and survey of provincial clerks; data adapted from Docherty 2005, 78

Resources available to Canadian provincial legislatures are displayed in Table 8.1. Constituency service in most provinces has become professionalized; budgets are available for both offices and staff in the riding, though clearly the size of the budget varies by province. New Brunswick is no different in this regard. In addition, most assemblies provide members with global allowances that permit each MLA to determine how and where to allocate staff. The noted exceptions to this practice are all in Atlantic Canada, specifically Newfoundland and Labrador and Prince Edward Island. In the case of Prince Edward Island, members have access to office space for appointments and other constituency duties through regional government offices, though they share this space with other MLAs. Given the smaller geographic size of the ridings and the smaller number of voters per district (just over 5,000) such a system makes sense. It is less feasible in just about every other province, including Newfoundland and Labrador where constituents can contact their MLA via toll free lines.

For those that do have global funding allowances, the allocation of resources is a good indication of the importance of local work versus capital duties. Of course the size of the global allowance will dictate much of the distribution of staff. The funding level in New Brunswick is much lower than provinces with similar constituency populations, such as Nova Scotia. As a result, New Brunswick MLAs have much less freedom to split resources between

Table 8.2: Allocations of staff in riding and time spent on constituency work by average size of provincial constituency

Constituency size	Staff in Riding (N = 100)	Time spent by MLA on Constituency work (n = 120)
Over 60,000	2.46	36.1%
20,000–60,000	0.63	30.2%
Less than 20,000	0.42	40.2%
New Brunswick	0.25	44.8%

Note: Included in these figures are cabinet ministers who may have additional staff assigned to constituency work. Also, the less-than-20,000 category does not include New Brunswick. For time spent on constituency work, we have used the 2004 Survey for New Brunswick MLAs, as the sample size by province in the 2002 survey is too small.

Source: Author's survey

Fredericton and their district, let alone have more than one assistant. New Brunswick legislators who responded to the 2002 survey of MLAs were quick to point out that the amount of their allowance was not nearly enough to properly meet the demands of their constituencies. Table 8.2 examines staff allocations in provincial constituencies controlling for the average size of a constituency in each province. It is hardly surprising that Ontario and Quebec, the two provinces with over 55,000 voters per constituency, have the largest constituency staffs. But comparing New Brunswick to other jurisdictions with comparably sized constituencies, we see that it lags behind. We caution that these numbers represent self-reporting by MLAs to a survey of how they allocate staff available to them. The question asked members about paid staff in the constituency, though some respondents may have included volunteers. However, we also note that the under-20,000 category includes MLAs from Prince Edward Island and Newfoundland and Labrador, where no constituency staff are provided by the legislature.

With fewer workers in the riding, New Brunswick MLAs might be expected to devote more of their own working day to local affairs. Typically, a member of a provincial legislature spends over a third (approximately 37%) of their working time on constituency matters and just under a third of their working time on legislative matters (policy development, party, and caucus work consume the remaining time). In New Brunswick, members spend slightly more time on constituency work than the typical Canadian MLA, even those with ridings of similar population sizes.

The slightly stronger attachment to constituency service in New Brunswick is due in part to its size. In general, the larger the province, the less time spent

Table 8.3: Constituency work in different ridings

	At least 25% unincorporated	All incorporated
Time devoted to constituency work (%)	46.5	40
Time would like to devote to constituency work (%)	51.5	48
Percentage of riding unincorporated	55	n/a
Percentage of constituency time devoted to work that would otherwise be handled by municipal officials	64	n/a
Time additional staff member would dedicate to constituency work (%)	85	80

Source: Author's survey

on constituency matters. Compared to the larger central and western provinces, there may be a greater local attachment in New Brunswick. But there may also be work to be done in New Brunswick.

It can be argued that the number of unincorporated areas within New Brunswick increases the workload significantly. Rural New Brunswick MLAs are not only the provincial member, but also act as the de facto local reeve or councillor, dealing with road and sewer issues that urban MLAs do not have to worry about. Rural MLAs do spend more time on constituency work. According to the 2004 survey of New Brunswick legislators, MLAs from predominantly rural ridings spend just over 45% of their working day on constituency work, compared to approximately 40% for predominantly urban MLAs.[2]

While this difference might not appear great, there is a substantial difference in the type of local service being provided by these members. In fact, members who have unincorporated areas within their ridings spend a disproportionate amount of time working on matters that urban MLAs never have to worry about. The 2004 survey of MLAs asked what percentage of a members' riding was unincorporated. Two-thirds of respondents indicated that at least one quarter of their riding had no local government.[3] Table 8.3 indicates some meaningful findings for these individuals.

It is hardly surprising that members with unincorporated areas devote more time to constituency service than urban members (or members with no unincorporated areas). While not a perfect linear relationship, the survey did find that the more a riding was unincorporated, the more time an MLA devoted to constituency work. Both types of members would prefer to devote more of their day to constituency concerns, and there is little difference between types in this regard.

The most telling finding is the type of constituency service provided. Those individuals with unincorporated portions of their district spend well over half of the time they can dedicate to constituency work on those issues that would normally be handled by municipal officials, such as road and sewer issues. The result is less time spent on constituency work that is more typical of Canadian MLAs, including issues such as health care, education, and social services.

This dedication to local service should not be seen as a revelation. All respondents to the survey, both rural and urban, indicated that a desire to serve their community was the single most important factor that caused them to seek office. This was a constant, not a variable. Not surprising, then, that when asked what they would do if they were provided with an additional full-time staff member, most indicated they would use this person as primarily a constituency assistant. There was no difference between MLAs from fully incorporated ridings and those serving some areas without municipal governments.

It is worth noting that the 2004 survey asked MLAs to describe the two most important reforms either inside or outside the legislature that would assist them in their role as a local representative. By far the most popular concern was the need for more staff. In the words of one MLA, they require "adequate funding for proper staff." Another responded, "More support staff for the constituency." A third responded, "Greater resources for my riding." These are typical of the reactions of most MLAs who responded to the survey.[4] There were some calls for fixed election dates. Others indicated that more free votes would better allow them to represent their electors. However, these calls were dwarfed by the request for greater constituency funding. The request for increased constituency resources is not dependent upon the type of riding a given members represents, but holds for both rural and urban members.

It is a truism that few Canadians know exactly what each level of government does. As a result, members of provincial and federal legislatures are often contacted about issues that rest outside their jurisdiction. The fact that rural MLAs are responsible for all local matters in some parts of New Brunswick muddies the lines of responsibility even more. According to the 2002 survey, Atlantic Canadian provincial representatives are far more likely than central or western Canadian MLAs to be contacted by voters on matters that are not a provincial responsibility. The 2004 survey of New Brunswick MLAs found that just over 60% of respondents indicated that their offices were contacted on a daily or weekly basis regarding a matter outside their jurisdictional authority. Members with higher percentages of unincorporated areas were more likely to be contacted about federal matters than were members representing urban and incorporated regions of the province.

When this occurs, there is a mixed response on the part of legislators: 29%

always forward the issue to the appropriate member of parliament, and only 11% never forward the matter along. Nearly half of all members indicated that they sometimes try to solve the problem through their own constituency office. In the earlier survey of provincial members, most individuals who said they actually responded to these "additional" requests tended to do so if the service was relatively easy to provide and would be less confusing for the constituent. If the constituent is simply requesting information that the constituency office knows, the simplest method of response is to answer the citizen. If the matter is more complicated, it tends to get passed along to the federal member. It is rarely about jurisdiction hopping, or stepping on someone else's toes.

In sum, MLAs in New Brunswick have fewer resources, both financial and human, to serve their voters than members in most other provinces. To make up for this, they spend more of their own time attending to constituency concerns. This is even more critical for rural MLAs, who represent large pieces of unincorporated land where they also act as local councillors. These individuals do additional constituency work that is of a more local nature, and it eats into the time that would be spent providing more traditional provincial constituency assistance on matters such as health care and education. The workload of New Brunswick MLAs is also increased by a large number of requests for assistance on matters that are not a provincial responsibility, though this occurs in most jurisdictions.

Implications of Electoral Reform on Constituency Service

Now that we have examined the present state of constituency service in New Brunswick, it is worthwhile to explore some potential implications of electoral reform. In particular, what impact would a move to a mixed-member system have on the level of constituency service in New Brunswick?

The first implication is that constituencies would be bigger. While New Brunswick has avoided the recent trend in other provinces to have fewer legislative seats (Docherty 2005), it is not clear that a move to a mixed-member system would mean a substantially larger assembly. Instead, some existing ridings would be amalgamated in order to produce list seats. The immediate impact of this would be larger constituency seats in terms of both size and population.

Among other things, this means more constituency work for already overburdened members. If there is a lack of adequate resources for this aspect of representation under present circumstances, we can assume that much greater funding would be required for larger ridings. There will be additional pressure on the legislature to provide increased constituency resources. This report will not make comment on the number of constituency seats versus list seats, or the appropriate number of voters per riding. Nonetheless, the information in Table 8.1 provides some guide as to how other Canadian jurisdictions fund the offices of MLAs with various constituency populations.

Constituency work depends on one important factor: having a constituency. Clearly members elected from a list will not require the type of funding that members elected from a geographic constituency will need. This means different levels of office funding for different members. In New Zealand and Scotland, there is an asymmetrical funding of members' offices so that members in constituency seats may have greater funding than members elected from a list. In the case of Scotland, the funding for list members is a function of the number of party members elected off of the list in any particular region (see www.scottish.parliament.uk/MSPAllowances/index.htm). Constituency members enjoy far greater funding and resources.

Asymmetrical funding among members is a viable option for jurisdictions considering electoral reform. For example, individuals who represent larger, rural (and perhaps unincorporated) areas of a province may require constituency funding that is greater than members who represent a similar number of people, but all within a more compact geographic location. As indicated above, members that serve as local councillors have their own challenges in meeting constituency demands. If these challenges are increased by both geography and population, some additional staffing and funding may offset these obstacles to effective representation.

The entire issue of providing additional resources for constituency service raises a more fundamental dilemma and question. Members elected from a list will not face the burden of constituency work. In New Brunswick this means freeing up more than a third of their working day. How do they plan to fill in the time?

There are two possible alternatives, each with potential ramifications for the legislature and a member's approach to their representation duties. First, one expects that they will engage in more legislative and policy work. From the standpoint of accountability and scrutiny, this should serve the legislature and province well. List members would have more time to become policy experts, keep the government accountable, and engage in proactive policy development. Opposition list members would be well prepared for question period, would be briefed on policies, and would theoretically have as much time to spend on their critic role as ministers spend on overseeing their departments. List members who are part of the government would have the luxury of developing their own policy expertise and engaging in policy and legislative initiatives that are often denied MLAs with demanding constituency concerns.

Of course, given the desire for premiers to appoint policy experts to cabinet,

Table 8.4: Size of assembly and cabinet 2004

	Members Constituency/List	Cabinet Constituency/List	Percent in cabinet Constituency/List
Scottish Parliament	73 / 53	9 / 2	12.3% / 3.7%
Welsh Assembly	40 / 20	9 / 0	22.5% / 0%
New Zealand HR	69 / 51	17 / 2	27.9% / 3.9%

Note: New Zealand's 69 constituency seats include 7 Maori seats. In addition New Zealand has six ministers who are not in cabinet, all of whom are constituency members and are not included in the cabinet total.

Source: Information in this table was taken from the websites of each of the three legislatures in August 2004.

government list members might be expected to have better chances of being selected for cabinet service. The fear under this scenario is that two classes of members would develop; list members who are policy experts and on a career ladder, and constituency members who are encouraged to spend as much time in their constituencies as possible. MLAs by their very nature are ambitious and most see cabinet as part of their goals. In the 2002 survey of MLAs, 70% of members indicated that serving in cabinet was important to fulfilling their career plans. This figure is very similar to the 2004 survey results. So the question remains, is there a career advantage to being a list member over a constituency member?

Table 8.4 examines the makeup of cabinets in Scotland, Wales, and New Zealand. As it turns out, the path to a seat at the cabinet table does not go through the list, but rather through a constituency. In all three jurisdictions, the vast majority of cabinet ministers are elected in constituencies and not from a list. Further, these results are not simply due to the fact that there are more constituency seats than list seats. As the final column in Table 8.4 indicates, there is a far greater proportion of constituency members in cabinet than there are list members.

Are these findings counterintuitive? Perhaps, but as observers of politics also understand, legislators are chosen for cabinet for a whole host of reasons—many of them have less to do with policy expertise and a lot more to do with politics (Smith 2000). In Scotland and New Zealand, region is very important. For example, it would be unthinkable to exclude the entire South Island from a New Zealand cabinet. Likewise, in New Brunswick it would be political folly to exclude certain areas from cabinet (assuming the governing party won constituency seats in that region). As a result, when leaders are constructing their cabinet they first make sure that every region is represented with a constituency member in the executive. In Scotland and Wales, list seats are distributed on a regional basis. However, government leaders are still far more hesitant to turn to list members for executive service.

From an academic perspective, this suggests that there exists a political calculus to cabinet selection. Turnover in Canada is high, at both the provincial and federal levels (Docherty and White 1999; Atkinson and Docherty 1992). However, cabinet ministers are more electorally secure than private members. Even when governments are defeated, private members are more likely to lose their seats than members of the executive (Docherty and White 1999). Voters intrinsically prefer to have a cabinet member represent them in the capital. Prime ministers and premiers would gain less by promoting a list member to cabinet than they would by selecting a member whose riding would show them gratitude at election time.

There is also an institutional explanation for these results. In mixed-member systems, the government tends to win more constituency seats than list seats. After all, the very nature of a mixed-member system is to provide additional seats to the constituencies to counteract the distortion of a single-member plurality system. In the case of New Zealand, this is explicit in the electoral formula. The number of top-up list seats varies from election to election and is dependent upon the number of party seats needed to reflect voting preferences.

In Scotland and New Zealand, constituency members are more likely to be selected to cabinet because constituency members are more likely to be in the government. Opposition parties make up the bulk of legislators selected from lists. Unless there is a coalition government, most list members are not even on the correct side of the speaker to be considered for cabinet.

This is also why we see more constituency members serving in lead legislative roles such as committee chairs. In Scotland and New Zealand standing orders regulate that some committees (beyond public accounts) be chaired by Opposition members.[5] In these cases, list members are more likely to serve as chairs. However, most committees that are chaired by members of the government party are chaired by constituency members.

From the perspective of an ambitious politician, there is a more utilitarian lesson. The path to cabinet does not lie on a list, but rather winds its way through local service. If individuals wish to be in cabinet, they must first get into the government. Political parties still win elections in the constituencies, not on the lists. The list generally serves as a top-up, and as a result list members are more likely to be on the opposition side of the benches. In this sense, there is little difference between the present single-member plurality system and a mixed-member system, in terms of cabinet formation.

Depending, of course, upon voting results, a mixed-member system in New Brunswick could produce results similar to those in New Zealand, Scotland,

and Wales, where the majority of list members would be in opposition. This suggests that list members would spend most of their time opposing the government. While this might not be an ideal situation from the government's perspective, it does suggest that the scrutiny function of legislators could be improved dramatically. After all, a legislature provides a venue for an alternative government to present themselves (Franks 1987).

Yet too often, particularly in smaller assemblies, Opposition members find themselves worn thin. They must serve as a critic as well as on standing and/or legislative committees. They deal with interest groups and other citizens. And finally, they have their own constituencies to serve. If some Opposition members are relieved of constituency concerns to concentrate on accountability and the development of public policy, then it is difficult to argue that the legislative process is suffering. List members who concentrate on legislation and scrutiny are supporting, not detracting from, the functions of a legislature, even if they are doing it from outside of cabinet.

A second alternative is that list members might spend a good portion of their time trying to get off the list and into a constituency. It is worth noting that all members might desire the electoral security of a constituency, where hard local work can be rewarded at election time. There is an added bonus that a nomination and electoral security in a riding might free a member from relying on their position on a list (open or closed) for their political future. There is less need to placate party leaders under such a scenario, as a member's electoral fortunes are up to local voters and not a strong relationship with the central party. If this were the case, one might expect to see list members begin to "poach" on ridings that are represented by constituency members. This would be the case particularly in competitive ridings, where a list member from one party might spend a great deal of time and effort on local work in a district held by another party's MLA.

This is the Scottish experience. List members actually target constituency ridings they wish to compete in, and place their resources specifically in these districts. List members are selected from regional lists and are expected to act as the voice of concerns from these regions in the legislature. However, many Scottish list members take an additional step and actually engage in one-on-one constituency service in one specific riding, the one they wish to win in an upcoming election.

This type of activity is termed "constituency shadowing" and occurs in most mixed-member systems. List members still feel the need to attend to local or group concerns. In Germany, this occurs but is not viewed as a crucial issue. There is not perceived to be a class distinction between list and constituency members, nor do constituency members react so negatively towards their list "shadows." By contrast, many Scottish and Welsh constituency members treat list members with "disdain" (Lundberg 2002).[6] These actions suggest that list members are seen by legislators themselves as second-class citizens, and hence they desire to get off of the list and into a riding. The notion of list members as second-class citizens is also present, though not as pronounced, in New Zealand (Ward 1998).

One could make the argument that this problem mostly affects citizens. In Scotland, the list and constituency members must also compete with Westminister MPs whose primary local duties were usurped with the creation of the Scottish Parliament. A Scot with a health care or education concern could end up having three elected members competing to be the first to solve the problem. This "open market" approach to constituency service may work for constituents, as it allows citizens more access to assistance. However, it also muddies the waters of responsibility. Who does one blame if the problem is not adequately addressed?

Further, this is hardly an efficient use of legislators' time. If members without a constituency spend a good chunk of their day working in one, it means they are neglecting part of their role, which is to represent a broader part of the population, those that supported a party that failed to win enough constituency seats. It is the job of these individuals to speak on behalf of under-represented individuals and to ameliorate the distortions of the single-member plurality system. Ignoring this task does not enhance the legislative and policy functions of legislatures. If this latter scenario were to develop, all members would sacrifice other work to concentrate almost entirely on scoring points at home, even if home is an aspiration, not a reality.

Implications for Legislative Representation and Opportunities for Reform of the Legislature

Changes to electoral systems can and will have consequences within the legislature. But that does not mean that the legislature cannot adapt to new ways of selecting members. Nor does it suggest that the legislature should be stagnant and wait for changes in electoral laws. In their survey responses, the members of the New Brunswick assembly have indicated a desire to increase cross-party cooperation and improve the quality of representation inside the assembly, though many admit the roadblocks to achieving this are considerable. The question is how to best get there, particularly under a renewed electoral system.

In addition to creating two types of legislators, mixed-member systems increase the likelihood that more political parties will be represented in the legislature. This also increases the propensity for minority governments. This latter result will pose significant challenges to the Westminster-styled New Brunswick assembly, which favours strong majority governments and efficient governments.

In Westminster parliamentary governments, the first minister must always be able to face the legislature knowing that he or she has the confidence of the majority of members. This is one of the first principles of parliamentary government (Franks 1987). If a leader does not have the confidence of the majority of the assembly, he or she can no longer lead. When this occurs, the lieutenant-governor or governor general has one of two choices: either someone else (typically the leader of the party with the second-most seats) can try and lead the house, or the legislature is dissolved and the public ultimately decides at the ballot box.

Traditionally, Canadian legislatures have employed strict notions of what constitutes confidence, and have tried to include all government legislation, not just campaign pledges, the speech from the throne, and budgetary matters (Docherty 2004). By contrast, the British Parliament in Westminster has a more open understanding of confidence, and uses a three-line whip system in which some government bills can be defeated without necessitating a change in government or an election. Only recently have Canadian legislatures begun to look to the UK as a model (Docherty 2004).

Of course, anything that makes a political party look strong will be promoted, at least by the party leader. If more matters are treated as confidence, there is less opportunity for dissent, particularly within the governing caucus. Not shocking, then, that premiers and prime ministers play up the importance of confidence and hence party solidarity.

Just as single-member plurality systems are more likely to produce majority governments, proportional representation systems are more inclined to produce minority governments. As a result, premiers in a mixed-member system will be less assured of the continual confidence of the assembly, even when they keep their own caucus onside.

The simplest way to deal with this is to change what constitutes confidence. This would require a different mindset among leaders. It certainly would be easier than continual elections or coalitions to create majority government conditions. Changing confidence would mean that a premier would have to indicate that if his or her government lost a vote on a piece of legislation, they would not dissolve parliament and seek a new mandate. Once notions of confidence are changed, a relaxation of party discipline may follow as members would feel freer to vote against their own party on occasion, secure in the knowledge that the government would survive.

Such a move would have resonance with the public. It also has appeal with members of provincial assemblies. The 2002 survey of provincial legislators in Canada found that over 80% of responding MLAs supported (either strongly or with some qualifications) more free votes. Further, the same survey found that nearly one-third of respondents felt present levels of party discipline prevented them from properly representing their constituents. There is strong support for changing present notions of party discipline inside most legislatures in Canada.

But the changing mindset on confidence must also occur with members, not just party leaders, and this is not as simple as one might imagine. Members, both on the government and opposition side of the speaker, must be willing to work with the understanding that defeated legislation does not mean a weaker government. The 2002 provincial legislators survey found that government backbenchers are less willing than opposition members to tolerate defeat on individual bills and still be seen as effective governors. Government MLAs may be suspicious of the motives of opposition members, fearing they will use defeat on legislation to paint the government as ineffective. In order to work, changes to relax confidence must be accepted by all members of the legislature.

As indicated in Table 8.5, New Brunswick MLAs have somewhat different views than other legislators, though the views were less distinct between the parties. According to the 2004 survey, nearly two-thirds of responding members supported more free votes on matters that were not viewed as questions of confidence. Interestingly, Opposition members were more likely to indicate that failure on only one or two bills would be enough to spark an election, and less than 30% felt that the government could continue to lose legislative votes and not be seen as weak. This suggests that while there is support for freer votes in the legislature, governments should do so with discretion. There will be little internal support for a government that does not manage victory on the major (and most of the minor) issues of the day.

In addition, over half of the New Brunswick MLAs responding to the 2004 survey indicated that an overt relaxing of confidence on government sponsored legislation would lead to at least "somewhat of an increase" in free, or non-whipped votes. Hardly surprising that members of an assembly, particularly private members, support more free votes. Interestingly, members who identified themselves as either past or present ministers of the crown were equally supportive of more free votes as were non-cabinet ministers. This suggests that there is general support within the present legislature for free votes that would not lead to changes in government or elections.

Further muddying the waters are the rather contradictory responses on two other questions. First, respondents to the New Brunswick survey were

Table 8.5: Legislators' perceptions of the impact of free votes

	2002 Survey of prov. legislators		2004 New Brunswick survey	
	Government	Opposition	Government	Opposition
Could only lose one or two (%)	14.5	4.1	0	18.2
Could govern but be weaker (%)	55	20.4	62.5	63
Could lose and not be weak (%)	29.5	75.5	37.5	29.6
Total	100% (61)	100% (41)	100% (16)	100% (11)

nearly evenly split on the impact of minority governments on public policy. Over half (56%) felt minority governments would "provide opportunities to produce better public policy," while approximately one-third indicated they would produce worse public policy. Just over 10% indicated there would be no impact on public policy.

Among those who felt minority government would help public policy, some indicated that minority government might be more efficient. In the words of one member, "too much time is wasted on estimates … minority government might produce efficiencies by prior negotiation among the parties." Another felt the "lack of stability" would actually make the government listen more closely to both the Opposition parties and the government's own caucus. A third member indicated that minority government would actually help instill a greater "sense of consideration and respect" from constituents, and that this could be used to develop more consensus policies. The need for consensus was raised by a number of respondents who looked favourably upon minority governments and policy development.

By contrast, those who felt that minority government would have a negative impact on policy development expressed concern over the need for parties to work out accommodations privately. One member felt minority government led to too many "backroom deals." Another felt that minority governments make it impossible to "advance government agendas," while yet another member commented that the role of opposition is to "question and oppose" the government; if they are supporting the government, they cannot do this "effectively." One member suggested that a minority government is less efficient than a majority, as it would require members to be "in or near the [legislative] building at all times, making it very hard to get other work done."

Second, many members were concerned about the impact that minority governments would have on party discipline. Understanding that minority governments tend to enjoy shorter terms than majority governments, and that such governments require all members to stick together, it should not be surprising that MLAs might envision an even tougher whip under such circumstances.

Some 60% of responding New Brunswick MLAs felt that minority government would increase the need for strong party discipline. These individuals felt that there would be pressure on government MLAs to stick together and pressure on Opposition MLAs to oppose the government. However, not all of these individuals think that this is by definition a bad thing. Some members indicated that minority government might make party leaders more responsive to members. If there were more democracy inside caucus, then party discipline would not be bad for the democratic process. Members would stick with their party on decisions they all had a hand in crafting. The government would be unified, but through a collective discussion and agreement, not via the whip. Approximately 30% felt it would actually decrease the need for strong party discipline, while the remaining 11% felt that minority government would have no impact on party discipline.

As a result, we begin to paint a rather confusing picture of members' attitudes towards both party discipline and the implications of electoral reform. On one hand, members generally support a move to have fewer pieces of legislation treated as confidence and thus have more free votes. But on the other hand, there is a concern that governments could only lose so many of these votes before their ability to govern would be openly questioned. Members are split on the impact of minority governments on public policy, but generally think that minority governments will increase the need for strong party discipline. Presumably this will allow governments to appear strong, but will not satisfy the desires of members to vote more freely on many issues. The key for many members is how to decrease the role of political parties in the day-to-day governing of the legislative assembly.

Just as members had strong ideas regarding increasing resources for local representation, so too do they have firm views on how the functioning of the present assembly might be improved. Not surprisingly, many of the proffered ideas are geared towards increasing the policy role of private members. The New Brunswick assembly, like many others, has been criticized in the past for focusing less on matters of critical provincial importance and more on being a forum for highlighting local festivals and events (Peterson 1989, 160–161). Of course, improving the role of private members in a Westminster parliament is hardly a novel idea. In Ottawa, every government from Lester Pearson on has allowed successive parliamentary committees to put forward ideas on how to provide a more meaningful legislative role for members. Attempts at reform are hardly novel, though the typical complaint has been that they are often done only to improve the efficiency of the executive and not necessarily the scrutiny function of private members (Docherty 1997; Jackson and Atkinson 1980; Jewett 1966).

So what changes do members themselves see as potentially beneficial?

Broadly speaking, the changes suggested by New Brunswick MLAs fall into one of two categories: modernizing the legislature and providing members more opportunities to engage in policy development on a non-partisan (or at least less partisan) basis.

Suggested reforms concerning modernizing the legislature focused on both resources and better usage of time. The thinking on resources was very similar to members' concerns about the lack of capacity to perform constituency duties. Members desire more staff, both in the constituency and to help them with legislative and policy work. There was a strong sentiment that their scrutiny function is compromised (particularly in opposition) when cabinet ministers have far more resources than non-cabinet ministers. In this regard, the concerns of MLAs are noteworthy, but hardly isolated to New Brunswick. The under-staffing of members is common in Canadian legislatures.

This desire for an increase in resources is not limited to human capital. Members also desired greater computer and Internet resources to assist them in their legislative roles. In particular, members felt better use of information technology and more use of Web pages could significantly help in serving constituents. Like many provincial assemblies' Web sites, the New Brunswick site has no links to members' individual sites. Constituents can find information about a member from the assembly page and can access MLAs e-mail addresses, but members do not have assembly-supported web sites to help constituents in a non-partisan manner.

Of greater concern (at least according to responding members) is the management of the legislative calendar. This was a common concern among members who were asked to name the "two most important reforms that would assist" them in "performing their scrutiny function." One member indicated that there should be limits on debate that "holds up House procedures" and thus wastes time. There were others who echoed these concerns.

The estimates process, where private members review government expenditures, was noted by many as a matter of some significance, and in need of reform. This can be included in the category of modernizing the assembly and time management, as many members indicated that this was a waste of time. There was a general call for a "revised process for estimates." The concern is that members have little ability to make substantive changes and are debating over money that has already been allocated. While this does actually serve the scrutiny function of holding ministers responsible for actions of their departments, it does little to increase the policy role of legislators, and indeed serves as a source of some frustration. Modernizing the estimates process was seen as an opportunity for committee work of a more non-partisan, and private member–driven nature.

Finally, more than one member noted that all legislators should have access to legislative council for assistance in drafting legislation. In the words of one member, a lack of access to council has the effect of "slamming shut the legislative door" on elected officials that are not in cabinet. There was no mention of challenging the parliamentary rule that only ministers of the crown be able to introduce "money bills." Simply, there was a call to provide all members with equal access to legislative council when it came to drafting bills.

In terms of changes designed to enhance opportunities for cross-party consensus building, more members focused their attention on legislative committees. There is little support for changes inside the formal legislature, where adversarial politics is seen as natural. But members from all parties felt some opportunities existed for positive and meaningful change outside the legislature. Responding MLAs were realistic. There is little chance of a true consensus approach to public policy in a party-dominated political process. However, there was genuine support for plausible changes that would foster an increased role for private members in all political parties.

As Table 8.6 shows, there was support to give more freedom to committees, but only in areas where the government was already committed to action. There was little support for committees to engage in the actual drafting of legislation, even if there was unanimous committee support for the legislation. There was slightly greater support among New Brunswick MLAs for adopting a move to secret-ballot election of committee chairs, something the federal parliament recently adopted. However, even here it was not universal. Less than one-fifth of responding MLAs strongly agreed with this idea, though a solid cohort (40%) somewhat agreed that this move could make committees more independent of government and opposition party leaders.

However, members did feel that moves to send government legislation to committees more quickly could be quite beneficial. At present, 5 of Canada's 14 elected legislatures have provisions in their standing orders to send legislation to committee after first reading, though many rarely use this procedure.[7] More than 80% of responding members felt this would be of some benefit. After second reading, partisan lines have already been drawn, as the bill has been voted on in principle. If a bill is sent earlier, any report of the committee is not as constrained by partisan ties to a previous vote. This allows members of the legislature to solicit public feedback to a matter that might not have initially been subject to a wider public discourse. In this case, the report of a committee might include sweeping amendments and a change in course that reflects public support.

One benefit of this form of pre-legislative scrutiny is that is does not diminish the power of the government to control its own agenda. If the government

Table 8.6: Support for committee reforms among New Brunswick MLAs

	Secret ballot election of chairs	Committees to draft legislation	Bills sent to committee after 1st reading
Strongly Agree (%)	18.5	17.9	22
Somewhat Agree (%)	40.7	39.3	64
Somewhat Disagree (%)	14.8	25.0	7
Strongly Disagree (%)	25.9	17.9	7
N	27	28	28

did not like the bill as reported back by committee, it could simply withhold voting on a bill. Pre-legislative scrutiny does not force a government's hand in calling for resolution on a bill. Nor does it force a government to retract from a public position. In fact, pre-legislative scrutiny of this kind can allow a government to put something on the public agenda without having all the details of the legislation worked out. It allows greater participation of members without the parties having staked out political positions.

The practicality of this reform may explain why it enjoys more support among New Brunswick legislators. It is realistic, and does not threaten to change our conventional understandings of parliamentary government in the way that having committees draft legislation would. At the same time, it is meaningful and could signal a changing approach to developing public policy through the legislature. It has the potential to be far more constructive than altering the selection method for committee chairs. And like all proposed reforms aimed at building cross-party consensus or at least minimizing partisan animosity, it can be undertaken anytime and is not tied to external changes in the electoral process.

Conclusion

If one theme emerges from this study it is that New Brunswick MLAs take both their constituency and capital duties seriously. They spend more time than most other MLAs in the former, though this is largely a result of the number of ridings in New Brunswick where the local member does double duty in unincorporated areas. Time spent on constituency work is largely demand-driven and does not signify a lack of interest in legislative affairs. For members of the New Brunswick assembly, the challenge is in finding ways to make their jobs both more effective and more efficient.

Even without significant electoral change, members believe that both their capital and constituency jobs could be improved with additional resources. There is little doubt that members feel increased human resources in both Fredericton and their ridings would assist them greatly. They are among the least resourced members in the provinces, and the unique nature of many rural ridings poses additional burdens on local service.

Beyond more personnel, members also believe that changes to the internal workings of the legislature could foster greater consensus among private members. MLAs are reasonable about these prospects. Changes in the internal structure of the assembly will not bring about the abolition of partisan politics in New Brunswick. Nor should they. But changes that might give members a greater stake in developing policy once it has been introduced, changes that do not violate the principles of parliamentary government, deserve serious consideration.

Like most elected officials in Canada, New Brunswick MLAs would welcome a relaxing of party discipline within the assembly, but recognize that this must be done in such a fashion that a government can pursue its agenda and not be held captive to opposition demands at every turn. It is here that concerns over more minority governments come to the fore.

This study admittedly focused its attention on the impact of a change in the electoral process to a mixed-member system, which the Commission on Legislative Democracy recommended in its January 2005 report. It is, of course, impossible to accurately predict the results of any reform. Similar electoral systems produce different outcomes in different jurisdictions, as they are influenced by political culture and party systems. However, a move to a mixed-member system is likely to have a greater impact on the legislature than changes to the electoral system that do not produce list and constituency members.

In terms of the makeup of the legislative assembly, the greatest impact of a move towards a mixed-member system would be the introduction of two types of members, list and constituency. The concern here is that two types of members might produce two classes of MLAs.

The animosity towards list members is more pronounced in New Zealand, Scotland, and Wales than it is in Germany. One obvious point to note is that the first three of these countries operate within a Westminster parliamentary system like New Brunswick. In addition, even though Scotland and Wales have new parliaments, their histories are with the single-member plurality system. Likewise, New Zealand moved from a riding-only to a mixed-member system. As a result, there is little reason to anticipate that similar problems will not beset jurisdictions that decide to pursue a mixed-member system. This is not to say that Canadian provinces should shy away from any reform for fear of creating a two-tiered system of lawmakers. Recognizing the potential drawbacks beforehand provides opportunities to minimize unwanted outcomes.

There is an argument that the problem is greatest in Scotland due to the use of regional lists. List members are from a specific geographic area, but without a riding. They naturally are more inclined to seek ties to the region. In addition, those elected from constituencies are more likely to see regional members as natural competitors, particular given the difference in political stripes. Further, if comparative experiences are any indication, we can take some comfort in knowing that list members will engage in representation outside the legislature. They will do some constituency shadowing or work with interest groups in communities across the province.

Beyond two classes of members, mixed systems also produce more minority governments. Members are split on the problem or potential of more minority governments. Some believe it would induce governments to listen to all members, those in cabinet, those in the backbenches, and those in opposition. Others felt it would increase the pressure on party solidarity and create even more incentives towards strict party discipline.

Yet concern over minority governments is not, by itself, a reason to fear changes to the electoral system. Internal changes to understandings of confidence can allow a government to operate effectively within a minority government framework while still providing the freer votes that many members seek. To see how this might work, we turn to the mother of all parliamentary governments, Westminster in London. At Westminster, the three-line whip system allows members the freedom to vote against their party on many matters that the government does not see as crucial to their success. Of course, on matters that have a three-line whip, all members on the government side are expected to support their leader.

In order to be successful, this system requires the government to openly state which items are considered so critical that their failure to pass would precipitate a change in government or an election. It also requires opposition parties to honour the system. If they try and make a government appear weak simply because a routine matter failed in the assembly, there will be no incentive for any government to treat any legislation as anything but a three-line whip. However, if properly administered and honoured, there is no reason to believe that governments cannot effectively lead in minority situations and still free up members to vote as they think best suits their constituents or conscience on many issues.

New Brunswick is well served by its MLAs. They are a dedicated and hard-working group of men and women who seek increased resources, not for their own self-interest, but rather to better serve their constituents. Changes made to the electoral system in New Brunswick will produce challenges to incumbent members. However, strong leadership and a commitment to improving resources and looking at ways to improve cross-party policy discussions can go a long way to improving legislative democracy. Further, while changes to the electoral system will have an impact on the legislature, moves to increase mechanisms for cross-party consensus can take place independent of any external reforms. Further, there is strong support from all members to make the legislature a more dynamic and effective arena for public discourse and decision making.

Notes

1. I use the term MLA (Member of the Legislative Assembly) when referring both to New Brunswick members and to legislators from other provinces and territories, recognizing that different jurisdictions use different titles for their sub-national elected officials.
2. The survey asked members if their riding was "predominantly rural or urban" as well as what percentage of their riding was unincorporated. The figures in this paragraph refer to the self-description, not the percentage that is used as the basis for Table 8.3.
3. No responding member indicated a percentage between 1% and 25% of their riding as unincorporated. In other words, one-third of respondents indicated no unincorporated areas and two-thirds indicated at least 25%.
4. As will be discussed later, there were a number of other suggestions geared towards internal reform of the legislature.
5. In addition, the New Zealand speaker chairs two legislative committees, one on house rules and the other overseeing officers of parliament.
6. There are few academic sources for the contention that list members in Scotland engage in "poaching." See also Cowley and Lochore (2000). In addition, interviews by the author with academics in Great Britain, Scottish members, and Westminster MPs from Scotland all confirm that this is a regular part of political life in Scotland.
7. This includes the House of Commons and the three territorial legislatures, as well as all provincial assemblies.

References

Atkinson, M., and D. Docherty. 1992. "Moving Right Along: the Roots of Amateurism in the Canadian House of Commons." *Canadian Journal of Political Science* 25(2):295–318.

Blais, A., E. Gidengil, R. Nadeau, and N. Nevitte. 2002. *Anatomy of a Liberal Victory.* Peterborough, ON: Broadview Press.

Boston, J. 2003. "Institutional Change in a Small Democracy: New Zealand's Experience with Electoral Reform." In *Reforming Parliamentary Democracy*, ed. F.L. Seidle and D. Docherty, 25–55. Montreal: McGill-Queen's University Press.

Cowley, P., and S. Lochore. 2000. "AMS in a Cold Climate: The Scottish Parliament in Practice." *Representation* 37(3/4):175–185.

Docherty, D. 1997. *Mr. Smith Goes to Ottawa: Life in the House of Commons.* Vancouver: UBC Press.

—. 2004. "Could the Rebels Find a Cause: House of Commons Reform in the Chrétien Era" *Review of Constitutional Studies* 9(1/2): 283–302.

—. 2005. *Legislatures.* Vancouver: University of British Columbia Press.

Docherty. D., and Graham White. 1999. "Throwing the Rascals Out: Backbench and Cabinet Defeats in the Canadian Provinces." Paper presented at the Annual Meeting of the Midwest Political Science Association, Chicago, April.

Hazell, R. 2003. "The UK's Rolling Program of Devolution: Slippery Slope or Safeguard of the Union?" In *Reforming Parliamentary Democracy*, ed. F.L. Seidle and D. Docherty, 180–201. Montreal: McGill-Queen's University Press.

Franks, C.E.S. 1987. *The Parliament of Canada.* Toronto: University of Toronto Press.

Jackson, R., and M. Atkinson. 1980. *The Canadian Legislative System.* 2nd ed. Toronto: Macmillan Canada.

Jewett, P. 1966. "The Reform of Parliament." *Journal of Canadian Studies* 1(3):11–15.

Lundberg, T. 2002. "Electoral System Effects on the Partisan and Constituency Roles of German Legislators: Lessons for Scotland and Wales?" Paper presented at the 52nd Annual Conference of the Political Studies Association, Aberdeen, April.

National Assembly for Wales. 2006. "About the Assembly." Retrieved from http://www.wales.gov.uk/pubinfaboutassembly/index.htm.

Peterson. D. 1989. "New Brunswick: A Bilingual Assembly for a Bilingual Province." In *Provincial and Territorial Legislatures in Canada*, ed. Gary Levy and Graham White, 156–165. Toronto: University of Toronto Press.

Scottish Parliament. 2006. "MSPs." Retrieved from http://www.scottish.parliament.uk/msp/index.htm.

Smith, D.E. 1995. "The Federal Cabinet in Canadian Politics." In *Canadian Politics in the 1990s*, ed. M. Whittington and G. Williams. 4th ed. Toronto: Nelson Press.

Smith, Jennifer. 1999. "Democracy and the Canadian House of Commons at the Millennium." *Canadian Public Administration* 42(4):398–421.

Ward. L.J. 1998. "Second Class Mps? New Zealand's Adaptation to Mixed-Member Parliamentary Representation." *Political Science* 49(1):125–152. Retrieved from http://www.parliament.govt.nz/en-NZ/MPP/.

CHAPTER NINE

Electoral Reform and Electoral Boundaries in New Brunswick

MUNROE EAGLES

Introduction

As PART OF the province's British parliamentary heritage, legislative districts or constituencies are the building blocks of representative democracy in New Brunswick. They are the sites in which elections—the central mechanism of political accountability in the province—are contested. As such, constituencies constitute the prime arenas of, and provide the raw materials for, partisan mobilization. Their characteristics, along with those of their residents, condition the representational relationship between electors and politicians. Elected members care deeply where these lines are drawn, for they define the constituents whose interests the members must take forward in the legislative process and to whose demands for service they must respond. Thus the nature of electoral districts comprising an electoral system—and the criteria used in their determination—profoundly shape the kind of political interests that are given privileged expression in the political process. The relative size of constituency electorates gives concrete expression to the achievement of political equality of citizens. For all these reasons, the process whereby the boundaries of electoral districts are determined and periodically modified is one of the most important and contentious processes in a democratic regime.[1]

Creating or revising an electoral map is something that can be done well or badly. This chapter seeks to advance quality electoral cartography by examining issues of process and principle. As I will discuss in greater detail in the next section of this chapter, drawing electoral boundaries well involves a complex and value-laden balancing of a wide variety of competing—if not contradictory—representational and districting principles. Balancing these principles in a way that is consistent with the values of a particular society is a profoundly political task—and the nature of the compromises reached in this process is closely revealing of the value structure of that society. Good boundary drawing also requires intimate and detailed knowledge of where things are in geographic space. Drawing different lines obviously has consequences for the composition and character of the electoral units that must be monitored through the process. As such, electoral cartography also represents a formidable technical challenge. Fortunately, this aspect of the process has been well addressed by the development and refinement of "geographic information systems" (or GISs for short). This kind of computer software is designed to store, analyze, and display many of the kinds of spatially referenced information that sound districting decisions require (see Eagles et al. 1999, 2000).

Over the past several decades, Canada's provinces have been undergoing a revolution in the way their electoral boundaries are being drawn (Carty 1985)—a revolution that in the first stage saw the timing and control over redistricting move from partisan to non-partisan bodies operating within a statutory framework. A second dimension to this revolution involved heightened concern for the political equality of voters. As we will see, New Brunswick has also been touched by these forces of change, albeit perhaps less completely than were other provinces. This situation is clearly changing, however, and the recent release of the report of the province's Commission on Legislative Democracy suggests that this province may well be joining the leaders in the area of electoral reform in Canada's provinces.

In this Chapter I examine the substantive and procedural challenges that attend the drawing of good electoral boundaries, both in general and specifically in terms of the distinctive features of New Brunswick. The analysis proceeds through four main sections. I begin with a discussion of the procedures best suited for successful electoral boundary adjustment in the first section, and move in the second to consider the general principles that guide the process of boundary determination. In the chapter's third section I briefly review the New Brunswick experience with both the process and the principles of electoral boundary determination. Electoral reforms aimed at reducing disproportionality require multimember districts, since allocating legislative seats in proportion to popular vote necessarily means that there is more than one seat in each district to be allocated. As such, in the fourth and final section of the Chapter I consider some specific challenges of determining electoral boundaries in a multimember district setting.

The Process of Electoral Boundary Drawing

Resolving differences over the competing representational and districting values that lie at the heart of electoral mapmaking is necessarily and unavoidably a political process. Until relatively recently, in most systems it was conventional that politicians retain control of the process, reflecting their inordinately high stake in the outcome of boundary adjustments. Risk-averse politicians typically prefer the status quo to uncertain alternatives. As such, left to their own devices, politicians often simply failed to revise electoral boundaries, with the result that population inequalities among ridings increased as a result of demographic shifts. Unfettered by governing statutes, the temptation for politicians to use the boundary adjustment process to achieve partisan advantage or to protect incumbents proved to be simply too strong to resist. In these cases, the electoral map might be actively gerrymandered by politicians to protect and enhance the control of the majority party.[2] Instances of the latter are the stuff of political lore in many jurisdictions. Naturally, under these conditions electoral mapmaking was a business to be conducted in the deepest of the smoke-filled backrooms. Beyond the public eye, politicians could manipulate the electoral map to either dilute the voting strength of their opponents by splitting it across districts ("cracking") or concentrate it in as few seats as possible in order to minimize its political impact ("packing"). They could even "kidnap" a district by ensuring that an unwanted incumbent would reside outside the lines of a redrawn district. Contorted district shapes, unequally sized electorates, and non-competitive (government-biased) election contests became the hallmark of such gerrymandered systems (Monmonier 2001).

Such, unfortunately, is the state of electoral cartography in America at this time (see Peck and Casey 2004; Richey 2003; Toobin 2003). Letting politicians design electoral districts allows them to reduce their vulnerability to defeat (or, to put it another way, diminishes their electoral accountability). For example, in the 435 congressional district elections in 2002, only 79 House seats were won by less than a 20% margin, fully 80 incumbents running for re-election faced no opponent, and only four incumbents were defeated. The American experience illustrates sharply that the potential for mischief in the process of drawing electoral boundaries escalates in proportion to the control exerted by partisan politicians. Improving the process of boundary adjustment has meant taking steps to reduce—or at the very least counterbalance—the partisan element.

Table 9.1: Provincial provisions for electoral boundary adjustment, 2004

Province	Frequency of redistribution	Composition of commission	Population or electors?	Allowable deviation from equality
Newfoundland	10 years	Judge and four members appointed by Speaker	Population	10% except 5 districts with larger tolerances
Prince Edward Island	After 3 elections	Judge or retired judge and two citizens, one nominated by government and other by opposition	Electors	None specified
Nova Scotia	10 years	Appointments made by order-in-council on recommendation of select committee representing recognized parties	Population	None specified
New Brunswick	As directed by order-in-council	As directed by order-in-council	Electors	25% except Fundy Isles
Quebec	After every 2nd election	Chief Electoral Officer, two others appointed by 2/3rds majority of the legislature	Electors	25% except for Isles de la Madeleine
Ontario		Uses federal electoral district boundaries		
Manitoba	10 years	Chief justice of MB, chief electoral officer, and president of the University of Manitoba	Population	10% south of 53rd parallel; 25% north of 53rd parallel
Saskatchewan	10 years	Judge and two residents named by order-in-council	Population	2 northern ridings preserved; 5% in south
Alberta	After every 2nd election	Chair appointed by order-in-council and four members appointed by the Speaker, two by government and two by opposition	Population	25%, except up to 50% in no more than 4 districts in sparsely populated areas ones containing concentrations of Aboriginal peoples/Métis
British Columbia	After every 2nd election	Judge or retired judge, chief electoral officer, and a third person named by the Speaker	Population	25% except in "extraordinary circumstances"

Source: Courtney 2001, table 6.2, 107–109; Blake 2001, table 1, appendix, 30

Because of their obvious vulnerability to changes in the electoral map, relinquishing control over boundary adjustment has been hard for politicians to do. Yet, the trend in Canada—as in Australia, the United Kingdom, and most other jurisdictions that retain a single-member electoral system (with the aforementioned exception of the US, and even there four states have removed control of the process from the politicians)—has clearly been in this direction. The first steps along this road were taken in the province of Manitoba. Its legislature passed the Electoral Divisions Amendment Act in 1955, providing for decennial revisions of the electoral map to be conducted by an independent three-member panel. While the panel issues a report to be considered by the provincial legislature, John Courtney notes that not a single detail of the five reports that these panels have prepared has been altered by the politicians (Courtney 2001, 44). De facto, if not de jure, control over electoral boundaries in that province rests with the panel. Federal legislation establishing independent electoral boundary commissions for each province was passed in 1964. Subsequently, all provinces have adopted reforms that reduce the role of elected politicians in the process, and introduced other improvements. At the time of writing in 2004, New Brunswick is the only province not to have established a fixed time frame for boundary adjustments. In addition, although an independent commission was responsible for the last set of electoral boundaries in the province, the composition of this body has not been fixed by provincial statute (Hyson 1999). In these respects, the revolution in boundary adjustment identified decades ago by Carty (1985) remains incompletely realized in this province.

The general and salutary effect of most provinces' reforms over the past several decades has been to routinize and depoliticize the boundary adjustment process by establishing independent boundary commissions to draw electoral maps.[3] However, there remain some significant interprovincial variations in how this has been achieved. There are four dimensions of differentiation—concerning when boundaries are adjusted, by whom they are adjusted, *how* these practices are accomplished, and how heavily the issue of equal population sized districts is weighed in the process. Table 9.1 summarizes the main features of provincial practices with respect to electoral mapmaking.

As the second column of Table 9.1 shows, New Brunswick is the only province not to have put the redistribution process on a regular cycle. All other provinces have routinized the timing of redistributions so that they will occur either after two or three elections (for maximum intervals of 10 or 15 years respectively) or after the decennial census. For our purposes, the important distinction is not which basis for the timetable is used (electoral or census), but rather whether such an automatic trigger for a redistribution exists or not. Moving to such a regular timetable removes any partisan advantage from the government as regards the timing of the revision of the electoral map. Moreover, it ensures that the demographic shifts that take place after a map is adopted are not allowed indefinitely to erode the equality of representation in a province by increasing the difference between large and small riding electorates. To illustrate, lacking such a regular timetable for revisions, the electoral boundaries in place in New Brunswick today received legislative approval a decade ago, and were first used in the provincial election of 1995. And at present it is not clear when the next adjustment of these riding boundaries will occur. As a result, significant shifts in population that have occurred since that time will continue to exacerbate imbalances in the size of constituency electorates. Some descriptive evidence showing the effect of less than a decade of demographic change on increased disparities in the size of constituency electorates will be given later in this chapter.

The third column of Table 9.1 illustrates interprovincial variations in the procedures for appointing those individuals who will be responsible for redrawing the electoral map. Here again New Brunswick's practice of *ad hoc* appointments by an order-in-council departs from the practices in other provinces (and at the federal level). In other provinces (and at the federal level)those jurisdictions, there are restrictions that are designed to limit or balance the impact of political partisanship on the commission. In five provinces, appointments to a boundary adjustment commission must include either a judge (active or retired) or the province's chief electoral officer. The expectation here appears to be that these professionals will be less susceptible to partisan political pressure than other kinds of appointees, and that they are perhaps uniquely equipped to adjudicate competing claims made before the commission. This kind of process attempts to subordinate partisanship to administrative discretion and technical expertise. Such an administrative approach is carried furthest by Manitoba, where the province's chief justice, the chief electoral officer, and the president of the University of Manitoba are designated as boundary commissioners. Success for provinces adopting a bureaucratic approach hinges, of course, on the non-partisanship of judges and chief electoral officers—something that cannot always simply be taken for granted (Courtney 2001, 105–106).

Other provinces attempt to control the pernicious effects of partisanship in the districting process by adopting regulations that ensure that no single party can control the process. These jurisdictions (Prince Edward Island, Nova Scotia, Quebec, and Alberta) make an effort to ensure that the boundary commission reflects at least two partisan views by ensuring that the main opposition party (or parties) has a role in suggesting, appointing, or approving potential boundary commissioners. Here the partisan nature of the process is implicitly acknowledged and inherent political interests are brought directly into the boundary drawing process. In six of the ten provinces (including all of those adopting the "administrative" approach to defining maps mentioned above) and at the federal level (and hence in Ontario), boundary commissions have only three members. In the others (Newfoundland, New Brunswick, Nova Scotia, and Alberta) the number of commissioners is either greater than three or not fixed by statute. In these latter cases, it is possible for provinces to fashion more socially and politically diverse boundary commissions. Opening up the cartographic exercise by increasing the size of the boundary commission can enhance mapmaking by ensuring that important interests are accommodated early in the process. Alternately, it may complicate matters by incorporating hostile political interests and values directly into the boundary adjustment process. An example of the latter can be found in Alberta during the early 1990s. At this time, the bipartisan nature of the commission's composition made agreement impossible and, as Keith Archer (1993, 189) has noted, the Alberta boundary commission "gained the dubious distinction of being the first electoral boundaries commission to file only minority reports."

Once a boundary commission has been appointed for a province, its task is to draw an electoral map that respects and balances competing representational principles (to be discussed in the next section). The districting plan devised by the commission is then typically submitted by the government to the provincial legislative assembly, where it will be debated, possibly amended, and ultimately adopted. Only in the case of the federal boundary commissions and the province of Quebec do commissions finally determine the electoral map. Federally, public and parliamentary hearings may suggest revisions to the maps originally proposed by the boundary commissions. Accepting or rejecting these revisions is the prerogative of the commissions and in the end the map comes into force through a representation order that automatically takes effect after the dissolution of parliament. Similarly, in Quebec the commission's proposed map comes into force following the dissolution of the second legislature elected on the old boundaries. In all other provinces the new electoral map must be adopted by an act of the legislature. Since this latter practice opens up opportunities for politicians (or more precisely, governments) to influence the map in their favour, Stewart Hyson (1999, 193) concludes his thorough review of the workings of the last New Brunswick provincial electoral boundaries commission by arguing that "in order to be perceived as being fair and thereby enhance the integrity of the process, future commissions in New Brunswick will probably need to have the final say in setting electoral boundaries." This may well represent the final extension of the as-yet unfinished electoral boundary "revolution" in Canada's provinces.

Finally, the right-most column of Table 9.1 shows interprovincial differences in the tolerable range adopted by each province for deviations in constituency population size around the mean for all ridings in the province. This indicates how seriously these jurisdictions value the equality of voting power of their citizens. Where there are large variations in constituency size, voters in different ridings will cast votes that differ commensurately in their power or decisiveness (see Eagles 1991, for a general discussion). On the other hand, constituencies of equal size result in citizens casting ballots that are of equal weight (hence the phrase, "one person, one vote, one value"). As this column shows, there is considerable range on this dimension across the provinces, with Nova Scotia and Province Edward Island failing altogether to specify a range. Other provinces adopt either +/−10% or +/−25% (the federal allowance) as acceptable ranges for variation in constituency size, but all allow for exceptions that justify larger deviations. These variations raise the more general question of the role of commissions in balancing equality with other considerations in the boundary adjustment process. This is the subject of the next section.

Evolving Principles for Electoral Boundary Determination

Boundary commissions, however they are constituted, confront a challenging exercise of balancing a host of broad, complex, and often contradictory districting principles in the design of an electoral map. Choices among these embody and reflect the particular values and political ideals and the geographic and demographic reality of the society they serve. Figure 9.1 provides a list of some of the most important districting *desiderata* as they have emerged in the experience of a number of Anglo-American jurisdictions. Among these contending districting principles, two—population equality and community of interest—have enjoyed particular prominence in the boundary adjustment practices of Canada and elsewhere, and for this reason they appear under "primary" considerations in Figure 9.1.

Reflecting the British tradition of representing communities (counties and burghs) rather than voters in the House of Commons, one foundational districting principle contends that—insofar as possible—district boundaries should define natural communities that share important sociological, demographic, or political characteristics. Such a commonality of interest enhances the accountability and representation process since it makes it easier for an elected representative to determine—and presumably act upon to promote—a common (or at least a majority) political perspective of his or her constituents.

Figure 9.1: Principles for designing good electoral districts

Primary	Secondary
"Community of interest"	Geographic contiguity
Population/Electoral equality	Geographic compactness
	"Manageable geographic size"
	Preservation of political boundaries associated with other jurisdictions
	Continuity with past boundaries

Source: Adapted from Butler and Cain 1992

By the same token, the vitality of political life within an electoral district that comprises a community (or communities) of interest could be expected to be greater than one in which residents shared little in common. For these reasons, then, good electoral districts were ones that respected natural boundaries and that grouped together residents who shared as many characteristics in common as possible.

Over time, as democratic practices and values became more entrenched, concern for the formal political equality of voters grew in significance. Of interest here were differences in the relative power of voters who resided in districts of varying population size, since the weight of a single citizen's vote increases in inverse proportion to the population size of the district. Discrepancies in the weight of votes were felt to violate the formal political equality values at the heart of democracy, and as a result, traditional districting practices based on "community of interest" have increasingly given way to an emphasis on the population or electoral equality of districts. The leader in this development has been the US, where a series of court cases in the 1960s struck down districting schemes that deviated from equal population size. Taken collectively, these court decisions constituted a "reapportionment revolution" that to this day makes it impossible to deviate even slightly from an exact standard of population equality in American electoral maps (Butler and Cain 1992).

Accordingly, the second aspect of the revolution in electoral boundary determination in Canada's provinces as identified by Ken Carty (1985, 285) was "a measurable change in the direction of greater equality" in provincial electoral maps (see also Pasis 1990, 251). This trend notwithstanding, Canadian electoral cartographers have conventionally been more tolerant of districts of highly unequal population than their counterparts in many other countries. As mentioned earlier, the federal statute in Canada gives boundary commissioners broad latitude to accommodate historical factors or communities of interest in electoral maps. They are required to define districts that "as close as reasonably possible, correspond to the electoral quota for the province," but are given a tolerance of +/−25% of the average district population size for their province in doing so. Additionally, in extraordinary cases, boundary commissions can recommend even larger deviations.

With the introduction of the Charter of Rights and Freedoms and its guarantees of the political equality of citizens in the mid-1980s, concerns were widely expressed about the constitutionality of districts that were far below or above average population sizes. To date, however, relatively few electoral maps have been challenged before the courts. Moreover, such litigation as has gone forward to the Supreme Courts has allayed fears that Canada would enter a "reapportionment revolution" similar to that which swept the United States and eliminated population differentials in the size of congressional districts within states. Madame Justice (as she was then) Beverly McLachlin made it clear when writing the Supreme Court's majority decision in the *Carter* (1991) reference case that Canadians were assured only of "relative parity of voting power." Rather than follow the American example of strict equality in voter populations, she made it clear that the Charter guaranteed not equal but rather "effective representation." According to McLachlin, in addition to population equality, the effectiveness of representation embodied in electoral maps would be evaluated according to geographic factors, community history, community interest, and minority representation. This list of considerations, she continued, "was not closed" (*Reference re Provincial Electoral Boundaries* 1991).

While community of interest may have lost some ground to equality claims in modern electoral boundary adjustment, there has simultaneously been an escalation in the demands of some social groups for explicit consideration as particular "communities of interest." During the 1990s round of redistricting in the United States, for example, attempts were made to redress past injustices done to racial minorities. Accordingly, where racial minorities were sufficiently geographically concentrated and when they were located in areas with identifiable patterns of racial bloc voting (the so-called Gingles test), they were recognized by the definition of "majority-minority" districts (e.g., see Grofman 1998). In some cases, the inclusion of racial criteria in the "affirmative gerrymandering" process produced districts with bizarre and highly non-compact shapes that were challenged and deemed unacceptable by the US Supreme Court. Aside from the provincial electoral map drawn up in Nova Scotia in the 1990s, in which the province's black and Acadian communities each received explicit attention in the boundary adjustment process (see Smith and Landes 1998), there has been little evidence of comparable developments in Canada. However, according to Bernard Grofman, a political scientist who has been very active in the American litigation on these issues, Canada's commitment to recognizing group rights in the Charter and elsewhere makes it very likely that groups will turn to the courts to press their representational claims. "I am also quite confident in predicting that Canada can look forward to a wave of future challenges to boundary distributions on the grounds that they discriminate against particular racial, linguistic, or political groups" (Grofman 1992, 171). An example of this kind of challenge arising in New Brunswick's case will be discussed briefly in the next section of this chapter.

In addition to the two primary factors of "community of interest" and "population equality," Figure 9.1 identifies a host of secondary considerations that have been developed as guidelines in the boundary adjustment process. Two geographic qualities—contiguity and compactness—have featured especially prominently, both as a diagnostic tool useful in identifying potential gerrymanders and as a positive districting virtue in their own rights. With respect to the former, non-contiguous, meandering, or irregularly shaped districts with unnatural looking boundaries have long been taken as an indicator that the boundaries reflect some nefarious purpose (Morrill 1981, 21–22; Altman 1998). More positively, these geographic qualities can serve as proxies for "community of interest"—a concept that is notoriously difficult to objectively define despite its significance to the districting process. Having districts defined in terms of contiguous territory and with compact dimensions maximizes the likelihood that residents of a district will share whatever political interests and values arise from their geographic location. The same can be said for compactness, since sprawling, irregularly defined territories may be less homogeneous in terms of their social, cultural, or economic composition. When compactness and contiguity are maximized, districts are more likely to include populations that share interests in such public goods as clean air and water, among other things (for a discussion of compactness in terms of recent federal maps, see Bélanger and Eagles 2001).

These geographic characteristics are frequently associated with other political implications that are considered in the boundary adjustment process. *Ceteris paribus*, more contiguous, compact, and centrally located territories will be relatively easier for elected politicians to service. Here the underlying concern is that some ridings—because of their sheer geographic expansiveness, the paucity of roads or other means of communication, or their remoteness from the capital or other population centres—may be more difficult to represent than others that are smaller and more centrally located. Reflecting the impress of Canada's unique geography, allowances have traditionally been made for the sprawling, remote, sparsely populated ridings of the country's north (as was evident in Table 9.1). In these settings, the challenges of representation have been considered pressing enough to justify significantly lower district populations. To a lesser extent, similar considerations have been used to justify the traditional practice of over-representing rural areas in legislatures across the country.

Finally, there has developed a tradition in electoral cartography of respecting wherever possible lower-order political boundaries. As a result, we have come to expect that political jurisdictions will "nest" cleanly within larger units of representation. This practice ensures that whatever communities of interest may be defined by municipal, county, or other jurisdictions will be wholly contained as well within the larger political units. Finally, because the practice of representation ultimately hinges on the development of a relationship between politicians and constituents, the boundary adjustment process should disrupt these ties as little as possible by maximizing the continuity of political boundaries. This will minimize the disruptiveness of the process to both politicians and citizens alike, thereby nurturing the interpersonal bonds that are at the centre of the representational relationship.

It should be obvious from this brief review of the principles underlying the construction of election districts that electoral map-making is a contentious, complex, and ultimately deeply political process involving multiple compromises and innumerable value judgments. The relative weight accorded to the various dimensions of the process depends on the values and interests prevalent in society. Maximizing one of these—say, population equality—will likely erode the achievement of others—say, community of interest, continuity, or manageable geographic size. Many of the factors defy easy or objective operationalization. Indeed, one of the seductive aspects of the value of population equality is that this one factor—more than any other—lends itself to objective and precise measurement.[4] Most districting claims are constructed and advanced in the process by political interests when it to their advantage, when they are often met by opposing claims and interests. Reconciling these contentious and contradictory principles in a particular setting is the specific challenge facing any boundary commission. In the next section I consider some of the distinctive features of the province of New Brunswick as regards electoral cartography.

Electoral Boundaries in the New Brunswick Context

New Brunswick's history and geography combine to present a very distinctive setting for electoral mapmaking. To begin, it is a relatively small province—demographically and geographically. There were 729,498 residents counted in the 2001 census (down 1.2% from the 1996 census estimate—all census figures taken from Statistics Canada's online website). Geographically, the province's

73,437 square kilometres are roughly square shaped. Demographically, the province more closely resembles a doughnut, with most of its population found on the perimeter surrounding the relatively sparsely populated wilderness centre of the province. More than 80% of its landmass is covered by forests (Dyck 1996, 167). Over half the population is rural and approximately 40% live in unincorporated rural areas (New Brunswick Department of Environment and Local Government 2001).[5] There are, however, three larger urban concentrations in the province. Of these, Saint John in the southwest has long been the largest city and the industrial centre of the province. Recently, however, Moncton, in the province's southeast, has been the most rapidly growing urban centre. Fredericton is the third largest city and the province's capital. New Brunswickers are generally more rooted in their communities than their fellow Canadians—according to the 2001 Census, fully 67.2% lived in the same home as they had five years ago compared to the national average of 58.1% (placing the province third in this category, behind only Newfoundland and PEI).

Culturally and linguistically, New Brunswick reflects almost exclusively the English–French dualism that has been characteristic of Canada's past. An anglophone majority comprises two-thirds of the province's population and a francophone Acadian minority accounts for most of the remaining third (the 2001 census reported that 66.7% of residents spoke English as their first language and 33.0% spoke French as their first language). Slightly more than half are Catholic. Reflecting centuries-old settlement patterns, the province is linguistically and socio-economically bifurcated by an imaginary diagonal running from the northwest to Moncton in the southeast. Acadian francophones, who are most often Catholic and less affluent, are concentrated north and east of this diagonal, while anglophones, mostly Protestants, who are generally better off, live beneath this hypothetical line. About 2%, or slightly fewer than 17,000, of the province's residents, are classed as aboriginal Canadians and less than 1%—9,420 residents—are visible minorities. Only 3.1% were born abroad (compared to 18.4% for the country as a whole), and only 1.2% of residents were non-citizens in 2001. All of these qualities—the smallness of size and intimacy, the close association of language and territory, and the relatively strong and enduring attachments to one's community—are of potential significance for electoral cartographers.

New Brunswick's long tradition of representative government began with the first election in the province in 1785 (a year after the territory was separated from Nova Scotia by British authorities). While a number of representation regimes have been implemented, since 1791 the primary basis of electoral representation has been the county (see Chapter 13 on the history of democratic reform in New Brunswick). After 1791 the Legislative Assembly consisted of

26 representatives from the 8 (original) counties that were then in existence, and 2 representatives for the city of Saint John. Since that time, the number of counties has increased as the population of the province has grown, to reach the current total of 15. Summarizing the historical background of democratic representation up to the end of World War II, Stewart Hyson (2000, 177) wrote that

> demarcation had traditionally coincided with county lines (as well as with those of the largest city, Saint John); multi-member representation was the rule with each constituency having two or more MLAs in approximation to its population size; new seats were always added to reflect population shifts rather than readjusting the existing seats or using a fixed number of seats; differential treatment of urban areas was adhered to; and heavy emphasis was placed on non-population factors such as territory.

The earliest electoral boundaries in the province, therefore, followed county lines wherever possible. The adoption of multimember districts between 1791 and 1967 largely followed county boundaries, with district magnitudes (DMs) varying from two to five members, roughly in line with differences in population (New Brunswick Representation and Electoral District Boundaries Commission [1992, 25] provides a summary table showing the evolution of seat distributions between 1791–1967). Over this period, electoral boundaries did not frequently change, but rather the allocation of MLAs to each county was periodically changed to reflect population differences. Electors were given as many votes as there were positions on the ballot, with parties supplying pre-marked ballots for those wishing to simply vote the party ticket. This system was criticized on a number of grounds. In part, it was felt that the multimember constituencies were too large, making it difficult for parties with locally concentrated support to win seats (ironically, the current single-member district system is also widely believed to penalize minor parties, albeit through different mechanisms). In part, critics felt that the ballot process was too demanding, unfamiliar, and therefore potentially confusing to voters (Thorburn 1961, 40–41). Accordingly, in 1974 the Representation and Electoral District Boundaries Commission divided each of the multimember electoral districts into 58 separate single-member districts, though they did not utilize a single, province-wide redistribution formula for this purpose (Hyson 2004). These districts remained in place almost two decades—until the Representation and Electoral District Boundaries Commission recommended new boundaries and reduced the size of the legislature from 58 to 55 members in time for the 1995 provincial election.

This map, which remains in place today, has been very well received. In part, the positive reception reflects the map's success in respecting vote equality. With the introduction of the Charter in the 1980s, electoral districts have been scrutinized as never before according to the equality guarantees set out in sections 1 and 15 most explicitly of the Charter. Subsequent judicial interpretation of these Charter guarantees in the context of electoral boundaries has clearly established that there is no absolute right to the kind of rigid vote equality found in the US since the reapportionment revolution of the 1960s (see the analyses in Courtney, MacKinnon, and Smith 1992). Rather, as noted above, the Charter has been interpreted by the Supreme Court to guarantee "effective representation" for all citizens, which suggests a relative not an absolute level of parity in the size of election districts. Although one riding recommended by the Representation and Electoral District Boundaries Commission—Fundy Isles—was 64% smaller than the provincial average in terms of electoral size, Donald Blake's comparison of provincial electoral maps in terms of their success in achieving "fairness" ranked New Brunswick third best in the country (Blake 2001, 11).

It is worth noting, however, that over time demographic changes inevitably erode the level of voter equality achieved by even the fairest of electoral maps. This is the case even in a province such as New Brunswick where intra-provincial geographic mobility and levels of migration from outside the province are—comparatively speaking—low. Evidence of the effect of demographic changes on voter equality since 1995 is shown in Figure 9.2. Whereas in the 1995 election the average deviation in constituency electoral size above or below the provincial mean was only 10.9%, by 2003 this figure had increased by half again to more than 15%. Figure 9.2 gives a graphic indication of the erosion of constituency equality over the past decade by presenting a simple histogram for 1995 and 2003 showing where constituencies fell in terms of the provincial mean. The left-most histogram shows a relatively tight clustering of constituencies near the mean (represented by the peak on the "normal curve" that is superimposed on the histogram), with only one highly negative outlier. While there remains a cluster of ridings that are very close to the provincial mean in terms of size, the distribution of ridings around the mean in 2003 is more dispersed than in 1995. The range of variation has been widened in the interim and the one negative outlier in 1995 (Fundy Isles) has been joined in 2003 by a positive one (Dieppe-Memramcook). This development reflects the population growth of the Moncton area between the two election periods. Clearly, even the best of maps requires periodic revision to ensure effective representation and maintain the relative parity of voting power.

Figure 9.2: Temporal erosion of electoral equality in New Brunswick, 1995–2003

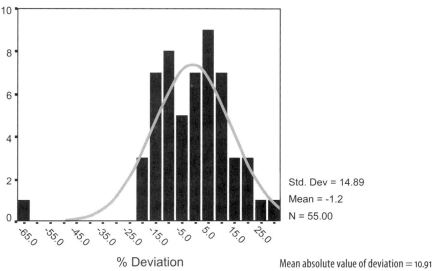

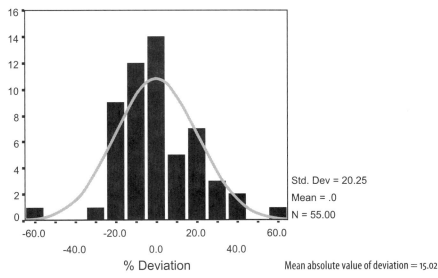

Source: 2003 riding election results retrieved from http://www.gnb.ca/elections/03prov/03recapsheet-e.asp (accessed August 2004); 1995 figures from Hyson 1999, 178–179.

In drawing the most recent map in the early 1990s, the New Brunswick Legislature's Select Committee on Representation and Electoral Boundaries gave the independent boundary commission a two-phase mandate: (1) to make recommendations on the number of electoral districts there should be, the average number of voters to be assigned to each district, the percentage variation from the average to be allowed, and the best approach to ensure aboriginal representation in a manner similar to that used in the state of Maine, and (2) to recommend a new electoral map (Hyson 1999, 183). The committee further instructed the commission to take account of the following factors when drawing the map: "linguistic composition, geography, community of interest, population, and growth patterns" (Hyson 1999, 184). In other words, the commission was charged to sort through the intellectual and political principles associated with boundary adjustment in general terms before turning to the specific challenges of realizing these values in the drawing of a revised electoral map for the province. According to Hyson (1999), however, the political background and experience of all seven commissioners made it impossible for them to separate consideration of the general principles from their particular consequences in terms of specific boundaries.

The commission's work was somewhat simplified by the select committee's removal of the charge to consider forms of aboriginal representation based on the Maine model. Since 1820, that state has guaranteed two representatives of aboriginal peoples, one each for the Penobscot and the Passamaquoddy tribes, to be elected as members of the state legislature. These representatives are not given a vote in assembly proceedings but can participate in the debates and vote on matters in legislative committees. Since they are, however, less than full members of the legislature, and because endorsing this form of participation in mainstream governance might be seen by some to weaken aboriginal claims for broader measures respecting their rights to self-determination, New Brunswick's aboriginal community expressed no interest in this form of representation (New Brunswick Representation and Electoral District Boundaries Commission 1992, 18). It was clear from the submissions to the commission, however, that there was considerable disagreement among First Nations in the province over the question of how any special representational measures that would give this community a voice in the legislative process would be implemented. The 1990s experience makes it clear that tokenism in this respect will be unacceptable. As such, the question of recognizing the special community of interest associated with aboriginal status in the province remains unresolved in the current electoral system. I will turn to a discussion of some of the challenges and options in securing aboriginal representation in the next section of this chapter.

More generally, drawing electoral boundaries in New Brunswick involves balancing all the conflicting and contested values discussed above. There are potentially many communities of interest that might expect to be recognized in the boundary adjustment process, including the province's language, religious, and aboriginal communities. The relatively compact geography of the province coupled with the comparatively wide dispersal of population makes it possible to minimize the problem of sparsely populated but geographically sprawling ridings of the sort found in the northern sections of the provinces west of Quebec. However, as noted in Chapter 8, the large number of residents living in unincorporated rural areas after the abolition of county government in the 1960s adds a distinctive challenge to MLAs since they are often approached by constituents with servicing demands that might otherwise be attended to by local government officials.[6] This fact provides a continuing rationale for the traditional practice of over-representing rural areas in order to compensate for the putatively higher levels of demand for the services of politicians representing these areas (Hyson 1999, 184–185). The boundaries commission estimated that the "ombudsman" role of MLAs in New Brunswick comprised on average between 60% to 80% of their workload (New Brunswick Representation and Electoral District Boundaries Commission 1992, 15). With comparatively small district electorates and a tradition of personalist politics, the representational relationship between politician and voter afforded by the current system is intimate. In the words of Hugh Mellon (2001, 75), "New Brunswickers are a people used to having access to their politicians.... Politicians deemed to have lost touch with the 'folks' back home can be candidates for a rude awakening at election time."

In terms of the process whereby the conflicting and contested value claims are weighed and determined in the creation of an electoral map, the New Brunswick experience in recent decades is quite instructive and different from the experience in other Canadian provinces and at the federal level. We have already seen that the province lags behind other jurisdictions in not having put the revision of the provincial electoral map on a regular timetable. More broadly, however, whereas at the federal level the province's electoral boundaries have been determined in accordance with the Electoral Boundaries Adjustment Act by three-member commissions headed by a provincial judge, the most recent provincial boundary commission was deliberately constructed so as to be more representative of the province's social and political diversity. These different practices reflect profoundly different conceptions of how the legitimacy of the boundary adjustment process—and hence the likelihood that the map that is produced from this process will be widely acceptable to the populace—is best achieved and maintained.

The federal boundary adjustment process is conducted in each province by a judge and two appointees of the Speaker of the House of Commons. These appointments have overwhelmingly been "white, urban males whose occupational training in law, political science, or election administration has signaled a professionalization of the boundary readjustment process" (Courtney 2001, 120). In Courtney's view, this manifestly unrepresentative (in the descriptive sense of representation) quality of boundary commissions is not problematic. Certainly, it appears that three-member federal boundary commissions have worked well and smoothly in drawing federal constituencies that are regarded as legitimate and acceptable in most provinces (though see Eagles and Carty 1999, for evidence that this may not always be the result). It is therefore worth quoting Courtney's argument on this point at length:

> In one sense, to attempt to mirror parts of the larger society in a commission's membership is arguably not what district boundary readjustments are about. They are after all responsible for crafting constituencies in a large and socially mixed country, which suggests that they ought to have the maximum degree of freedom and independence to so. Engaged in a complex endeavour which requires both considerable distance from openly partisan interests and the freedom to conduct their business, commissioners should be able to serve as "transactional representatives" whose authority to act independently of particular social interests derives from the fact that they are both knowledgeable about the subject matter and non-partisan. More than anything, they must have a demonstrated ability to weigh competing representational claims and to resolve them as fairly and as equitably as each particular situation allows. Constructed at the beginning of what will eventually be a long representational process, their principal responsibility is to fulfill their legislative mandate and in so doing to define the "public interest" of the jurisdiction for which they are responsible (Courtney 2001, 120).

In stark contrast to the experience of other provinces, the last two federal electoral maps drawn in New Brunswick have been associated with considerable controversy, both within the boundary commissions themselves and more broadly among citizens, regarding the appropriate representation of the province's sizeable francophone minority. In the 1990s round, the federal commission was unable to reach a consensus on a map. One member, Professor Roger Ouellette, issued a dissenting opinion, charging that the reduction in the number of francophone majority districts from three to two would seriously erode the political representation traditionally accorded to this community. Being only one of the three commissioners, however, Professor Ouellette was unable to prevent the implementation of the map agreed to by the other two members. Reflecting these underlying issues, once the map was promulgated, the Société des Acadiens et Acadiennes du Nouveau-Brunswick launched a complaint with the Official Languages Commissioner in Ottawa and challenged the boundaries in court (Courtney 2001, 141-42). In addition, although the most recent federal boundary commission report was based on an agreement on the "broad picture" of the proposed districts, it also included a minority opinion from one member based on a "difference of opinion only on the boundaries of the three southern electoral districts" (Elections Canada 2003).

By contrast, in the highly successful provincial boundary adjustment exercise during the early-to-mid-1990s, the commission was led by two co-chairs who were both judges of the Court of Queen's Bench, one from the (anglophone) south of the province and the other from the (francophone) north. In addition, five commissioners were individuals drawn from different regions, both genders, and different but clearly identified partisan backgrounds (two were known Liberals, with one each coming from the Conservative, NDP, and CoR parties). Attention was drawn to the balanced composition of the commission in its report and at public hearings (New Brunswick Representation and Electoral District Boundaries Commission 1992, 9; Hyson 1999, 181–82). The representative nature of its membership did not appear to compromise its independence and willingness to compromise in the interests of drawing a fair map. As Stewart Hyson has noted, "much of the success is ... attributable to the professionalism and impartiality shown by the commissioners. There was no evidence of partisanship on the part of the commissioners to gerrymander the results" (1999, 193). Perhaps the practical political backgrounds of the commissioners that Hyson describes also contributed to a sense of pragmatism in the process that was helpful in identifying compromises where they were necessary.

The New Brunswick experience suggests that one model or approach to the constitution of electoral boundary commissions may not be suitable for all the varied situations encountered across Canada. Though defending the federal practice of small, professional, and non-representative commissions, Courtney (2001, 120–121) also concedes that there is no "necessary contradiction" between balanced professionalism in a commission's performance and its diverse social or political composition. In New Brunswick's case, the long tradition of accommodating linguistic and cultural diversity through inclusion and negotiation (see Aunger 1981) suggests that a larger, more representative boundary commission than the three-person federal model may be best able to come up with an electoral map that enjoys broad legitimacy among the province's residents.

Drawing Boundaries in a Reformed New Brunswick Electoral System

To this point our discussion has been centred on the principles and processes of electoral boundary adjustment in single-member district systems. For several reasons, boundary determination achieves its greatest importance in these settings. First, and most obviously, there are simply more boundaries to draw in single-member systems, and hence the scale of the cartographic undertaking is larger than in multimember settings. Second, in a single-member district system demographic changes cannot be accommodated by simply adding members to or removing members from electoral units; rather, the equality of the vote can only be maintained through periodic boundary adjustments. As a result, in order to preserve relative vote equality, boundary issues arise more frequently in single-member district systems. Finally, and most importantly, elections in single-member districts confer a representational monopoly for a period of time to the winner of the seat. As such, it is important for quality representation that the district be as meaningful—sociologically and/or politically—and as geographically manageable as possible. Too heterogeneous a district would make it extremely difficult for a single elected member to act on behalf of her/his constituents in the legislative process, whereas a heterogeneous multimember district could have its various component communities effectively represented by different politicians. In general, then, the significance attached to the boundary adjustment process—and the importance of the constraints represented by the various principles of boundary determination we have discussed in the second section of this chapter—tends to decrease across different electoral systems in rough proportion to increases in district magnitude. Obviously, these considerations disappear entirely in pure list PR systems such as those in Israel and the Netherlands, where the DM equals the total size of the legislature. The important exception here is the principle of voter equality. Regardless of what the DM for constituencies is, in the post-Charter era the ratio of population to elected politicians in these constituencies cannot vary widely across electoral districts.

Although the importance of traditional districting principles diminishes in relation to increases in DM, the general principle of constructing districts that are as sociologically and/or politically meaningful as possible remains a sensible goal for mapmakers when defining multimember districts. There is, however, no single best solution to identifying the boundaries of multimember districts,

Figure 9.3: County boundaries in New Brunswick

Source: http://new-brunswick.net/new-brunswick/maps/nb/nbmap.html

and there are several options for this that are immediately apparent. However, some general comments may be helpful in framing some of the underlying boundary issues. Most fundamentally, electoral cartographers may proceed to draw multimember districts according to the traditional districting principles, or they might decide that there are grounds for adopting the boundaries of sub-units already in existence. Obviously, drawing special electoral districts has the considerable advantage of ensuring an optimal balancing of population, community of interest, geography, and other factors. Over time, new and larger districts would establish themselves in the hearts and minds of citizens, further contributing to their legitimacy.

The main alternative to drawing new electoral boundaries for multi-member districts would be to adopt existing boundaries of other—possibly non-electoral—units for the purposes of political representation. In this case, the attractiveness of any particular set of boundaries depends on the degree to which they define or embody meaningful communities of identity or interest. A brief discussion of several specific options of this sort in the New Brunswick case may be useful in illustrating this more general principle. One potentially attractive choice in that setting might be to return to the long tradition of using the 15 counties of the province as units of electoral representation, a choice that would necessitate varying DMs to account for population differentials among counties (see Figure 9.3) and periodically redistributing MLAs across counties to reflect demographic changes. While the county level of government was abolished in the 1970s, these units are still widely recognized by the public and their visibility and popular resonance would enhance their legitimacy as units of political representation. However, some of the counties have very small populations and therefore the DMs of these counties would be correspondingly low. In fact, because it was home to fewer than 12,000 residents in 2001, Queens County would likely either be combined with Sunbury County (2001 population: 25,776) or remain a single-member district in the reformed system. In this situation (since the proportionality profile of an electoral system is a direct function of its DM), the gains in proportionality resulting from adopting counties as multimember electoral districts would remain modest unless the politically unpalatable step of increasing the size of the legislature were to be contemplated as part of the reform package.

An alternative way to generate multimember districts would be to distribute seats to pre-existing regional units that have been defined for some purpose, such as the eight regional health districts shown in Figure 9.4. In terms of program expenditure, health care is the single largest and most rapidly growing responsibility of the provincial government, accounting for 34.7% of total spending in the 2003–2004 provincial budget (New Brunswick. Department

ELECTORAL REFORM AND ELECTORAL BOUNDARIES IN NEW BRUNSWICK

Figure 9.4: Regional Health Authority boundaries in New Brunswick
Source: Statistics Canada, http://www.statcan.ca/english/freepub/82-221-XIE/01103/images/jpg/nb.jpg

of Finance 2002). The delivery of quality health care consistently ranks among the highest and most important policy concerns among Canadians. Therefore, the boundaries of these functional units, though perhaps not as grounded as other alternatives in sociological communities of interest as some others under consideration, would embody the considerable political community of interest residents share in enjoying quality health care. With a smaller number of larger (in geographic size and DM) sub-provincial electoral units, the gains in proportionality for the system as a whole would be greater than they would be under the county option.

Still another option might be to adopt the 10 federal electoral districts shown in Figure 9.5 to define multimember provincial constituencies. The federal boundary commissioners periodically undertake to balance population equality with other considerations in the constitution of these units, and to the extent that they are successful, the districts they design will be meaningful for citizens. Beginning with the provincial election in 1999, Ontario has simply adopted the federal districts for use in provincial elections. There the relatively large number of federal seats (after the 2003 provincial election, Ontario had 103 provincial MLAs) makes such an option more feasible. Moreover, there was no increase in proportionality associated with Ontario's reform. In New Brunswick it would be necessary to assign multiple seats to the federal ridings for provincial purposes, but since the federal units are drawn to respect population equality, it might be feasible to have all provincial multimember districts adopt a constant district magnitude. However, whereas adopting counties or health authority districts as ridings would result in relatively stable and unchanging boundaries, federal riding boundaries will themselves be adjusted every ten years.

Finally, multimember district boundaries might be determined by aggregating existing contiguous provincial electoral districts (see Figure 9.6), with the internal boundaries among component ridings simply erased. In all of these procedures, communities of interest defined by (in the case of health authorities) or contained within the pre-existing boundaries would be respected in the new multimember districts.

With the increasing popularity worldwide of mixed-member proportional (MMP) representation systems, a potentially attractive option for New Brunswick might be a combination of single-member and proportional representation systems. MMP systems vary in terms of the number of seats assigned in single-member districts by the plurality rule as opposed to the number assigned to overlapping multimember districts to be assigned in proportion to a party's vote (see Shugart and Wattenberg 2001). For example, in the (original) German model, the two systems allocate the same number of seats, while in

ELECTORAL REFORM AND ELECTORAL BOUNDARIES IN NEW BRUNSWICK

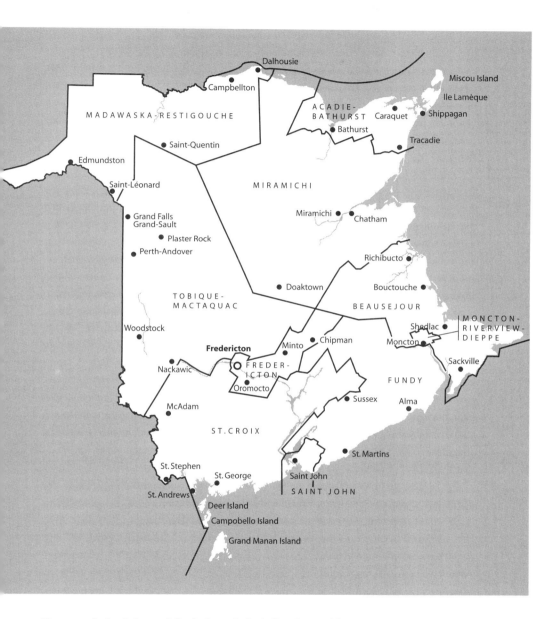

Figure 9.5: Federal electoral district boundaries in New Brunswick, 2004
Source: http://www.elections.ca/cir/rid/13901_e.html <TBC>

the New Zealand case following its 1996 electoral reform, 69 of its 120 MPs (57.5%) have been elected from single-member districts, while 51 (42.5%) were added from national party lists to ensure that the party composition of the legislature reflected the shares of the vote received by each party at the election (I will discuss New Zealand's Maori seats shortly). Obviously, in such systems voters can readily identify a legislator who is their constituency servant for ombudsman-like duties, but they are also able to approach legislators drawn from the list should they choose.

These hybrid systems can claim therefore to embody the strengths of both the single-member and the proportional electoral systems. The boundaries for the single-member districts must, of course, be periodically adjusted to account for demographic changes, ideally by independent commissions as discussed earlier. The assignment of top-up members from party lists can take place at the province-wide level, in which case no sub-provincial districting would be required beyond that needed to define the single-member districts. This would be comparable to the system in New Zealand, which allocates these seats from a single 59-member national constituency. Alternately, the party lists might be drawn up at a regional level, with additional members drawn from these lists as needed to balance the composition of the total legislature, as in Germany where the party lists are developed for each *Land* or province in the federal system. In New Brunswick, if a decision were made to allocate the proportional seats at a sub-provincial level, the most obvious choices regarding the possible sources of boundaries for these units are the same as for a full-blown PR electoral system as discussed above, that is, the counties, health authority (or some other functionally defined) districts, the federal ridings, or aggregations of existing provincial electoral districts.

A vexing problem facing many jurisdictions in Canada and elsewhere concerns the under-representation of aboriginal or First Nations peoples in legislatures. The problem is exacerbated in New Brunswick's single-member electoral systems by the relatively small number and the relatively wide geographic dispersal of First Nations residents. In this case, "affirmatively gerrymandering" a single electoral district that would have a majority of First Nations residents would be extremely difficult and non-compact. Similarly, the province's proposal in the 1990s to create a special aboriginal seat (or two) along the lines of Maine's model was, as we have seen, unacceptable. Similar conundrums arising elsewhere in Anglo-American systems have encouraged research and experimentation with systems of dedicated seats set aside to enhance the presence of aboriginals in legislatures (Magallanes 2003). One of the most successful and long-lived of these attempts has been the experience of the New Zealand Maori, who after 1867 were given (initially on a temporary

Figure 9.6: Provincial electoral district boundaries in New Brunswick, 2004

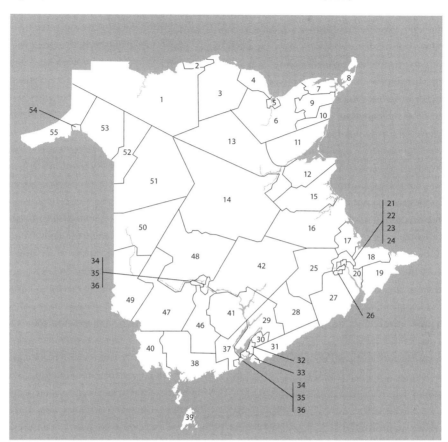

1 Restigouche West
2 Campbellton
3 Dalhousie-Restigouche East
4 Nigadoo-Chaleur
5 Bathurst
6 Nepisiguit
7 Caraquet
8 Lamèque-Shippagan-Miscou
9 Centre-Péninsule
10 Tracadie-Sheila
11 Miramichi Bay
12 Miramichi-Bay du Vin
13 Miramichi Centre
14 Southwest Miramichi
15 Rogersville-Kouchibouguac
16 Kent
17 Kent South
18 Shediac-Cap-Pelé
19 Tantramar
20 Dieppe-Memramcook
21 Moncton East
22 Moncton South
23 Moncton North
24 Moncton Crescent
25 Petitcodiac
26 Riverview
27 Albert
28 Kings East
29 Hampton-Belleisle
30 Kennebecasis
31 Saint John-Fundy
32 Saint John-Kings
33 Saint John Champlain
34 Saint John Harbour
35 Saint John Portland
36 Saint John Lancaster
37 Grand Bay-Westfield
38 Charlotte
39 Fundy Isles
40 Western Charlotte
41 Oromocto-Gagetown
42 Grand Lake
43 Fredericton North
44 Fredericton-Fort Nashwaak
45 Fredericton South
46 New Maryland
47 York
48 Mactaquac
49 Woodstock
50 Carleton
51 Victoria-Tobique
52 Grand Falls Region
53 Madawaska-la-Vallée
54 Edmundston
55 Madawaska-les-Lacs

basis) five seats in the country's legislature. These seats eventually were reduced in number by one, but were made permanent. After 1976, Maori were given the option of enrolling either in the regular constituency electorate or on the Maori rolls. In 1990, the number of Maori seats in the legislature was made proportional to the number of registrants on the Maori rolls. As a result of these initiatives, and in part as a function of the introduction of MMP in 1996, there were 18 Maori MPs in the New Zealand legislature—seven of whom are from the dedicated seats—a figure almost exactly proportional to their share of the general population.

The New Zealand experience has largely been viewed as a successful instance of integrating an indigenous community into the system of parliamentary representation. Yet the system has not been without its critics. Some have argued that the system was ineffective in protecting Maori interests, while others have noted that the unwieldy size of the Maori electorates has made them difficult for their elected representatives to service. Some contend that Maori MPs took the blame for all the problems of the system, and still others complained that having special set-aside seats implied that "regular" MPs were responsive only to non-Maori voters. Despite these criticisms, however, the most recent (2001) review of the New Zealand system of representation for the Maori could not come up with any recommendation for change (Magallanes 2003, 7–8).

Emulating this experience in New Brunswick would be difficult, however, since the province's aboriginal community is considerably smaller as a proportion of the overall population than the Maori in New Zealand. Indeed, the aboriginal community is so small as to qualify it for only one to two seats unless permitted to deviate considerably below the average size of provincial electorates. Even if two districts were "set aside" as "majority aboriginal" in nature, they would be even more open to criticism along all the lines that have been advanced in the New Zealand case. Moreover, it is far from clear that the province's First Nations would accept these measures, since they have in the past rejected electoral reforms on the grounds that accepting these might compromise their claims for more sweeping measures of self-determination. Therefore, although such seats might have some symbolic value, it is difficult to see such a concession as contributing significantly to the quality or effectiveness of aboriginal representation in the province's legislature.

Conclusion

This chapter has focused on the theory and practice of determining electoral boundaries in New Brunswick and elsewhere. As Gail Campbell's chapter in this volume outlines, New Brunswick has experienced a variety of representational systems over the course of its history with parliamentary government. The current single-member plurality electoral system, comprised of 55 constituencies, is relatively new, having been in place only since 1974. The SMP system has its supporters and detractors in New Brunswick and elsewhere. The province's long and generally successful experience of multimember districts should allay some concerns that such systems would be regarded as foreign or unnatural. Indeed, a carefully implemented proportional or mixed electoral system might well be simpler in practice for voters and politicians than the version of multimember representation practised for generations in New Brunswick.

In many aspects of the processes of electoral boundary adjustment, the province has lagged behind in the revolution witnessed in recent decades in other provinces, most particularly in not having put the cycle of refreshing the electoral map on a regular basis. The province's recent experience with independent boundary commissions differs significantly from the federal model—and those adopted in many provinces—in that New Brunswick's boundary commission is at once both larger and more explicitly representative of the province's main features of social and political diversity. In light of the more positive public reaction to the provincial as opposed to the federal electoral map, it is tempting to suggest that having the boundary commission play a more political role in brokering compromise in the boundary adjustment process is better suited to the province's quintessentially accommodative political traditions and culture.

In terms of the principles of electoral districting, New Brunswick's experience appears to fall closely into line with that of other provinces in that equality considerations have emerged more centrally in the complex balancing of rival representational values as a result of the Charter's equality guarantees. As in most other jurisdictions, voter equality as a representational value was conditioned by a variety of other districting considerations, including respect for communities of interest, history, geographic size and manageability, and the like. Although the boundary commission produced a map that has been judged to be one of the fairest in terms of its achievement of relative vote equality, the fact that it has not been readjusted to account for population shifts since the mid-1990s means that this initial achievement has been eroded. The relatively small size of the current electoral districts—on average with only just over 10,000 electors—means that New Brunswickers enjoy a highly intimate representational relationship with their politicians, one that has led them to expect personally attentive and accessible politicians.

As New Brunswick and other jurisdictions contemplate electoral reforms embracing a stronger commitment to proportionality in legislative representation, their prior experience with determining boundaries for single-member districts will serve the province well. Boundary determination in mixed-member or multimember districts follows the same basic principles as it does in the case of single-member districts, only the significance of these values as constraints on boundary commissions tends to diminish in line with increases in the district magnitude of electoral units. In other words, the more members elected from the units (and commensurately the larger the geographic size), the more the various districting principles—with the exception of relative vote equality—can be relaxed. A range of alternatives can be imagined for determining the boundaries of multimember districts necessary for implementing fully proportional or perhaps mixed-member systems. Boundaries for such units could be generated from those of other pre-existing units, such as counties or regional health districts, or they could be determined specifically for this purpose, either by amalgamating pre-existing units or by drawing new boundaries using an independent boundary commission struck specifically for this purpose. In mixed-member systems, of course, it will be necessary to draw—and periodically revise—the boundaries of the single-member components of the hybrid electoral system. If this system is adopted, the boundary adjustment process ought to be put on a regular timetable, the commissioners' credentials and appointment process publicized and made regular, and steps taken to ensure that the maps recommended by the independent commission will not be subject to subsequent amendment by politicians.

While there is considerable interest in measures designed to enhance the place of aboriginal Canadians in the legislature (evident in the province's recent boundary adjustment experiences), the relatively small proportion of residents in New Brunswick who fall into this category makes it difficult to increase the numbers of aboriginal legislators without running afoul of commitments to vote equality for all citizens. It may be possible to affirmatively gerrymander the map to create majority (or perhaps near majority) aboriginal districts, or perhaps special seats could be set aside—with substantially smaller population sizes than other constituencies. Whether the public interest in having our First Nations more thoroughly represented in the legislative process is sufficient to counter-weigh the equality claims on the part of other communities of interest in the province is something that would in all likelihood be determined by judges in a Charter-based challenge to such recommendations. While anticipating the outcome of such an uncertain process is perilous, the Canadian Supreme Court has certainly made it abundantly clear that it will not adhere slavishly to arithmetic notions of vote equality when it hears electoral boundaries cases. In general, this judicial latitude or restraint ought to embolden electoral cartographers to experiment with innovative electoral reforms motivated by a desire to strengthen and invigorate the representational process.

Notes

1. In the US, for example, Andrew Gelman and Gary King (1994, 541) have written, "In total, legislative redistricting is one of the most conflictual forms of regular politics ... short of violence."
2. A gerrymander occurs when a geographic area is divided into voting districts so as to give unfair advantage to one party in elections. The term derives from an electoral map of Massachusetts drawn in 1812 on behalf of then-governor Elbridge Gerry, in which his opponents were concentrated in a contorted district that resembled a salamander.
3. In this context, "independent" does not mean non-partisan or apolitical, but rather that the members of the boundary commission will not themselves be directly effected by the particular electoral boundaries they determine, and that their deliberations will not be subject to political interference.
4. Though even here there are debates about whether total population (including non-citizens and under-age citizens) or electors should form the basis of population counts. For a general discussion of this controversy, see Eagles (1991).
5. Richard and Susan Tindal, citing a 1977 study by Harley d'Entremont and Patrick Robardet, suggest that the proportion living in non-incorporated rural areas is 30%. See Tindal and Tindal (1995, 114).
6. Reinforcing the workload of MLAs is the fact that New Brunswick has the highest number of provincial government employees per capita in Canada and the lowest proportion of municipal employees per capita (Dyck 1996, 170).

References

Altman, Michah. 1998. "Modeling the Effect of Mandatory District Compactness on Partisan Gerrymandering." *Political Geography* 17:998–1012.

Archer, Keith. 1993. "Conflict and Confusion in Drawing Constituency Boundaries: The Case of Alberta." *Canadian Public Policy* 19(June): 177–193.

Aunger, Edmund. 1981. *In Search of Political Stability: A Comparative Study of New Brunswick and Northern Ireland*. Montreal: McGill-Queen's University Press.

Bélanger, Paul, and Munroe Eagles. 2001. "The Compactness of Federal Electoral Districts in Canada in the 1980s and 1990s: An Exploratory Analysis." *The Canadian Geographer / Le Géographe canadien* 45(4):450–460.

Blake, Donald E. 2001. "Electoral Democracy in the Provinces." *Choices* 7(2):1–37.

Butler, David, and Bruce Cain. 1992. *Congressional Redistricting: Comparative and Theoretical Perspectives*. New York: Macmillan.

Carty, R. Kenneth. 1985. "The Electoral Boundary Revolution in Canada." *American Review of Canadian Studies* 15(3):273–287.

Courtney, John. 2001. *Commissioned Ridings: Designing Canada's Electoral Districts*. Montreal and Kingston: McGill-Queen's University Press.

Courtney, John, Peter MacKinnon, and David E. Smith, eds. 1992. *Drawing Boundaries: Legislatures, Courts, and Electoral Values*. Saskatoon: Fifth House.

Dyck, Rand. 1996. *Provincial Politics in Canada: Towards the Turn of the Century*. Scarborough, ON: Prentice-Hall.

Eagles, Munroe. 1991. "Enhancing Relative Vote Equality in Canada: The Role of Electors in Boundary Adjustment." In *Drawing the Map: Equality and Efficacy of the Vote in Canadian Electoral Boundary Reform*, ed. David Small, 175–200. Research Studies of the Royal Commission on Electoral Reform and Party Financing, volume 11. Toronto and Ottawa: Dundurn Press.

Eagles, Munroe, and R. Kenneth Carty. 1999. "MPs and Electoral Redistribution Controversies in Canada, 1993–96." *Journal of Legislative Studies* 5(2): 74–95.

Eagles, Munroe, Richard S. Katz, and David Mark. 1999. "GIS and Redistricting: Emergent Technologies, Social Geography, and Political Sensibilities." *Social Science Computer Review* 17(1):5–9.

—. 2000. "Controversies in Political Redistricting: GIS, Geography and Society." *Political Geography* 19(2):135–260.

Elections Canada. 2003. *Federal Representation 2004: New Brunswick—Report and Further Comments from Commission Member John P. Barry, QC*. Retrieved December 2003 from www.elections.ca/scripts/fedrep/newbruns/report.

Gelman, Andrew, and Gary King. 1994. "Enhancing Democracy Through Legislative Redistricting." *American Political Science Review* 88(3): 541–559.

Grofman, Bernard. 1992. "What Happens After One Person—One Vote? Implications of the United States Experience for Canada." In *Drawing Boundaries: Legislatures, Courts, and Electoral Values*, ed. John Courtney, Peter MacKinnon, and David E. Smith, 156–178. Saskatoon: Fifth House.

—, ed. 1998. *Race and Redistricting in the 1990s*. New York: Agathon Press.

Hyson, Stewart. 2000. "Electoral Boundary Redistribution by Independent Commission in New Brunswick, 1990–1994," *Canadian Public Administration* 42(3):174–197.

—. 2004. Presentation to a Roundtable Discussion. New Brunswick Commission on Legislative Democracy, University of New Brunswick, Fredericton, NB, 28 April.

Magallenes, Catherine Iorns. 2003. "Dedicated Parliamentary Seats for Indigenous Peoples: Political Representation as an Element of Indigenous Self-Determination," *E Law: Murdoch University Electronic Journal of Law* 10(4):1–28.

Mellon, Hugh. 2001. "The Challenge of New Brunswick Politics." In *The Provincial State in Canada: Politics in the Provinces and Territories*, ed. Keith Brownsey and Michael Howlett, 75–109. Peterborough, ON: Broadview Press.

Monmonier, Mark. 2001. *Bushmanders and Bullwinkles: How Politicians Manipulate Electronic Maps and Census Data to Win Elections*. Chicago: University of Chicago Press.

Morrill, Richard. 1981. *Political Redistricting and Geographic Theory*. Washington, DC: Association of American Geographers.

New Brunswick. Department of Environment and Local Government. 2001. *Opportunities for Improving Local Governance in New Brunswick: Report of the Municipalities Act Review Panel*. Retrieved August 2004 from www.gnb.ca/0009/0005-e.asp.

New Brunswick Department of Finance. 2002. *Budget 2003–2004*. Retrieved December 2004 from www.gnb.ca/0024/index-e.asp.

New Brunswick Representation and Electoral District Boundaries Commission. 1992. *Towards a New Electoral Map for New Brunswick: First Report*. July.

Pasis, Harvey E. 1990. "Electoral Distribution in the Canadian Provincial Legislatures." In *Representation and Electoral Systems: Canadian Perspectives*, ed. J. Paul Johnston and Harvey E. Pasis, 251–252. Scarborough, ON: Prentice-Hall.

Peck, Don, and Caitlin Casey. 2004. "Packing, Cracking, and Kidnapping: The Science of Gerrymandering." *The Atlantic Monthly* (January/February): 50–51.

Reference re Provincial Electoral Boundaries. 1991. 2 SCR 158. (Commonly referred to as the *Carter* reference of the Supreme Court of Canada.)

Richey, Warren. 2003. "Rigging Election Boundaries: When Does it Go Too Far?" *The Christian Science Monitor* (December 10): 2.

Shugart, Matthew Soberg, and Martin P. Wattenberg, eds. 2001. *Mixed-Member Electoral Systems: The Best of Both Worlds?* New York: Oxford University Press.

Smith, Jennifer, and Ronald G. Landes. 1998. "Entitlement versus Variance Models in the Determination of Canadian Electoral Boundaries." *International Journal of Canadian Studies* 17(1): 19–36.

Statistics Canada. 2001. *2001 Census Highlight Tables*. Retrieved August 2004 from www12.statcan.ca/english/census01/products/highlight/index.cfm.

Thorburn, Hugh G. 1961. *Politics in New Brunswick*. Toronto: University of Toronto Press.

Tindal, C. Richard, and Susan Nobes Tindal. 1995. *Local Government in Canada*. 4th ed. Toronto: McGraw-Hill Ryerson.

Toobin, Jeffrey. 2003. "The Great Election Grab: When Does Gerrymandering Become a Threat to Democracy?" *The New Yorker* (December 8): 63–80.

CHAPTER TEN

Fixed-Date Elections under the Canadian Parliamentary System

DON DESSERUD

"People like to know when the elections are going to be."
Premier Bernard Lord, May 2003

Introduction: Manipulating Election Calls

UNDER THE CANADIAN parliamentary system, governments can time their election calls to coincide with improvements in economic performance, favourable opinion polls, the completion of capital projects, the disarray of opposition parties, or practically anything that strikes their fancy. Critics complain that this gives the party in power an unfair advantage. In the words of one intervener to the 1991 Royal Commission on Electoral Reform and Party Financing:

> I believe only the systems based on the British parliamentary system have the situation now where the government can be opportunistic in that they can call an election when things look good. And they can manipulate the system, so they can basically do all sorts of unpopular things, have a cooling-off period, and then call an election.
> (Royal Commission 1991, 4:110)

The solution, according to many, is to hold elections on fixed dates after specific periods, an idea that appears to be enjoying growing support. In 2000, the Institute for Research on Public Policy (IRPP) found that 54% of respondents supported fixing election dates (Howe and Northrup 2000). Four years later, and just a week before Prime Minister Paul Martin called the 2004 Canadian general elections, the Environics Research group found that 81% of Canadians preferred that elections be held at specific and fixed times instead of "whenever the party in power wants to call it."[1]

With such popular support, it is not surprising to find that politicians from both the left and the right and at both the federal and provincial levels have jumped on the fixed-date election bandwagon (Nystrom 2000; New Brunswick Votes 2003; Progressive Conservative Party of New Brunswick 2003; Office of the Premier of Ontario 2004; Mackie 2004; Seskus and Baxter 2004; Taft 2004). Nor is support for fixed-date elections confined to those most often frustrated by the unpredictability of election calls. At the provincial level anyway, even governments—the very people supposedly advantaged by the present system—have come onside: Ontario's Liberal government has introduced legislation to fix election dates in that province; the province of British Columbia already has such legislation; and, at the time of writing, the governments of New Brunswick, Nova Scotia, and Newfoundland are all considering the option.

Surprisingly enough, little hard evidence exists that strategic election calls really do help the party in power (Balke 1990; Smith 1996 and 2003; Roper and Andrews 2002; Strøm and Swindle 2002; Blais et al. 2004a). However favourable the election conditions at the moment the election is called, party fortunes can and do change over the course of a campaign (Jenkins 2002). Even so, surely few governments purposely call elections for dates they know to be disadvantageous. It is easy, then, to believe that the ability to call an election at a date of the government's choosing constitutes some advantage for the party in power. If so, then the ability of our political system to renew itself may be undermined by re-electing governments that might otherwise be defeated. Furthermore, continually frustrating the ambitions of opposition parties must have a detrimental effect on their ability to attract candidates, raise funds, and generally be effective in their role.

The solution, then, seems to be to fix election dates so that governments can no longer call elections whenever they like. However, fixing election dates under Canada's system of parliamentary government poses serious challenges. In fact, without a radical and probably unpalatable transformation of the Canadian parliamentary system, entrenching fixed-election dates so that no government could alter or manipulate them is not possible. As the Lortie Commission made clear, a government could always "take steps to engineer its own defeat in the House of Commons if it judged that the timing of an election would serve its interests" (Royal Commission 1991, 2:78). Furthermore, reforms affecting how elections are called may well undermine the constitutional principles upon which our parliamentary system is based, and possibly create an unworkable hybrid. By solving one problem, fixed-date elections may well cause other, perhaps more serious ones.[2]

This chapter analyzes the possibility and practicality of fixing election dates under the Canadian parliamentary system.[3] It discusses, first, some of the advantages that might come from fixing election dates. It then argues that constitutional and practical problems render such advantages moot. Finally, the paper concludes with an analysis of why fixed-date election reform has become such a popular topic, and suggests that there may be other, more practical and realizable means of reforming the current system to address the problems fixed-date elections are thought to resolve.

Fixed Dates and Fixed Terms

Fixed-date elections are those in which the election date for government and representatives is established by law, usually through a constitutional provision. The best-known example, for Canadians at any rate, is probably the date in November fixed for the election of the president and Congress in the United States. Fixing an election date means more than simply placing a limit on how long a government can be in office before it must face its electorate; most systems without fixed-date elections, including the Canadian parliamentary system, already have such limits.[4] Rather, fixing election dates means also fixing the term of office, so that governments and assemblies can neither choose nor be forced to face an election except at the fixed date. Such a system is quite different from the British parliamentary system, also known as the Westminster model, which provides the basis for most systems of government in the British Commonwealth, including that of Canada.[5] The key difference between the two lies in how they attempt to prevent political power, particularly power in the hands of the executive, from being abused. As Aucoin, Smith, and Dinsdale (2003, 19) explain,

> In the Western world, there are only two democratic devices used to restrain the power of the executive: the American congressional system of checks and balances and the British system of responsible government. The former separates the executive from the legislature; the latter makes the executive part of the legislature and responsible to it.

FIXED-DATE ELECTIONS UNDER THE CANADIAN PARLIAMENTARY SYSTEM

In the American example, the president cannot dissolve Congress, nor can Congress defeat the government and force an election. Together with the judiciary, these branches of government are constitutionally separated from one another. In theory, anyway, this is meant to provide a check and balance on the power of each branch. Under the Westminster model, on the other hand, the executive and legislative branches are entwined. They are not, however, unified into a single office or assembly; rather, the two branches are, to borrow a famous image, "buckled" together (Bagehot, quoted in Dawson 1970, 168). What this means is that under the Westminster model, both the executive and legislative branches can wield certain essential powers with regard to the other. These include the ability of the legislative branch to withdraw support from the government, and so force an election, as well as the power of the prime minister (or premier) speaking for the government to resign or to seek a new mandate from the people when he or she desires.

Why Fix Election Dates?

Limiting the Power of the Prime Minister
The system described above evolved in British North America in the first half of the 19th century, following similar reforms that had occurred in Great Britain. Responsible government, as the collective reforms became known, was meant to place certain restrictions on the colonial governors, particularly their discretion in appointing ministers and dissolving the legislative assembly (Craig 1963; Mallory 1971, ch. 1; Reesor 1992, ch. 2; Hogg 2003, ch. 9). As in Great Britain, the end result of these restrictions in Canada has been a division of the executive into a formal or ceremonial office on the one hand, and a political or pragmatic one on the other, with the governor general holding the former, and the prime minister the latter.

Over the years, however, the political executive has become so powerful and concentrated into the person of the prime minister that it is a legitimate question whether responsible government still exists in Canada. The arbitrary power once wielded by the colonial governor to appoint and fire ministers, dissolve the legislature and so on, is now a certain characteristic of the office of the prime minister (Savoie 1999, 2003). This power is now greater than that once held by the old colonial governors; the governors, at least, had to contend with an often stubborn and obstructionist elected assembly. The prime minister, on the other hand, is normally the majority leader of that assembly and hence is rarely so opposed. The call to fix election dates, then, can be seen as an attempt to limit what is now regarded as unfettered power in the hands of the prime minister. In turn, limiting the prime minister's power is meant to restore responsibility and responsiveness of the executive to the legislature.

One example of how the prime minister can exploit his or her power to call elections is in the exercise of party discipline. The obligation imposed on government MPs to always support the government impedes their ability to voice concerns or even oppose their government's policies: the prime minister declares all votes confidence votes, threatening to call an election if government MPs should break ranks (Royal Commission 1991, 4:111). Few MPs, particularly backbench MPs on the government side, look forward to elections: there is little to gain and much to lose. Under the present regime, it is argued, many backbench MPs find such a role limiting and unrewarding. However, if dissolution only occurred at fixed dates, then prime ministers would be unable to threaten sudden dissolutions. No longer fearful that they might force an election they do not wish to fight, backbench MPs should become more empowered, and quite capable of voting against their party if they so wished (see Chapter 8). Under such conditions, prime ministers would have to pay closer attention to MPs' opinions and views, and be more cognizant of their own need for the support of the legislative assembly.

Citizen Engagement

Restoring the responsiveness and responsibility of the executive to the legislature is also seen as a means of redressing another related problem: the public's apparent loss of confidence in the parliamentary system, and its general disengagement from the electoral process. Numerous studies have noted the general decline in civic engagement and public confidence in Western democracies, including Canada (Nevitte 1996; Blais, Howe, and Johnston 1999; Blais et al. 2004b). Fixed-date elections are thought to improve citizen confidence and participation in the political process. First, if the public regarded elected representatives as less restricted by party discipline and more responsive to constituency interests, then voting turnout should improve. As it is, one reason for the declining voting turnout is that voters don't see much point in electing representatives who have little or no voice once elected (LCC 2002; Docherty and White 2004). Second, if elections themselves were accepted as fairer contests and not manipulated events, then this should also increase voting interest (Royal Commission 1991, 2:6).

Fixing election dates is also seen as a means of encouraging more people to seek office. Surely all but the most intrepid potential candidates would be deterred if they believed the odds were stacked against anyone who might wish to challenge the party in power. As well, there are significant practical and logistical problems to be overcome before a citizen enters the political arena. Arrangements with one's employer and reorganization of family responsibilities, to mention just two concerns, take time and planning. This seems particularly true for potential candidates who are female. New Brunswick's Advisory Council on the Status of Women has argued that a flexible election date system "tends to disadvantage women and others who need to plan for new or modified responsibilities." A fixed-date election system would permit "candidates and politicians [to better] reorganize their paid work and family commitments to meet their political obligations" (NBACSW 2004, 31).

Administration and Bureaucracy

Finally, fixing election dates is also seen as a means by which government administration can become more efficient. Administering elections themselves would improve under a fixed-date system: enumeration and other aspects of election organization could become easier to plan (Royal Commission 1991, 4:110). Other government services, particularly the planning and development of large-scale projects, would improve, as government departments would have a much better sense of the life of the current government, and could therefore budget and create realistic timelines, free from the concern that their projects might be undermined by an unexpected election call. Once again, improving government efficiency should also improve public confidence.

Problems of Fixing Elections in Parliamentary Systems

A fixed-date election system, then, might produce some advantages, even significant ones. Further, there are other potential benefits not discussed here, including, for example, improving youth turnout by fixing election dates at a time less likely to be disrupted by school schedules. However, several practical problems would have to be overcome before Canada could fix its election dates, some of which might well be insurmountable. As well, important constitutional barriers would hinder most attempts at fixing election dates. Hence, discussions of benefits that might be accrued with a fixed-date system could well be moot.

Practical Problems

Canada, following the practice of Great Britain, already limits parliamentary terms to five years,[6] so fixing election dates is not meant to prevent governments from staying in power beyond their mandate. Instead, fixing election dates is supposed to prevent governments from resigning or seeking dissolution too early. If such a reform was successful, it would create another problem. Some means would have to be found to maintain a government in the wake of a deadlocked or impotent legislature, perhaps following of a vote of non-confidence or the resignation (or threatened resignation) of the government itself. Under such circumstances, someone must govern, and someone must be able to govern.

It is true that the resignation of a government does not in itself necessitate an election. However, government cannot proceed unless someone is able to pass legislation, and it cannot pass legislation without the support of the majority of the legislature. Elections, then, become a means not only to refresh a mandate or to replace a tired government, but to overcome and resolve a parliamentary stalemate, or to find someone capable of leading and willing to lead a majority in the assembly. However, if election dates are fixed absolutely, then the term of the assembly is also fixed. With such fixed terms, finding a majority in the wake of a prime minister or premier's resignation would be difficult if not impossible. The governor general or lieutenant-governor could, as happened in Ontario in 1985, ask another leader to seek the confidence of the legislature and form a government (Aird 1985; Speirs 1986). However, such a solution would only succeed if another workable majority existed, and this is an exceedingly rare occurrence in Canada at either level of government. If no other workable majority existed, then the assembly would be faced with a government without majority support, and so no means to pass legislation. Perhaps, under such circumstances, parties would be forced to compromise and cooperate. But perhaps instead, government would simply come to a standstill, with no party capable of forming a majority. Legislation would not be passed, and governments would administer rather than govern.

This is why those provinces that have tried to fix elections and terms have also provided some failsafe measure to avoid such a deadlock. British Columbia's fixed-date election legislation states, while "a general voting day must occur on May 17, 2005 and thereafter on the second Tuesday in May in the fourth calendar year following the general voting day for the most recently held general election," this stipulation is subject to the following clause: "The Lieutenant-Governor may, by proclamation in Her Majesty's name, prorogue or dissolve the Legislative Assembly when the Lieutenant-Governor sees fit" (RSBC 1996). Similarly, Ontario's Bill 86, Election Statute Law Amendment Act, 2004, fixes election dates "subject to the Lieutenant Governor's existing power to dissolve the Legislature whenever he or she sees fit." Indeed, British Columbia and Ontario could do nothing else, as they do not have the legal power to override the lieutenant-governor's prerogative as entrenched in the present Canadian constitution. However, the presence of such a provision undermines the claim that the election date is fixed at all. Except under very unusual circumstances, under the conditions of responsible government the lieutenant-governor invariably "sees fit" when the premier so requests.

Perhaps, then, the answer is to allow the governor general or the lieutenant-governor to dissolve the assembly when required, but to carefully define what those conditions would be. Perhaps the head of state should not be permitted to accept advice for dissolution unless the government were defeated by an explicit vote of non-confidence, or in the wake of a repeated failure to discover a majority. Requests made under any other circumstances would be turned down. To so limit the powers of the head of state would be constitutionally difficult, but not logically impossible.

However, as the Lortie Commission made clear, even if such restrictions were put into place, governments would nevertheless be able to force elections if they wished. Surely if the governor general refused a request of a prime minister to dissolve Parliament, the prime minister and cabinet would resign. Then the governor general would be forced to try to appoint a new government. If the former government had been in a majority situation, then the new government would be unlikely to secure majority support. Either the same deadlock described above would occur or the majority party, now in opposition, would simply vote non-confidence in their replacement. Now the governor general would have the appropriate request for dissolution and, with an election called, the wishes of the former government would be finally realized.[7]

It is difficult to understand why this convoluted set of events would be an improvement over the current system. Political parties would likely find the temptation to exploit this strange situation irresistible, thereby entangling the head of state in unseemly political controversy. More important, all these scenarios force governors general and lieutenant-governors to make many more decisions about who governs, and for how long, than most Canadians would find palatable.

Precluding governments from overstaying their mandate is a relatively simple matter, and the present system contains a means for preventing this from happening. But stopping a premier or prime minister from resigning is impossible. However, unless premiers or prime ministers can be forced not to resign, then no measure under the current system will prevent governments finding a way to force elections for dates other than those supposedly fixed.

Constitutional Problems

This is not to say that there is no way to reform our system such that election dates become fixed; however, to do so would require a radical reform of the present system. Specifically, the only sure way to prevent legislative deadlocks or governments from ignoring the fixed dates is to separate the executive powers from the legislative. This way, the government would no longer require the confidence of the legislature to govern, nor would the executive possess the authority to dissolve the legislature. This is not precisely the same as saying that the government would no longer be responsible to the legislative branch, as it would still require that any measure or legislation that it proposed be accepted and passed with a majority in that assembly. However, defeats in the legislature would not require new governments or elections. This, of course, is how the American congressional model works.

As interesting as this proposition is, surely such reforms would be challenged on the grounds that they would transform the Canadian parliamentary system into something resembling the American congressional system.[8] Aside from the problems of selling such a radical reform to the public, moving Canada from a parliamentary to a republican system of government would require a comprehensive and probably unachievable set of constitutional amendments.[9]

Even if such radical reforms were possible on a national level, they would be beyond the legal competence of a province acting alone. Canadian courts have ruled against reforms that, in their judgement, have threatened such principles as parliamentary privilege (Heard 1993) and responsible government.[10] Consider the Supreme Court's ruling in *Ontario v. OPSEU* (1987). Although this case dealt with the right of a provincial government to restrict civil servants from participating in federal politics, the Court made it clear that provinces lacked the authority to alter the fundamental principle of responsible government:

> The fact that a province can validly give legislative effect to a prerequisite condition of responsible government does not necessarily mean it can do anything it pleases with the principle of responsible government itself. Thus, it is uncertain, to say the least, that a province could touch upon the power of the Lieutenant-Governor to dissolve the legislature, or his power to appoint and dismiss ministers, without unconstitutionally touching his office itself. The principle of responsible government could, to the extent that it depends on those important royal powers, be entrenched to a substantial extent. *The power of constitutional amendment given to the provinces by s. 92(1) does not necessarily comprise the power to bring about a profound constitutional upheaval by the introduction of political institutions foreign to and incompatible with the Canadian system* [emphasis added].

Therefore, any province contemplating reforms of a type that threaten to compromise essential principles of the Canadian constitution should expect to receive a rough reception in Canadian courts.

Fixing Election Dates through Ordinary Legislation

Regardless of these obstacles and concerns, several provinces have fixed, or are attempting to fix, election dates. Despite the recommendations of this author, New Brunswick's Commission on Legislative Democracy (2004, 5) has recommended fixing the election date at four years, every October, while Ontario and British Columbia have introduced legislation to fix election dates. However, Ontario's fixed election law is a product of ordinary legislation; that is, the law fixing election dates has been passed by the Legislative Assembly of Ontario but not entrenched in the Canadian Constitution. Although British Columbia professes to have entrenched its fixed-date election law in its provincial constitution, from a constitutional standpoint it too is merely a product of ordinary legislation, as is the BC Constitution Act itself, for that matter.[11] Any subsequent government in Ontario or British Columbia can pass legislation either exempting itself from the law's provisions or repealing it entirely; such a government could even simply pass legislation that contradicts the earlier, and have that legislation prevail (Hogg 2003, 12.3, p. 289). In any case, neither fixed-date election law prevents elections from being called if a government should lose a vote of confidence.

Regardless, the fundamental problem with using ordinary legislation to fix election dates is that the law is unenforceable. We have already discussed the constitutional difficulty of restricting the power of the governor general to dissolve parliament. The same problems exist at the provincial level. As well, consider the consequences if a premier should choose to simply ignore fixed-date legislation and request a dissolution anyway. Under the terms of responsible government, the lieutenant-governor would almost always be constitutionally bound to agree with the request. Could a court then turn back the dropping of the writs, or overturn the election itself? Would the premier who called an election outside the parameters of the law be dismissed or called on to resign, thereby forcing the very result the legislation is meant to prevent? What possible sanction could be imposed to punish a transgressor of a fixed-date election law? The implications are bizarre.

Attempting to fix election dates through ordinary legislation, then, must be understood as merely a means by which the government signals its good intentions to restrict election calls to an orderly and predictable schedule, and not a serious limitation of the powers and discretion of prime ministers, premiers, governors general, or lieutenant-governors. Indeed, the BC experience suggests that even using a provincial constitution to fix election dates is no guarantee they will not be tampered with: after the last provincial election, the premier of British Columbia floated the idea of moving elections to a more convenient date (Meissner 2004). Still, the presence of legislation in Ontario and British Columbia might at least regularize election calls. If regular election calls became a parliamentary or constitutional convention, then it is possible that premiers or prime ministers would be reluctant to ignore them; they would at least need to explain why if they did. However, neither the convention nor the explicit law would be binding. The law could always be overturned or simply ignored. As for the convention, no one should assume that the self-interest of a governing party would be constrained by such a measure, no matter how long the convention had been in place. To paraphrase Geoffrey Marshall, parliamentary conventions are binding except when they are ignored (Marshall 1984, 54, quoted in Reesor 1992, 74).

What Is the Problem for Which Fixed-Date Elections Are the Solution?

The call to fix election dates seems to have support across the country, from left to right, from government to opposition. However, what precisely is the problem for which fixed-date elections would be the solution? Clearly, the public is frustrated with what it perceives to be overt and unfair manipulation of election dates by the party in power. However, the party in power is quite capable of avoiding the temptation to so orchestrate opportunistic election calls. Therefore, a government serious about assuaging the public's concerns could simply insist on calling its next election on the anniversary date. Save for the rare votes of non-confidence, few measures if any currently prevent a premier or prime minister from waiting for the four-year anniversary date before calling an election.

That this is not seen as sufficient raises two questions. First, are those governments that have declared their interest in fixing election dates merely doing so because they expect to garner public favour, all the while knowing full well that no measure would truly force them to comply? Or are they frustrated themselves with the pressures and dangers of trying to determine exactly when would be the best time to call an election? Perhaps such pre-election strategizing becomes exhausting and distracting for governments trying to implement complicated policy agendas. These are understandable motives for wanting to persuade the public that election dates will be fixed. However, they have the potential to create worse problems. First, the measures, as explained above, may well lead to a dysfunctional system of legislative government. Second, attempts to create a fixed-date system may force the government to engage in costly and ultimately futile legal battles. Third, the public could decide that the fixed-date election reforms were hollow and impotent, thereby increasing its cynicism.

Under the Westminster model, election dates cannot be fixed, at least not in any meaningful sense. The constitutional and practical problems would overwhelm any attempts to do so, and in any case, one province could not accomplish such reforms by itself. At best, election calls can become more predictable, orderly, and regularized. In any case, although some people grumbled about the calling of both the 2000 and 2003 federal elections, there is little evidence that election calls in Canada at either level are anything but orderly and regularized. Still, certain measures could be put into place that would, in the opinion of this author, go a long way to restoring the confidence the public has lost in the integrity of the electoral and legislative process.

If we take as a premise that what the public really objects to is not the fact that elections are unpredictably held—sometimes in the spring and sometimes the fall—but that the government in power holds an unfair advantage, then focussing on precisely why the advantage is seen as unfair might help determine what the public's real concern is, which seems to be that elections are not fair contests. If they were, then the election date and even its unpredictability would hardly be a cause for worry. Therefore, measures that improved the competitive nature of election contests would certainly go a long way towards alleviating public dissatisfaction. It is beyond the scope of this paper to delve into these measures in any detail; however, other papers in this collection do.

Second, the convenient myth that all legislative defeats are by necessity votes of non-confidence should be dispelled. As Philip Norton has written, "the belief that a government defeat necessarily entails resignation or a dissolution has influenced significantly parliamentary behaviour. [Yet], it is a perception which rests upon no continuous basis of practice or upon any authoritative original source and one which is belied by the experience of both the 19th and 20th centuries" (Norton 1986). It is worth asking, then, why this belief that a government defeat necessarily entails resignation or dissolution persists. Perhaps it is because it is in the interest of the party in power to maintain the fiction, as such a belief becomes a powerful disciplinary tool. However, if backbenchers called the government's bluff more often, they could work to dispel the myth. Freed from the worry that defeats in the legislature invariably mean an election, government backbenchers might be more willing to vote against party discipline. The public, then, may well see its faith in the importance of backbench MPs and MLAs restored, and with it, its confidence in the parliamentary system. But parliament can accomplish this without fixed-date election reform.

Conclusion

Fixed-date elections are an inappropriate and overly simplistic solution to a more difficult and complex problem: the decline in public confidence in the parliamentary system and in civic engagement in general. As well, fixed-date election reforms risk making this problem worse than it is. Such reforms will not limit the government's advantage in its ability to call elections at dates of its choosing; they may well convince the government to ignore the legislature even more than it does now, and they will likely increase the public's cynicism towards what they already see as a cumbersome and inefficient parliamentary system. While it seems possible that, were Canada to adopt a very different system, fixed-date elections could generate certain advantages, these advantages cannot be realized without such radical reform. The constitutional obstacles would overwhelm any attempt to truly fix election dates, and other means, such as ordinary legislation, simply do not work.

On the other hand, if governments truly believe that holding elections at fixed dates is important, then they should exercise the appropriate discipline and only hold elections on their four-year anniversary date. They already possess all the power they need to ensure this takes place. Resisting the temptation to call elections at opportune times will go much further in restoring the public's confidence than empty legislation or reckless constitutional reforms.

Notes

1. The survey, commissioned by CBC, was conducted between 12 and 18 May 2004; the election was called on 23 May. The actual question was: "Do you agree or disagree with each of the following statements?" followed by six questions concerning electoral procedures in Canada. The sixth was: "Federal elections should be held on a fixed date every four years instead of whenever the party in power wants to call it."
2. On the difficulties of reforming parliament, see Mallory (1979) and Sutherland (1991).
3. For the most part, unless stated otherwise, the reader can assume that conditions and constitutional provisions that apply to the governor general and prime minister also apply to the lieutenant-governors and premiers.
4. Sec 50, Constitution Act 1867: "Every House of Commons shall continue for Five Years from the Day of the Return of the Writs for choosing the House (subject to be sooner dissolved by the Governor General), and no longer." Sec 4, Constitution Act 1982: "No House of Commons and no legislative assembly shall continue for longer than five years from the date fixed for the return of the writs of a general

election of its members."

5. For an overview, see Verney (1959) and Birch (1964). For comparisons of parliamentary systems in Western Europe, see Strøm (1995). For comparison of the principles of parliamentary versus republican governments, with special reference to Australia, see Uhr (1993).
6. Sec 50, CA 1867: "Every House of Commons shall continue for Five Years from the Day of the Return of the Writs for choosing the House (subject to be sooner dissolved by the Governor General), and no longer." Sec 4, CA 1982: "No House of Commons and no legislative assembly shall continue for longer than five years from the date fixed for the return of the writs of a general election of its members." In Great Britain, the mandates are limited to five years by the 1911 Parliament Act.
7. This scenario is not entirely hypothetical, as a similar set of events took place in Newfoundland in the first decade of the 20th century. See Noel (1971, 68ff.)
8. Indeed, electing the governor general is a key plank in the Citizens for a Canadian Republic's platform (Citizens for a Canadian Republic 2004).
9. On the necessity of a formal constitutional amendment for such radical changes (although not specifically for fixed-date elections), see Heard (1994).
10. In *New Brunswick Broadcasting Co. v. Nova Scotia*, [1993] 1 SCR 319, the Court did recognize that "The Constitution of the United Kingdom recognized certain privileges in the legislative body. This suggests that the legislative bodies of the new Dominion would possess similar, although not necessarily identical, powers." However, it insisted that the basic features of the Westminster model, including, for example, parliamentary privilege (the issue at hand in New Brunswick Broadcasting) must be included in any definition of "similar in principle." For criticism of the Court's overall ruling in *NBBC v. NS*, see Bonsaint (1997).
11. The BC Supreme Court has ruled that province's Constitution Act is not a constitution in the strict sense of the word, and therefore has no power beyond that of ordinary legislation [*Dixon v. AGBC* (No. 2) (1989), 59 DLR (4th) 247 (BCSC)].

References

Aird, John. 1985. *Loyalty in a Changing World: The Contemporary Function of the Office of the Lieutenant-Governor of Ontario, As Interpreted by the Honourable John Black Aird*. Toronto: Office of the Premier.

Aucoin, Peter, Jennifer Smith, and Geoff Dinsdale. 2003. *Responsible Government: Clarifying Essentials, Dispelling Myths and Exploring Change*. Ottawa: Canadian Centre for Management Development.

Balke, Nathan S. 1990. "The Rational Timing of Parliamentary Elections." *Public Choice* 65:201–216.

Birch, A.H. 1964. *Representative and Responsible Government*. Toronto: University of Toronto Press.

Blais, André, Paul Howe, and Richard Johnston. 1999. "Strengthening Canadian Democracy: A New IRPP Research Project." *Policy Options* 20(9):7–9.

Blais, André, et al. 2004a. "Do (Some) Canadian Voters Punish a Prime Minister for Calling a Snap Election?" *Political Studies* 52(2):307–323.

—. 2004b. "Where Does Turnout Decline Come From?" *European Journal of Political Research* 43(2):221–236.

Bonsaint, Michel. 1997. "Parliamentary Privilege: The Impact of New Brunswick Broadcasting Co. Versus Nova Scotia." *Canadian Parliamentary Review* 19(4): 26–35.

CBC News. 2004. "Canadians want fixed election dates." Retrieved from www.cbc.ca/story/election/national/news/2004/05/24/elecpoll040524.html.

Citizens for a Canadian Republic. 2004. "Proposal for Electing the Governor General Announced." Retrieved from www.canadian-republic.ca/media_release_3_18_04.html.

Craig, G.M., ed. 1963. *Lord Durham's Report: An Abridgement of Report of the Affairs of British North America*. Toronto: McClelland.

Dawson, R. MacGregor. 1970. *The Government of Canada*. 5th ed., rev. by Norman Ward. Toronto: University of Toronto Press.

Docherty, David, and Stephen White. 2004. "Parliamentary Democracy in Canada." *Parliamentary Affairs* 57(3):613–629.

Heard, Andrew. 1993. "The Supreme Court Entrenches Parliamentary Privilege Out of the Charter's Reach: Donahoe v. CBC." *Constitutional Forum* (4):102–105.

—. 1994. "When Must Constitutional Innovation be Achieved by Formal Amendment?" Paper presented at the Annual Conference of the Canadian Political Science Association, Calgary, Alberta.

Hogg, Peter W. 2003. *Constitutional Law of Canada*. Scarborough, ON: Carswell.

Howe, Paul, and David Northrup. 2000. *Strengthening Canadian Democracy: The Views of Canadians*. Ottawa: Institute for Research on Public Policy.

Jenkins, Richard W. 2002. "How Campaigns Matter in Canada: Priming and Learning as Explanations for the Reform Party's 1993 Campaign Success." *Canadian Journal of Political Science* 35(2):383–408.

Law Commission of Canada. 2002. "Renewing Democracy: Debating Electoral Reform." Discussion paper, Law Commission of Canada, Ottawa.

Mackie, Richard. 2004. "Ontario goes to polls on Oct. 4, 2007." *Globe and Mail Update*, 1 June. Retrieved from www.theglobeandmail.com/servlet on 4 December 2004.

Mallory, J.R. 1971. *The Structure of Canadian Government*. Toronto: Macmillan of Canada.

—. 1979. "Parliament: Every Reform Creates a New Problem." *Journal of Canadian Studies* 14:26–34.

Marshall, Geoffrey. 1984. *Constitutional Conventions: The Rules and Forms of Political Accountability*. Toronto: Oxford University Press.

Meissner, Dirk. 2004. "B.C. Premier Muses about Changing Fixed Election Date after May 2005 Vote." *Canadian Press News Wire*, 12 July.

New Brunswick Advisory Council on the Status of Women. 2004. "Women and Electoral Reform in New Brunswick." Brief presented to the New Brunswick Commission on Legislative Democracy.

New Brunswick Commission on Legislative Democracy. 2004. *Options: A Progress Report to New Brunswickers*. Fredericton, NB: New Brunswick Commission on Legislative Democracy.

New Brunswick Votes. 2003. "Tory platform offers fixed date votes." Retrieved from nb.bc.ca on 27 May.

Nevitte, Neil. 1996. *The Decline of Deference: Canadian Value Change in Cross-national Perspective*. Peterborough, ON: Broadview Press.

Noel, Sidney, J.R. 1971. *Politics in Newfoundland*. Toronto: University of Toronto Press.

Norton, Philip. 1986. "Government Defeats in the House of Commons: The British Experience." *Canadian Parliamentary Review* 8(4):6–9.

Nystrom, Lorne. 2000. "Spinning election rumours: Why don't we have fixed election dates?" *National Post*, 12 October, A19.

Office of the Premier of Ontario. 2004. "McGuinty government takes bold action to strengthen our democracy: Historic New Legislation Would Fix Dates For Future Elections." Press release, Toronto, 1 June. Retrieved from http://ogov.newswire.ca/ontario/GPOE/2004/06/01/c9898.html.

Ontario [Attorney General] v. OPSEU [1987]. 1987. 2 S.C.R 2; (July 29, 1987).

Progressive Conservative Party of New Brunswick. 2003. *Reaching Higher. Going Further. 2003–2007*. Retrieved from www.pcnb.org/media/BernardLordPlanEN.pdf.

Reesor, Bayard William. 1992. *The Canadian Constitution in Historical Perspective*. Scarborough, ON: Prentice-Hall.

Roper, Steven D., and Christopher Andrews. 2002. "Timing an Election: The Impact on the Party in Government." *The American Review of Politics* 23:305–318.

Royal Commission on Electoral Reform and Party Financing. 1991. *Reforming Electoral Democracy: Final Report*. 4 volumes. Ottawa: Ministry of Supply and Services.

RSBC. 1996. Constitution Act, Chapter 66: Sec 23 (1).

Savoie, Donald J. 1999. *Governing from the Centre: The Concentration of Power in Canadian Politics*. Toronto: University of Toronto Press.

—. 2003. *Breaking the Bargain: Public Servants, Ministers and Parliament*. Toronto: University of Toronto Press.

Seskus, Tony, and James Baxter. 2004. "Carve election dates in stone, Grit leader: Klein timing vote to avoid 'perfect storm.'" *Calgary Herald*, 19 June.

Smith, Alastair. 1996. "Endogenous Election Timing in Majoritarian Parliamentary

Systems." *Economics & Politics* 8(2):85–110.

——. 2003. "Election Timing in Majoritarian Parliaments." *British Journal of Political Science* 33(3):397–418.

Speirs, Rosemary. 1986. *Out of the Blue: The Fall of the Tory Dynasty in Ontario.* Toronto: Macmillan.

Strøm, Kaare. 1995. "Parliamentary Government and Legislative Organization." In *Parliaments and Majority Rule in Western Europe*, ed. Herbert Döring, 51–82. New York: St. Martin's Press.

Strøm, Kaare, and Stephen M. Swindle. 2002. "Strategic Parliamentary Dissolution." *American Political Science Review* 96:3:575–591.

Sutherland, Sharon L. 1991. "Responsible Government and Ministerial Responsibility: Every Reform Is Its Own Problem." *Canadian Journal of Political Science* 24(1):96–97.

Taft, Kevin. 2004. "Alberta Liberals would hold fixed elections every four years, says Taft." *Canadian Press News Wire*, 18 June.

Uhr, John. 1993. "Instituting Republicanism: Parliamentary Vices, Republican Virtues?" *Australian Journal of Political Science* 28:27–39.

Verney, Douglas V. 1959. *The Analysis of Political Systems.* London: Routledge & Paul.

CHAPTER ELEVEN

The Referendum Experience in New Brunswick

CHEDLY BELKHODJA

Introduction

THIS CHAPTER EXAMINES the referendum experience in New Brunswick. Recourse to direct democracy is not common practice in a province often characterized by a political culture steeped in elitism and parliamentary tradition (Adamson and Stewart 1991). It is necessary to go far back in the province's history to find fleeting examples of direct participation by citizens in local decision making, in the tradition of the town hall meetings that were introduced by immigrants from New England but quickly supplanted by the British representation model (Krueger 1970, 52–53). These days, however, it seems that referendums have become a popular and indispensable tool in the effort to regain public trust. Many studies report an increase in the number of referendums since the 1960s, and especially since the 1990s (Leduc 2003; Morel 2001; Butler and Ranney 1994; Mendelsohn and Parkin 2001b). Referendums are more common today, particularly in Europe, as evidenced by the many plebiscites on EU membership (Morel 2001, 51; Leduc 2003). A number of European countries have held referendums on moral and political issues: for example, Ireland on abortion (1983, 1992, and 2002) and divorce (1986 and 1995), Sweden on nuclear energy (1980), and Spain on NATO (1980). There are also certain countries that have a referendum tradition, such as Switzerland (optional referendum and the popular initiative), Italy (abrogative referendum on laws), and France (Bonapartist and Gaullist plebiscite tradition). In North

America, states in the United States (California, Colorado, Vermont) have been holding referendums and popular initiatives since the 1700s, but the federal government has yet to stage a national referendum (Piott 2003; Dunsmuir 1992).

For its part, Canada has had a very prudent approach, with only three national referendums in the country's history (1898, 1942, and 1992). The first referendum took place in 1898, when the federal government decided to act on the lingering issue of prohibition. The result was not very convincing, with only a 44% participation rate. A second referendum was held in 1942 on the divisive question of sending conscripts to Europe during World War II. The results showed the profound solitudes of the two linguistic and religious communities of Canada. The most recent national referendum was held in 1992 on the constitutional agreement known as the Charlottetown Accord. Provinces have used referendums and initiatives more frequently.

The provincial experience with referendums could be characterized by two waves: a "first wave" occurred during the beginning of the 20th century when provinces were faced with the issue of prohibition, and a "second wave" has occurred since the end of the 1980s, as provinces have held more referendums on various questions such as a unified school system in Newfoundland (1997), a fixed link between PEI and New Brunswick (1988), abortion funding in Saskatchewan (1991), and equal representation in the first legislative assembly of Nunavut (1997) (Mowrey and Pelletier 2001). All provinces have also adopted legal provision for referendum legislation, the most recent one being Ontario.

One of the terms of reference of the New Brunswick Commission on Legislative Democracy was "to examine and make recommendations on enhancing direct democracy by proposing a New Brunswick Referendum Act that sets out the rules and procedures for allowing province-wide, binding referendums on significant public policy issues." New Brunswick is not alone in that regard, as the Canadian government and most of the provinces have set up commissions charged with examining democratic practices in the country and considering reforms in a number of areas. Often included in these democratic reform initiatives is consideration of direct-democracy processes, even though these are often perceived negatively by the media and a cynical general public. Examples are the recall and citizens' initiatives in California (such as the one that led to the election of Arnold Schwarzenegger) and referendums on moral issues suggested by the Reform Party and the Canadian Alliance.

Over the past decade referendums have been presented as a mechanism capable of redressing the democratic deficit. Some observers argue that direct democracy gives more scope for citizen participation in the political process and educates the general public on important policy matters. Referendums are also touted as a way to reinforce a community's sense of identity. Others make numerous objections to the use of referendums in a democratic society. They point to low voter turnout rates, complex wording of questions, weakening of political parties, manipulation by elites, inadequate information for voters, the role of special interest groups, the right of minorities, and the exacerbation of social and ethnic tensions brought on by referendum use (Leduc 2003, 31; Mendelhson and Parkin 2001b). Beyond the advantages and disadvantages associated with the use of direct democracy, some more fundamental questions need to be asked. Why do governments undertake public consultations by way of referendum? Can referendums help resolve the democratic malaise? Can referendums restore trust between voters and their politicians? Are referendums effective tools in plurinational societies such as Canada and New Brunswick?

In this chapter, we attempt to answer those questions by taking a more socio-historical approach. Starting from different referendum practices in New Brunswick's political life, we want to go a little more deeply into the province's political culture to identify certain interesting characteristics specific to New Brunswick. The first section presents some general considerations outlining the argument that the current enthusiasm for direct democracy stems from the infusion of populism into the political life of democratic societies. The second section looks at the lessons learned from three provincial referendums, namely, municipal referendums on prohibition in the early 1900s, the 1967 plebiscite on the voting age, and the 14 May 2001 referendum on video lottery terminals. The 2001 popular consultation will be analyzed in greater detail, since it constitutes a recent exercise that the government of New Brunswick hopes to repeat. Lastly, the third section of this chapter analyzes two major issues concerning referendums, namely, the pivotal role of political elites in the referendum process and the protection of minorities.

Populism and Referendums

Populism can be defined as a technique for mobilizing people through political action around an ideal aimed at breathing new life into democracy. Through reforms such as the decentralization of power, the use of referendums, and the provision of e-services by institutions, many countries are now experimenting with local, direct, and virtual democracy, evoking a more active role for individuals in the democratic process (Chandler 2001; Gibbins 2000). But what does populism actually mean? On the one hand, in a rather pragmatic fashion, by directly enlisting the individual's capacity to speak out, the populist movement has adopted as its own a classic criticism against the "undemocratic foundations" of representative democracy (Urbinati 1998). In a progressive tradition, particularly in the United States, populism has frequently portrayed itself as the missing link in true democratic participation, whose aim is to eliminate the gap between voters and elites. This "positive" take amounts to turning populism into a way of doing politics differently, a form of direct democracy that will help to bring the people and political authority closer together. On the other hand, populism can also reveal an entirely different meaning with a more "negative" face, namely, manipulation of the electorate, the personalization of power, and demagogic and authoritarian conduct. It is important to be mindful of these two facets of contemporary populism.

Several reasons can account for the general trend in favour of populism. First, numerous studies have reported a shift in politics towards the inclusion of public participation and debate, the result of the emergence of a "new politics" in advanced democratic societies beginning in the late 1960s (Dalton 2004; Nevitte 1996). Citizens are increasingly mistrustful of institutions and the traditional political elites and are more cynical about the political process. At the same time, citizens are expressing a desire to be better informed and to play a more active role politically through more democratic mechanisms, such as popular initiatives, recalls, and referendums (Norris 1999).

Second, in the late 1980s, the emergence of new right-wing populist parties brought about a major ideological upheaval. Until the 1980s, the words "populism" and "populist" were employed in a quite precise and specific way. They were used chiefly and almost exclusively to refer rather pejoratively to such historical movements as the radical racist right in the United States and the charismatic and authoritarian populism of Latin-American leaders (Mény and Surel 2001). Over the past 20 years or so, populism seems to have been growing, owing notably to the electoral successes of new so-called extreme right-wing political parties as well as right-wing neo-populists and populists (Ihl et al. 2003; Betz and Immerfall 1998). Over and above the electoral success of those groups, populist culture has become more widespread, shifting from the radical right to a more acceptable ideology in the middle of the political spectrum (Betz and Immerfall 1998). Lawrence Leduc (2003, 20) notes, "Indeed, there is little doubt that a once-radical view associated with a more populist form of democracy has found new favour throughout the world today." Nowadays, populism is no longer a foreign concept, nor is it associated with extremism. It reflects a democracy that promotes the principle of being more in touch with the people than with the elite (Papodopoulos 1998; Canovan 1999). Mény and

Surel (2001) also find a substantial shift from an institution-based democracy to a more popular democracy.

Third, direct democracy draws on the practice of a culture of choice, which tends to glorify the democratic individual and gives the impression that the individual is at the crux of the political decision-making process. All the individual has to do is choose from among several options. One example of this culture of choice would be the innumerable surveys featured by on-line newspapers, those instant polls that ask readers their opinions on all sorts of issues. This consequence of the surge of individualism in our democratic societies raises certain concerns over the simplification of politics and its adaptation to practices based more on consumerism than on citizenship. This populist culture will put the emphasis more and more on individuals in order to erase differences between them. The broad appeal to the people is made in a way that we are talking of one single group of people, "the People" (Canovan 1999).

In Canada, many observers have referred to a new wave of populism that emerged in the 1990s, the likes of which the country had not seen in 70 years (MacDonald 1991, 339). At that time, citizens were becoming more demanding and more critical of the political elites. A number of major political events that came along signalled a fairly significant change in Canada's political culture. Some observers speak of a break in the country's political evolution (Nevitte 1996). The constitutional debate (Meech Lake and the Charlottetown Accord), the Citizens' Forum on Canada's Future (Spicer Commission), the Canadian Royal Commission on Electoral Reform and Party Financing (Lortie Commission), and the birth of the Reform Party in 1987 and the Bloc Québécois in 1991 heralded disenchantment with the traditional mechanisms of politics and representative democracy. A clear message was heard during the hearings of the Spicer Commission when citizens expressed their disengagement with the political system (Marquis 1993, 5). During those years, the political situation in New Brunswick as well was favourable to the emergence of a populist actor able to reach people who were frustrated with the traditional party system.

The establishment of the Confederation of Regions (CoR) Party in the late 1980s aptly illustrates the appearance of populist forces (Belkhodja 1999). Through its ideology, CoR is reminiscent of the discourse of various extremist anti-francophone movements of the 1960s and 1970s, such as the Canadian Loyalist Association. The party had one principal goal—the abolition of the 1969 Official Languages Act, which guaranteed language rights to the francophone minority. However, CoR's electoral success in the 1991 provincial election was not solely the result of an anti-French backlash. The success of the party in New Brunswick can also be portrayed as the result of strong frustration with the rule of traditional parties (Belkhodja 2002). Drawing on some fairly standard tenets of populism, CoR portrayed itself as the only party made up of citizens serving ordinary citizens ("We the People") and as the defender of the interests of the individual (the common citizen). In the party's program, the ideal of proximity takes the form of a popular movement, composed of "little people" wanting to be heard by a political system seen as impersonal and distant: "Past governments of this Province have believed that election victory is a mandate to rule and to regulate. CoR-NB believes that election victory should be a mandate to represent all citizens, with fair treatment to all. Today, this Province is run by a corporate hierarchy" (*The Philosophy, Principles, and Policies* 1995, 3). The CoR Party also championed another facet of populism, namely, the desire for fundamental reforms in parliamentary institutions through the introduction of direct-democracy processes such as the loosening of party discipline in the House, the use of referendums on moral issues (abortion, capital punishment), and the recall of MPs and MLAs in their ridings. "The Confederation of Regions-NB Party supports a return to responsible government through the principle of initiative referendum on issues of importance, a fixed four-year term for government, and a recall procedure whereby the electorate may cause an early end to the term of a politician who fails to represent them to their satisfaction" (*The Philosophy, Principles, and Policies* 1993, 8; 1995, 11).

The CoR experience seems interesting to us for two reasons. First, the party was part of a populist tradition that had already asserted itself in the political culture of some anti-establishment groups in New Brunswick.[1] Second, the folding of the CoR party did not signify the end of right-wing populism in the province. On the contrary, there is a link between the solid populist organization established by the CoR party in some Anglophone regions of the province and the relative success of the Reform Party at the time of the 1993 and 1997 federal elections, followed by the Canadian Alliance in the November 2000 general election.[2] The rebirth of the Conservatives in New Brunswick in 1997 under the direction of the party's young new leader, Bernard Lord, is noteworthy in that the Conservatives welcomed former CoR militants and adopted certain populist ideas and practices, notably a rhetoric of "getting back to the people" (Poitras 2004).

In the provincial election on 22 June 1999, the Progressive Conservative Party trounced the Liberal Party, putting an end to 12 years of Liberal government in New Brunswick. Under the direction of Bernard Lord, the Conservatives portrayed themselves as a force of change as opposed to a worn-out government that had been in power since 1987. During the 1999 election campaign, the party came to the defence of the "little people," severely chastising the Liberals for having governed the province with no regard for its citizens. In its speeches, the party often referred to the lack of public participation in the existing government and the need to revisit the relationship between the political system and the "people of New Brunswick." It was against this backdrop that Bernard Lord called for renewed civic participation in several spheres in society: health, education, and the legislative process. In its electoral platform titled *New Vision New Brunswick*, the Conservative Party pledged to involve New Brunswickers and made the promise of holding a referendum: "We will empower people and communities across New Brunswick by allowing New Brunswickers to determine the future of video lottery terminals in the province by holding a referendum on VLTs at the time of the next municipal elections."

The Referendum Experience in New Brunswick

New Brunswick has had a few experiences with referendums, which are governed by two main pieces of legislation: the Municipalities Act and the Elections Act (Chapter 9, sec. 129).

Towards the end of the 19th century, New Brunswick experienced a series of progressive and reform movements similar to what was going on in the United States and Europe. In that era of prohibitionist movements, reformers, evangelists, and suffragettes became the mouthpieces for a reformist political culture, proposing alternatives to the capitalist model of industrialized societies (see Chapter 13). These movements demanded that government play a greater role in society and aid the most disadvantaged. A rather eloquent example of the social malaise at the time can be seen in the struggle by the Temperance League movements to have alcohol banned in the province. Most anglophone counties in the province invoked the Canada Temperance Act of 1878 and organized referendums on prohibition. The act provided for the holding of local referendums subject to a petition requiring the signatures of one-quarter of local electors. It is interesting to note that the counties were split along linguistic and religious lines (Couturier 1987, 109–115). The Protestant anglophone counties became prohibition zones, while the francophone counties did not. The province's Catholic and Acadian population did not show much enthusiasm for the issue of prohibition. This was the case until 1917, when province-wide prohibition was enacted.

Second, as part of the provincial election of 26 October 1967, the Liberal government of Louis J. Robichaud held a plebiscite on the voting age. New Brunswickers were asked how they felt about a proposal to lower the voting age from 21 to 18. The consultative nature of the plebiscite was in no way binding on the government, which, when apprised of the somewhat surprising results (69.5% of New Brunswickers were opposed to lowering the voting age, with 30.5% in favour), chose to wait several years before enacting legislation to lower the voting age. Interestingly, the results of the plebiscite were not made public until March 1968.

Lastly, the referendum of 14 May 2001 on video lottery terminals was a true exercise in direct democracy. The outcome, while hardly conclusive, provides us with some interesting lessons for the future. When asked whether the province of New Brunswick should continue to permit the legal and regulated operation of video gaming devices, the Yes side at 53.23% (118,574) defeated the No side at 46.77% (104,191). The participation rate was fairly low at 44.5%. To gain a better understanding of this direct-democracy experience, we analyze two aspects, namely, adoption of the referendum bill and the arguments presented in the media during the campaign.

Adoption of the Referendum Bill

The Conservative government tabled the draft Video Lottery Scheme Referendum Act, which was passed by the Legislative Assembly in December 2000. The act stipulated that a single referendum was to be held on a specific issue, video lottery schemes, with the result to be binding. A clause also stipulated that the act was to expire after one year, on 14 May 2002. Lastly, the act was subject to the provisions of the Municipal Elections Act. Cabinet was responsible for drafting the referendum question. In actuality, the act did not say much, limiting itself to simply describing the holding of a referendum as part of the municipal elections of 14 May 2001. It contained no provisions governing the amount of money that groups and individuals could spend on the campaign.

In the Legislative Assembly, debate revolved around the following issues: the wording of the question, the lack of any real debate in the assembly on the bill, the fear of splits between communities, and the lack of financing rules for the referendum. What may be surprising about the New Brunswick case is the disconnect shown by the Conservative government in encouraging the public to participate in a genuine democratic exercise while striving to maintain close control over the referendum process. Camille Thériault, leader of the Opposition, stated in the legislature: "This government professes itself to be one that is open and transparent, yet, when, for the first time in 40 years, it decides to go ahead with a referendum in New Brunswick, it decides that it will decide the question behind closed doors" (New Brunswick Legislative Assembly 2000c). The Liberals maintained that referendums were not common practice in the context of representative democracy and that a referendum would likely create conflict and tension between the parties concerned and introduce a politics of emotion. In the words of MLA Shawn Graham, "The concern we have in the opposition, and I myself feel, when one begins to govern by referendum, it also creates many splits and divisions within the community. We see households divided on issues; we see people becoming emotionally involved and often not able to separate the emotion from the reality of the problem" (New Brunswick Legislative Assembly 2000c).

In any referendum, the wording of the question is pivotal and can be contentious. The Quebec case is often cited. In New Brunswick, the opposition criticized the government for not including the question in its bill and for not allowing a real debate in the legislature. As MLA Bernard Richard put it, "What concerns us is that we are being asked to approve a piece of legislation that does not contain the question. We believe that if we are to approve this legislation, we should as well as legislators be given the opportunity to approve the question that will be asked" (New Brunswick Legislative Assembly 2000c). Generally speaking, however, a referendum initiated by a government remains under its control. As Mollie Dunsmuir (1992) writes: "the question arises as to whether the actual wording of the question is included in the statute, or is left to the executive." In New Brunswick, Justice Minister Brad Green noted that, in the case of several consultations by referendum on the same type of issue in Alberta and Saskatchewan, the question was not included in the respective bills. He also indicated that his government's actions were consistent with the "referendum experience in Canada." Lastly, he maintained that the referendum exercise was in keeping with the notion of calling directly upon the people: "What we are doing is taking this issue to the one forum in the province of New Brunswick that is above our own here in the Legislative Assembly. We are taking this question to the people" (New Brunswick Legislative Assembly 2000c). The question seemed simple enough: Should there be video gambling in the province of New Brunswick or should there not? Some said the question had to be very straightforward, i.e., "Do you want VLTs in New Brunswick?" (*Telegraph Journal* 2000).

On 3 April 2001, the government unveiled the referendum question: "Should the Province of New Brunswick continue to permit the legal and regulated operation of video gaming devices?" The campaign began on 5 April as part of the municipal elections process.

The Referendum Campaign
A review of the main dailies in the province reveals[3] the various arguments in the debate over video lottery terminals. At the start of the campaign, public opinion seemed to be in favour of withdrawing the gaming devices, as gam-

bling was seen as a societal problem for moral reasons. The public had heard about the damaging effects of the machines, about the sad cases of families that had been devastated by them. A study by the Canada West Foundation in June 1999 detailed anti-VLT sentiment in New Brunswick: "One of the strongest conclusions coming out of the study is that Atlantic Canadians are much more anti-gambling and specifically anti-VLT than the rest of the country" (Canada West Foundation 2001). During the campaign, the media painted a clear-cut struggle between two groups, presented as a David and Goliath–type battle. On the one hand, supporters of the machines—owners of licensed establishments and manufacturers—formed a well-organized committee and had substantial financial resources, with a $1.2-million advertising campaign in newspapers and in the media, a web site, and consultants. The owners devised a strategy based on economic arguments that proved to have a positive impact: withdrawal of the machines would result in $50 million in lost revenue for government, higher personal taxes, the loss of more than 1,000 jobs, and the re-emergence of a black market in the form of the infamous grey machines: "There will be grey (illegal) machines owned by the biker gangs from Quebec and the government will get no money from them," stated Gerry Lowe, president of the New Brunswick Licensees Association. Lisa Poirier wrote: "Tories warned VLT ban could lead to black-market problems" (*Telegraph Journal*, November 21, 2000, A1).

On the other hand, opponents of video lottery terminals consisted of individuals whose only weapon was emotion. They were not as well organized and would most often meet in churches and at community centres. Their arguments, which appeared in letters to the editor, were moral ones of a personal and emotional nature, such as the case of Don and Sandy Bishop, whose son Eric committed suicide in August 1998 as a result of his addiction to gambling and video lottery terminals. Churches were also very active in the debate as evidenced by the statement of Reverend O'Coin, pastor of Calvary Temple in Saint John: "We oppose it because of the addictive nature and because it preys often on those who can afford it the least. We also oppose it on the Christian principle of having to work for a living rather than trusting luck to be your provider (*Saint John Times Globe*, May 1, 2001, A1).

What can be learned from this referendum? This first exercise in direct democracy in New Brunswick remains rather inconclusive in that it reveals a certain naïveté on the government's part in making good on an election promise without clearly thinking through the referendum itself. One is left with the impression of a disconnect between the government's desire to involve the citizenry and its attachment to a more traditional decision-making process. Stewart Hyson (2001, 22) notes that the elitist element seems to have taken the upper hand. Nonetheless, the current government plans to repeat the exercise. During the last election campaign, in 2003, Premier Bernard Lord promised to adopt a permanent Referendum Act and to allow the holding of referendums on "important issues." The Premier wants to see a clearly defined legislative framework that would set forth certain rules in terms of referendum dates, financing, and the kinds of questions that could be asked (Ricard 2003, 4).

Discussion

There is no doubt that referendums can breathe new life into representative democracy. These days, it seems that they have become the panacea for the infamous "democratic deficit." However, it is necessary to proceed with caution and be mindful of certain issues associated with the use of referendums.

Political Commitment
The main challenge facing democratic societies is the need to rethink the relationship of trust between citizens and political elites. Aside from the issues involved, referendums can be an exercise in participatory democracy provided they engage the political authority in a consultative process with the populace as a whole. Accordingly, such a process must be conducted in a spirit of transparency and goodwill on the part of the political elites. Referendums may help build a "strong democracy" and link up with the idea of a "path" as espoused by Benjamin Barber (1997, 138–139), that is, a democracy that is experienced primarily as an educational exercise or a path, not simply a destination to be reached.

Put more pragmatically, governments therefore have responsibilities and obligations when it comes to the smooth running of a referendum. One of these is to establish clear and transparent rules for the process. In the case of the referendum of May 14, the Lord government's claim that it would remain neutral and that the debate would take place through the free play of the forces of civil society appears to have been ill-founded. Such rhetoric is risky, because it allows the strongest and best-organized groups to hijack the referendum process or more simply, to "buy the referendum outcome." The government did not limit spending on the campaign, a position that gave the impression that it was supporting the Yes side, which had far more financial resources. Moreover, it should be mentioned that the government did intervene in the campaign, through the comments of certain ministers, particularly Finance Minister Norm Betts and Justice Minister Brad Green, who voiced concern about the prospect of having to get by with less revenue and face an increase of taxes: "There will have to be an increase in revenues from taxes and a decrease in expenditures or a combination of the two, because deficits are not an option, said the finance minister" (*The Daily Gleaner*, May 4, 2001 A3).

In the case of government-initiated referendums, such as the New Brunswick case, clear and strict guidelines should be set out in the enacting legislation. Existing referendum legislation in Canada, particularly at the federal level with Bill C-81, has put in place rules to ensure a fair process. Mendelsohn and Parkin (2001a) identify four types of arrangement "that make it easier for voters to make good choices." First, referendum legislation must allow for parliamentary debate on the referendum question. It must specify the length of debate in the Legislative Assembly to allow the political parties to voice their opinions on the question. In our view, this first debate is fundamental in order to bring legitimacy to the referendum process, especially when the government controls the agenda. Second, citizens must feel involved in the referendum process with a process that will allow them to voice their opinions. Third, it is necessary not only to encourage debate within society but also to ensure balanced dissemination of information, such as pamphlets produced by the government. Fourth, financing rules are fundamental to the process of a fair referendum and must contain the following elements: specific criteria for interest groups (referendum committees), financing rules (ceiling, disclosure of sources), publication of government expenses (e.g., like the UK government, which provided £125,000 in grant money to coordinating groups during the 1975 British referendum on membership in the European Common Market; Quebec took the same approach in its 1978 Referendum Act).

Furthermore, it is important to acknowledge the role of political elites at the centre of the referendum process. In view of the risk of the privatization of politics as a result of demands formulated by special groups, which tends to be the case more in referendums initiated by citizens (the most extreme case being California, with a staggering number of citizens' initiatives [Bowler and Donovan 2000]), political elites must be involved and may be able to counter the negative effects of referendums, namely, manipulation by private groups and neglect of minority interests (Morel 2001).

The Issue of Minorities

Aside from the rather classic argument that referendums are detrimental to representative democracy and can result in tyranny of the majority, we must be mindful of the potential negative impact of referendums on the rights of minorities, especially in a society such as New Brunswick where there are historical religious and linguistic cleavages between a majority (anglophones) and a minority (Acadians). Many analysts are clear on this point. Direct democracy has a strong tendency to be abusive of majority rule. Bowler and Donovan's study of citizen's initiatives (2001, 125) underlines the danger of majority rule in three ways. First, a majority can draft and implement laws. Second, a majority may be intolerant of minorities and civil rights. Finally, voters, when given a chance to express their choices, tend to be intolerant. The popular or citizen initiative is the more extreme version of direct democracy and can put minorities at risk. For example, in Switzerland and in the US a number of recent initiatives were seen by some to be anti-immigrant and anti-gay (Bowler and Donovan 2001). There are also some ways of avoiding injustices to minority rights, such as indirect initiatives, double majorities systems (Switzerland and Australia), and a fair legislative process. But, as noted by Bowler and Donovan (2001, 127), referendums alone do not necessarily put minorities at risk: "Despite these long long-standing concerns, it has not been empirically established that direct democracy necessary produces outcomes that are decidedly more anti-minority than those produced by legistatures." The outcomes depend more on the role of political elites and the political context, whether it is conflictual or conciliatory, than a general theory.

It should also be noted that referendums are less of a threat to rights that minorities have already obtained, in the form of acquired rights that are constitutionally protected. Any infringement of those rights will trigger a reaction and result in legal recourse, which francophone minorities have traditionally availed themselves of. However, referendums can be a threat to minorities seeking new rights, such as gays and lesbians. In a recent study, Avigail Eisenberg (2004) draws an important distinction between two types of minorities: national minorities, which are intent on protecting specific rights such as language, and equal minorities, who seek to obtain recognition of equality with the majority, such as gays and lesbians seeking marriage rights. In the case of national minorities, Eisenberg notes that the use of referendums could possibly widen the gap between the majority and the minority in plurinational societies. According to the author, it is necessary to pay close attention to the threat of rifts caused by the use of referendums: "Referendums were an effective way to involve citizens in a form of 'participatory ethnic posturing'" (Eisenberg 2004, 14). Let us consider some extreme but rather revealing cases. In the United States, the English Only lobby movement has put forward popular initiatives in several states and municipalities aimed at curtailing the linguistic rights of Hispanic and aboriginal minorities. In the former Yugoslavia, referendums were used in an effort to break up the federation and encourage strongly aroused nationalist sentiments in the early 1990s. In Canada, the holding of some 30 municipal referendums in Manitoba in 1983 on the language issue did more to allow a few individuals to continue their fierce activism against the minority

Table 11.1: Results of the 1942 and 1992 referendums in New Brunswick

1942 Ridings	Yes (%)	No (%)	1992 Ridings	Yes (%)	No (%)
Restigouche (F)	40	60	Restigouche (F)	76	24
Gloucester (F)	41	59	Gloucester (F)	87	13
Northumberland	71	29	Miramichi	57	43
Westmorland	69	31	Beauséjour (F)	75	25
Kent (F)	31	69	Moncton	61	39
Royal (A)	88	12	Fundy-Royal	47	53
Saint John (A)	87	13	Saint John	47	53
York-Sunbury (A)	86	14	Fredericton (A)	49	51
Charlotte (A)	87	13	Carleton-Charlotte	48	52
Victoria-Carleton (F)	12	88	Madawaska (F)	82	18

F = majority francophone
A = majority anglophone

francophone community than to give populist impulse to an exercise in direct democracy (Hébert 2004).

Even though the question at issue in the referendum on video lottery terminals seemed far removed from traditional splits based on language and religion, the exercise revealed differences in perception between anglophones and francophones. Voting played out along religious and linguistic lines. Voters in the francophone regions of northeastern and northwestern New Brunswick were more detached and even indifferent towards this moral issue. In contrast, the more Protestant anglophone counties in southwestern New Brunswick were distinctly opposed to the VLTs, considering them a scourge on society; voters there let their social conservatism show. The outcome would appear to confirm a historical divide between anglophone and francophone regions in the province, taking us back to a time of "mutual incomprehension" between English Canadians and French Canadians (Mallory 1971, 395).

Similar federal examples are the linguistic and religious splits witnessed in the national referendums of 1942 (conscription) and 1992 (Charlottetown Accord). Table 11.1 presents the results of the two referendums in New Brunswick and the largest gaps between anglophone and francophone ridings. In 1992, New Brunswick was one of a few provinces that voted in favour of the Charlottetown Accord, but many anglophones rejected the deal, and the No side had a strong showing in four of the province's 10 federal ridings. We need also to remember that the only provincial committee campaigning for the No side was led by the CoR Party (Belkhodja 2002, 101). This outcome was not really expected by a government whose message was more focused on avoiding any references to the duality of the province and using the referendum as a populist way of reaching out to undifferentiated citizens. Drawing on the study of Avigail Eisenberg (2001) on the outcome of referendums, we find this aspect even more concerning for the rights of minorities. We need to be asking another question: what is the ideological reason behind the decision to use referendums?

Conclusion

This chapter has focused on the experience of direct democracy in New Brunswick. Three arguments can be made. First, it is important to acknowledge the complexity of the concept of populism. It is quite clear that populism is in vogue, thanks to what Bernard Manin (1995) calls the "democracy of the public," meaning a democracy that is strongly characterized by the principles of proximity and closeness (rapprochement). By using direct-democracy mechanisms, political elites are seeking first and foremost to connect with the people. However, we must not lose sight of the inherent risks of such an approach, namely, manipulation and personalization of power. We must remember that populism is not shielded from demagogic and manipulative behaviours and that it can be a way of overstepping the democracy of traditional mechanisms of representation.

Second, there is no question that referendums can divide populations or even exacerbate the isolation of and misunderstandings between communities. More and more, democratic societies will have to find ways to manage the very broad cultural, linguistic, ethnic, and religious diversity of their citizens. Consequently, the use of referendums can lead to an intensification of conflicts, which tend to take shape along new lines that are based more on ethnicity and identity, and much more divisive. In the end, the referendum process also has a tendency to obliterate or reduce the complex reality of a political situation to nothing more than a quick and effective choice and to make reconciliation difficult. In New Brunswick, many observers refer to a tradition of elite accommodation that has been responsible for the political stability enjoyed since the end of the 19th century. The Acadian community has been very much a part of political, economic, and cultural life in the province since the 1960s. It struggled to obtain recognition from the majority. The major reforms that were introduced by the Liberal government of Louis J. Robichaud and continued under the Conservative government of Richard Hatfield considerably altered the political landscape in the province. The modernization of government and the recognition of the language rights of the Acadian minority are the products of that culture of accommodation. However, the possibility of more extremist confrontation along those cleavages is not all that far removed from the province's political culture (Thorburn 1958; Aunger 1981; See 1993).

Lastly, it is important to question the true intent of governments in holding referendums. Is it for pragmatic or ideological reasons? The general perception is that referendums are more a pragmatic tool for obtaining a sense of public opinion on sensitive issues that governments have difficulty resolving. Referendums are a sort of democratic "valve" allowing for more direct and spontaneous consultation. If they are poorly structured, they can tarnish the legitimacy of the political process at the centre of democracy by allowing the message of politics to become overshadowed by other discourses, mainly those of economics, identity, and ethnicity (Mongin 1998). Referendums should be used cautiously and not for every passing issue. Referendums must be part of a fair and transparent process requiring public or civic participation. In our view, the decision of the Lord government to have only binding referendums seems restrictive. Consultative referendums are more common in the Canadian context and, as things stand now, all referendums are somewhat binding, as they compel governments to take the popular will into account.

Notes

1. A good example would be the United Farmers of New Brunswick movement, which, in the 1920s, succeeded in electing nine of its members to the provincial legislature. There is also the Acadian Party, which was founded in the 1970s.
2. Even though the Reform Party did not manage to get a single MP elected in the Atlantic Region, it nevertheless tried to become established in Nova Scotia and in New Brunswick especially. In the latter province, the party saw its popular support rise from 8.5% in 1993 to 13.1% in 1997. Also in 1997, the party obtained its highest standings in the anglophone ridings of New Brunswick, capturing more than 20% of the votes cast (Tobique-Mactaquac: 27.7%; Fundy-Royal: 22.9%; Fredericton: 21.8%; and Charlotte: 21.1%). In the last election, the Canadian Alliance continued to mobilize, capturing 15.7% of votes cast. See the *Report of the Chief Electoral Officer of Canada on the 37th General Election Held on November 27, 2000*.
3. *L'Acadie Nouvelle, Times & Transcript, Telegraph Journal, Daily Gleaner*.

References

Adamson, Agar, and Ian Stewart. 1991. "Party Politics in Atlantic Canada: Still the Mysterious East?" In *Party Politics in Canada*, ed. Hugh Thorburn, 507–521. Scarborough: Prentice Hall.

Augers, François-Albert. 1942. "Un vote de race." *L'Action nationale* 19:299–312.

Aunger, Edmund. 1981. *In Search of Political Stability: A Comparative Study of New*

Brunswick and Northern Ireland. Montreal and Kingston: McGill-Queen's University Press.

Barber, Benjamin. 1997. *Démocratie forte*. Paris: Desclée de Brouwer.

Belkhodja, Chedly. 1999. "La dimension populiste de l'émergence et du succès électoral du Parti Confederation of Regions (CoR) au Nouveau-Brunswick." *Revue canadienne de science politique* 32(2):293–315.

—. 2002. "Populism and Community: The Cases of Reform and the Confederation of Regions Party in New Brunswick." In *Political Parties, Representation, and Electoral Democracy in Canada*, ed. William Cross, 92–112. Toronto: Oxford University Press.

Betz, Hans-Georg, and Stephan Immerfall, eds. 1998. *New Politics of the Right: Neo-Populist Parties and Movements in Established Democracies*. New York: St. Martin's Press.

Bowler, Shaun, and Todd Donovan. 2000. "California's Experience with Direct Democracy." *Parliamentary Affairs* 53:644–656.

—. 2001. "Popular Control of Referendum Agendas: Implications for Democratic Outcomes and Minority Rights." In *Referendum Democracy: Citizens, Elites, and Deliberation in Referendum Campaigns*, ed. Matthew Mendelsohn and Andrew Parkin, 146–225. London: Palgrave.

Boyer, Patrick. 1992. *Direct Democracy in Canada: The History and Future of Referendums*. Toronto: Dundurn Press.

—. 1992. *The People's Mandate: Referendums and More Democratic Canada*. Toronto: Dundurn Press.

Budge, Ian. 1996. *The New Challenge of Direct Democracy*. Cambridge: Polity Press.

—. 2001. "Political Parties in Direct Democracy." In *Referendum Democracy: Citizens, Elites, and Deliberation in Referendum Campaigns*, ed. Matthew Mendelsohn and Andrew Parkin, 67–87. London: Palgrave.

Butler, David, and Austin Ranney, eds. 1994. *Referendums around the World: The Growing Use of Direct Democracy*. Washington: American Enterprise Institute.

Canada West Foundation. 2001. *Gambling in Canada Special Report: Video Lottery Terminals in New Brunswick*.

Canovan, Margaret. 1999. "Trust the People! Populism and the Two Faces of Democracy." *Political Studies* 47(1):2–16.

Chandler, David. 2001. "Active Citizens and the Therapeutic State: The Role of Democratic Participation in Local Government Reform." *Party Politics* 29(1):3–14.

Couturier, Jacques-Paul. 1987. "Splendeur et misère du sentiment prohibitionniste: Étude des référendums sur la prohibition locale dans le comté de Westmorland, N.-B., 1879–1899." *Revue de l'Université de Moncton* 20(1):99–118.

Dalton, J. Russell. 2004. "Advanced Democracies and the New Politics." *Journal of Democracy* 15(1):124–138.

Dunsmuir, Mollie. 1992. *Referendums: The Canadian Experience in an International Context.* Ottawa: Law and Government Division, Library of Parliament.

Eisenberg, Avigail. 2001. "The Medium is the Message: How Referendums Lead us to Understand Equality." In *Referendum Democracy: Citizens, Elites, and Deliberation in Referendum Campaigns,* ed. Matthew Mendelsohn and Andrew Parkin, 147–164. London: Palgrave.

—. 2004. "When (if Ever) Are Referendums on Minority Rights Fair?" In *Representation and Democratic Theory,* ed. David Laycock, 3–22. Vancouver: UBC Press.

Gibbins, Roger. 2000. "Federalism in a Digital World." *Canadian Journal of Political Science* 22(4):682–684.

Hahn, Harlan. 1968. "Voting in Canadian Communities: A Taxonomy of Referendum Issues." *Canadian Journal of Political Science* 1(4):462–469.

Hébert, Raymond. 2004. *Manitoba's French Language Crisis: A Cautionary Tale.* Montreal and Kingston: McGill-Queen's University Press.

Hyson, Stewart. 2001. "New Brunswick's Gamble on VLTs: Was This the Way to Conduct a Referendum?" *Canadian Parliamentary Review* 24(4):19–26.

—. 2003. "*New Brunswick's VLT Gambling Policy: Morality Politics and the Legitimization of Vice.*" Paper presented to the annual meeting of the Canadian Political Science Association, Dalhousie University, Halifax, Nova Scotia.

Ihl O., et al. 2003. *La tentation populiste au cœur de l'Europe.* Paris: La Découverte.

Johnston, Richard, et al. 1996. *The Challenge of Direct Democracy.* Montreal and Kingston: McGill-Queen's University Press.

Krueger, R. Ralph. 1970. "The Provincial-Municipal Government Revolution in New Brunswick." *Canadian Public Administration* 13(1):51–99.

LeDuc, Lawrence. 2003. *The Politics of Direct Democracy: Referendums in Global Perspective.* Peterborough: Broadview Press.

Macdonald, David. 1991. "Referendums and Federal General Elections in Canada." Research Studies, vol. 10, Royal Commission on Electoral Reform and Party Financing, 339–383.

Mallory, James R. 1971. *The Structure of Canadian Government.* Toronto: Macmillan.

Manin, Bernard. 1995. *Principes du gouvernement représentatif.* Paris: Calmann-Lévy.

Marquis, Pierre. 1993. *Referendums in Canada: The Effect of Populist Decision-Making on Representative Democracy.* Ottawa: Library of Parliament.

Mendelsohn, Matthew, and Andrew Parkin. 2001a. "Introducing Direct Democracy in Canada." *Choice* 7(5):3–35.

—. 2001b. *Referendum Democracy: Citizens, Elites, and Deliberation in Referendum Campaigns.* London: Palgrave.

Mény, Yves, and Yves Surel. 2000. *Par le peuple, pour le peuple: Le populisme et les démocraties.* Paris: Fayard.

Mongin, Olivier. 1998. *L'après 1989: Les nouveaux langages du politique.* Paris: Hachette.

Morel, Laurence. 2000. "Vers une démocratie directe partisane." *Revue française de science politique* 50(4–5):765–778.

———. 2001. "The Rise of Government-Initiated Referendums in Consolidated Democracies." In *Referendum Democracy: Citizens, Elites and Deliberation in Referendum Campaigns*, ed. Matthew Mendelsohn and Andrew Parkin, 46–64. London: Palgrave.

Mowrey, Tim, and Alain Pelletier. 2001. "Referendums in Canada: A Comparative Overview." *Electoral Insight* 3(1):18–22.

Nevitte, Neil. 1996. *The Decline of Deference*. Toronto: Broadview Press.

New Brunswick. Legislative Assembly. 2000a. *Excerpts from Hansard*, 8 December.

———. 2000b. *Excerpts from Hansard*, 12 December.

———. 2000c. *Excerpts from Hansard*, 20 December.

Norris, Pippa. 1999. *Critical Citizens: Global Support for Democratic Government*. Oxford: Oxford University Press.

Papadopoulos, Yannis. 1998. "Démocratie directe, mobilisation, intégration." In *L'ignorance du peuple: Essais sur la démocratie*, ed. Gérard Duprat, 79–125. Paris: Presses universitaires de France.

Piott, L. Steven. 2003. "Giving Voters a Voice: The Origins of the Initiative and the Referendum in America." Columbia, MO: University of Missouri Press.

Poitras, Jacques. 2004. *The Right Fight: Bernard Lord and the Conservative Dilemma*. Fredericton: Goose Lane.

Ricard, Philippe. 2003. "Lord promet plus de référendums dans un 2e mandat." *L'Acadie Nouvelle*, 28 February, p.4.

Rosanvallon, Pierre. 2000. *La démocratie inachevée: Histoire de la souveraineté du peuple en France*. Paris: Gallimard.

See, W. Scott. 1993. *Riots in New Brunswick: Orange Nativism and Social Violence in the 1840s*. Toronto: University of Toronto Press.

Telegraph Journal. 2000. "VLT Voters Need Options." 12 December, A4

Thorburn, Hugh. 1958. *Politics in New Brunswick*. Toronto: University of Toronto Press.

Urbinati, N. 1998. "Democracy and Populism." *Constellations* 5(1):110–124.

Urquart, Mia. 2001. "The VLT Debate." *Saint John Times Globe*, 1 May, A1.

⊰ CHAPTER TWELVE ⊱

Voter Participation in New Brunswick and the Political Disengagement of the Young

PAUL HOWE

Introduction

GROWING CONCERN ACROSS the country about declining participation rates in elections has lent impetus to the wave of democratic reform initiatives currently underway in various provinces and at the federal level. In New Brunswick, the first significant move on this front was the creation of the Commission on Legislative Democracy by the Conservative government in early 2004. The commission was asked, among other parts of its broad mandate, to "examine and make recommendations on increasing voter turnout in provincial general elections, particularly amongst young New Brunswickers." This chapter describes voter participation patterns in New Brunswick and Canada, assesses different ideas about why turnout has been declining, and suggests potential ways of addressing the matter.

The chapter provides a broad overview of competing explanations for the drop in voter turnout, with a particular focus on reasons for the withdrawal of younger voters from electoral politics. In part, this entails synthesizing research previously done on the topic. It also involves assessing particular hypotheses that have been advanced using survey data on the attitudes and behaviour of electors. While the issue of declining turnout is hardly unique to New Brunswick, it is nevertheless useful and appropriate to verify whether ideas and hypotheses meant to explain the phenomenon at large do, in fact, apply to this province. Most surveys on political matters do not contain sufficient numbers of New Brunswick respondents to permit such analysis. Fortuitously, however, a survey of New Brunswickers with a number of questions relevant to the issue of declining turnout, and a sample size of just over 1,000, was carried out in mid-2003—the New Brunswick Social Capital Survey, or NBSCS. This is the principal data source used in the analysis below. It is supplemented in places with Canada-wide surveys that address areas not covered in the New Brunswick study or which allow for more reliable analysis because of their larger sample sizes.[1]

Four sections follow. The first briefly sets the stage by reviewing trends in voter participation over time and age differences in turnout. The second considers a variety of societal patterns and trends that have been identified as factors contributing to declining turnout. Political and institutional explanations for the phenomenon are taken up in the third section. Having canvassed a wide range of hypotheses and explanations for declining turnout, possible solutions and recommendations are presented in the fourth and final section.

Trends in Voter Participation

The general pattern of declining voter participation in recent times is familiar to most observers of the Canadian political scene. Salient nationwide trends, as well as important particulars on the New Brunswick case, can be captured in a few key points:

- Turnout in Canadian elections has been dropping steadily over the past 15 years. At the federal level, turnout fell from 75.3% in 1988 to 60.9% in 2004, recovering slightly in 2006 to 64.7%.[2] Similarly in New Brunswick provincial elections, turnout has slowly slipped from 82.0% in 1987 to 68.7% in 2003, falling further still in 2006 to 67.5%.[3]

- One key reason for lower turnout overall is the reduced participation of young Canadians in elections. While there has long been a tendency for younger people to vote less than their elders, the participation gap between young and old has become particularly pronounced in recent years (Blais et al. 2004).

- While this general pattern is clear, the precise participation rate of different age groups has been subject to considerable debate, owing to the significantly inflated estimates of voter participation produced by survey-based methods. A recent study by Elections Canada based on a different methodology—a sampling of 95,000 voters list records from the 2004 federal election—has provided definitive estimates for the first time. Participation in that election among first-time voters, those aged 18 to 21.5, is estimated at 38.7%. Among second time voters, the estimate is 35.4%. At the other end of the scale, the highest estimated participation rate is 75% for those aged 58 to 67 (Elections Canada 2005, 5).[4]

- At this point, no such definitive estimate is available for voter participation rates in New Brunswick. However, the survey on which much of the later analysis in this paper is based does reveal a significant age gap for voter turnout in the 2003 provincial election. Table 12.1 shows the results. Turnout is estimated at 59.4% among those aged 18 to 24, 76.3% among those 25 to 29, and 90.8% among those 60 and older.[5] These numbers are similar to *survey-based* estimates for the 2004 federal election (relevant figures appear later in this chapter). It is reasonable to assume, therefore, that the *true* participation rate by age group in the 2003 New Brunswick election would broadly mirror the figures produced by Elections Canada for the 2004 federal election—that is to say, a participation rate under 40% for the youngest voters and a gap in participation of roughly 40 points between the youngest group and older citizens.

Explanations for Declining Turnout: Social Trends

Voting is first and foremost a political act and it is therefore natural to assume that the reasons for declining turnout must lie in the realm of politics. In particular, it is tempting to presume that declining voter turnout must be related to that other striking feature of contemporary Canadian democracy, the deep and widespread cynicism about politics and politicians that has come to the fore in recent years. Canadians themselves tend to believe this: when asked about declining turnout, "negative public attitudes toward ... politicians and political institutions" are identified by the majority as the reason why many of their fellow citizens are failing to vote (Pammett and Leduc 2003, 7). However, there are important schools of scholarly thought that suggest that reduced participation in elections is not a product of political discontent. Instead, it derives from long-term social changes, largely divorced from the political realm, that have altered society in subtle but important ways with significant consequences for political participation. This is an important alternative perspective—or rather set of perspectives—that should be given due consideration before turning

Table 12.1: Voter turnout in 2003 New Brunswick provincial election							
	Age						
	18–24	25–29	30–39	40–49	50–59	60+	Total
Voted in 2003 (%)	59.4	76.3	80.7	87.9	89.6	90.8	85.4
(N)	(64)	(59)	(135)	(224)	(211)	(251)	(944)

Source: Author's calculations based on 2003 NBSCS

to what may seem the more likely causes of voter withdrawal in the political realm.

The Erosion of Social Capital

One prominent account of long-term social changes affecting the quality and character of modern democracy is found in Robert Putnam's widely acclaimed book, *Bowling Alone*. Putnam's focus is the United States and the evolution of American society over the past 40 years. The argument, in a nutshell, is that a valuable social commodity referred to as "social capital"—broadly defined as the "connections among individuals," and more specifically as "social networks and the norms of reciprocity and trustworthiness that arise from them" (Putnam 2000, 19)—has diminished. The most important reason is the changed attitudes and behaviour of young Americans. On virtually every measure of social capital, younger generations are less involved and less connected with their fellow citizens than older generations were at the same age. As these generations have come to represent a larger proportion of the population, the stock of social capital in the United States has suffered gradual and continual erosion.

Putnam's sweeping account has caught the attention of many outside the United States, who have wondered whether his diagnosis of social malaise holds true elsewhere. In Canada, there has been no study of the same scope, but the relevant concepts have been invoked and applied to see whether the arguments can help explain salient features of contemporary Canadian society.

For Putnam, local and voluntary forms of association are the critical wellsprings of social capital. The relatively intimate connections established in face-to-face contacts foster norms of trust and social interaction that carry over into the more formal political realm to acts such as voting. Two key measures of social capital are involvement in associations of various kinds and the interpersonal trust that develops between people as a result of their involvement with others. The relevant question in considering the utility of Putnam's thesis is whether or not linkages exist between these measures of social capital

Table 12.2a: Measures of social capital by age, New Brunswick, 2003

	Age					
	18–29	30–39	40–49	50–59	60+	Total
Belong to three or more associations (%)	13.5	23.7	30.9	36.2	38.6	30.5
Believe that "most people can be trusted" (%)	49.6	62.8	58.8	61.1	65.5	60.2
(N)	(141)	(137)	(228)	(216)	(249)	(971)

Source: Author's calculations based on 2003 NBSCS

Table 12.2b: Social capital and voter participation, New Brunswick, 2003

	Voted in 2003 (%)	(N)
Number of associational memberships		
Three or more	90.9	(296)
Two	83.5	(224)
One	80.2	(247)
None	82.5	(177)
Interpersonal trust		
Believe that "most people can be trusted"	87.7	(575)
Believe that "you cannot be too careful in dealing with people"	81.2	(330)

Source: Author's calculations based on 2003 NBSCS

and electoral participation. Also relevant to consider is whether or not young people in New Brunswick lag behind older people on these barometers of social capital, as they do in the United States.

The relevant results, shown in Tables 12.2a and 12.2b, mirror what others have found: while some components of the argument hold up, it is difficult to pin much of the age gap in voter participation on factors related to social capital. Young people are less involved in associations[6]—only 14% of those under 30 belong to three or more, compared to 39% of those 60 and over—and they are less trusting of others, though here the difference between young and old is rather small. The weaker link, however, is that between these measures of social capital and voter participation, as shown in Table 12.2b. The relationships are in the anticipated direction—those active in associations and trusting of others are more likely to vote—but the turnout differences are relatively small, too small to explain a significant portion of the age gap in voter turnout. The social capital theory, whatever its other merits, does not appear to tell us a great deal about voter participation.[7]

Changing Values

Another perspective on social change potentially relevant to the issue of declining voter turnout is the theory of post-materialism developed by American political scientist Ronald Inglehart. Like Putnam, Inglehart identifies evolutionary changes rooted in intergenerational patterns that are gradually transforming the social and political landscape. His argument starts from the premise that basic value priorities form early in an individual's life, are shaped by prevailing conditions at that time, and remain relatively stable thereafter. Applying the theory in the first instance to post-war Western Europe, Inglehart reasoned that those who came of age before, during, and shortly after World War II would have experienced significant security concerns and economic hardship, causing them to value order and material well-being above all else. Younger generations who came of age in more stable and prosperous times would have tended to take order and prosperity for granted and come to place greater value on post-materialist values, such as personal autonomy and quality of life concerns. Drawing on survey data gathered over a long period, Inglehart showed that younger generations in Western Europe did indeed subscribe to post-materialist values in greater numbers than older citizens. Moreover, he linked these changing value priorities of younger generations to a variety of important political developments, including the salience of new issues, such as environmentalism, the rise of new parties promoting said causes (e.g., the Greens), and the increasing use of unconventional forms of participation, such as protests and petitions (Inglehart 1977, 1990).

The theory has attracted wide attention and certainly resonates with elements of the Canadian experience. Canadian politics, relatively tradition-bound, has witnessed, over the past 30 years or so, the emergence of many movements seeking to push new issues on the agenda, often circumventing traditional channels in favour of unconventional methods of citizen mobilization. The realm of party politics has also been affected, perhaps most notably in the 2004 federal election, which saw Green Party support rise to 4.3% nationwide. Survey evidence, as well as anecdotal reports, suggest that young people and previous non-voters figured heavily among its supporters.[8] The implication would seem to be that if there were more space still for alternative ideas and approaches, more young people would be drawn back into electoral politics. If the necessary reforms are not forthcoming, however, the theory also offers the consolation that young post-materialists, if not involved in electoral politics, are active on other fronts, finding alternative ways to make their views known and thereby exercise some influence on public opinion and policymaking.

The empirical support for the post-materialist assessment of declining turnout is, however, weak. In the first place, there are not higher numbers of

Table 12.3: Post-materialist values and behaviours by age, New Brunswick, 2003

	Age 18–29	30–39	40–49	50–59	60+	Total
Subscribe to post-materialist values (%)	16.9	11.1	20.6	17.8	22.8	18.6
Signed petition directed at government in past 5 years (%)	39.3	50.0	54.8	54.6	30.2	45.5
Attended protest meeting or demonstration in past 5 years (%)	14.9	16.5	20.0	18.1	11.1	16.0
(N)	(136)	(135)	(214)	(208)	(228)	(921)

Source: Author's calculations based on 2003 NBSCS

post-materialists among young New Brunswickers, using one variant on the conventional method of categorizing people as such.[9] As Table 12.3 indicates, about 17% of those under age 30 fall into this category, slightly below the figure of 18.6% for the sample as a whole. Nor, as Table 12.3 also demonstrates, are young people in New Brunswick particularly likely to engage in unconventional forms of political action such as signing petitions or attending demonstrations and protests.

It might be noted, however, that the gaps between young and old are much more pronounced when it comes to more traditional forms of political participation—voting in elections for one, but also joining political parties. A number of recent works have highlighted the dearth of young members in Canada's political parties, both federal and provincial (Cross and Young 2004; Cross 2004; Howe and Northrup 2001). Thus, it would appear that young people who are involved politically have a *relative* preference for unconventional forms of participation (O'Neill 2000, 13). But this does not alter what is perhaps the more critical pattern for current purposes: the bulk of those 18 to 29, as in older age categories, do not participate politically in unconventional ways.

In addition, further analysis of the 2003 NBSCS (not shown here) reveals that those New Brunswickers who do engage in unconventional political action are just as likely or more likely to vote than those who do not, undermining the notion that unconventional actions represent a substitute to traditional participation. The flip side of this is that non-voters in New Brunswick are not especially likely to participate in less conventional ways. The overall assessment emerging from these observations is that the value of post-materialist theory lies in identifying changing patterns in the issues and modes of political involvement for the *minority of young people* who do become involved politically.

Table 12.4a: Perceived duty to vote by age, New Brunswick, 2003

	Age					
	18–29	30–39	40–49	50–59	60+	Total
Strongly agree (%)	49.3	74.5	79.4	80.8	80.7	75.1
Somewhat agree (%)	27.5	16.1	11.8	11.2	10.8	14.3
Disagree (strongly or somewhat) (%)	23.2	9.5	8.8	7.9	8.4	10.7
(N)	(138)	(137)	(228)	(214)	(249)	(966)

Source: Author's calculations based on 2003 NBSCS

Table 12.4b: Perceived duty to vote and voter participation, New Brunswick, 2003

	Voted in 2003 (%)	(N)
Duty to Vote		
Strongly agree	91.1	(720)
Somewhat agree	72.0	(132)
Disagree (either strongly or somewhat)	62.0	(79)

Source: Author's calculations based on 2003 NBSCS

It does not, however, appear to explain the significant increase in the numbers who choose not to be involved in any way whatsoever.

There is, however, a related line of thought concerning changing values that provides a more promising explanation for declining turnout. Neil Nevitte's *The Decline of Deference* (1996) builds on Inglehart's ideas about intergenerational differences in basic values. The title captures the essence of his argument: young Canadians, in common with young people in other advanced industrial democracies, are less deferential to authority, less accepting of traditional norms and practices, than older generations. Like Inglehart, Nevitte sees this as a phenomenon long in the works, deriving from the formative experiences of today's younger generations. Critical influences include changing authority structures within the family and evolving norms and practices in the workplace, non-political realms of socialization that have produced a generation of young people more inclined to question political authority and tradition (Nevitte 1996, 279–280).

Nevitte's study has direct relevance to a factor that has been singled out as an important factor in voting: civic duty (Blais 2000, 92–114). It is this type of traditional norm that less deferential young people are likely to reject. The survey evidence here is quite supportive of the theory. As Table 12.4a shows, while most people in New Brunswick strongly believe that voting is a citizen's duty, young people are considerably less likely to share that view. Furthermore, this attitude does have a significant effect on voting, as shown in Table 12.4b: only 62% of those who disagree that voting is a civic duty cast a ballot in the 2003 provincial election, compared to 91% who believe strongly that it is. These findings are consistent with what has been found for Canada as a whole (Blais et al. 2004, 227–229), as well as other countries that have experienced a decline in voting among young people, such as Britain (Clarke et al. 2003).

A word of caution should be added to these results, however, concerning potential over-reporting of voting by survey respondents. Over-reporting is produced by respondents indicating they voted in a particular election when in fact they did not, and it is one of the factors that contributes to inflated estimates of voter participation in survey-based research. In trying to determine why respondents sometimes misrepresent their behaviour, it has been found that over-reporting is most prevalent among those who feel the greatest *social pressure* to vote (Bernstein, Chadha, and Montjoy 2001).[10] It is reasonable to speculate that one key element behind such pressure would be a perceived duty to vote. Therefore, it is possible, indeed likely, that over-reporting is particularly common among those who feel that voting is a civic duty. If this is the case, then differences in voter participation between civically minded citizens and their less conscientious counterparts will be overestimated.

The Rise of Individualism and the Decline of Community
A third distinct explanation for declining turnout emerges out of a common thread running through the social capital and post-materialist accounts of the evolution of contemporary society. Implicit in both theories is a refrain about the decline of community and the rise of individualism. People nowadays, young people especially, are less apt to concern themselves with the values and priorities of the communities they live in and more likely to put stock in their own ideas and concerns. Evaluations of this development differ—Putnam clearly laments the loss of interpersonal connection and community, whereas Nevitte and Inglehart seem to celebrate the newfound autonomy implied by the change—but they share this common thread in their characterization of the changing temper of modern times.

The notion of ascendant individualism certainly has a ring of truth to it and is potentially quite relevant to voter participation. For, whereas it has been argued by some that people have good reasons for *not* voting—the individual vote carries little weight and has a vanishingly small chance of actually making a difference to the election outcome[11]—others would contend that this thinking fails to appreciate the complex motivations that bring people to vote.

Election day, they would contend, is not just about picking a government; it also serves as an occasion for the people of a nation or province to affirm the bonds of community by coming together in a common endeavour. Thus voting, as André Blais argues, is partly a way of "expressing one's sense of belonging to the larger community" (2000, 52). If this reasoning is correct, a decline in community sentiment and a concomitant rise in individualism could be a significant factor behind declining turnout among younger citizens.

The empirical evidence here does support the theoretical reasoning, with both of the necessary relationships holding. Young people do have a weaker sense of attachment to community, a variable from the NBSCS that is based on combining measures of respondents' attachments to "their local community" and to "New Brunswick." Only 45% of those under 30 report strong attachments, compared to 73% of those 60 and over (Table 12.5a). Meanwhile, strength of attachment to community is a fairly significant predictor of voting. Among those with strong attachments, 90% indicate they voted in the 2003 provincial election; among those with weak attachments, the figure is only 67% (Table 12.5b). Individualistic attitudes among the young do seem to play some role in declining turnout.

Attention to Politics: Civic Literacy, Political Interest, and Media Consumption

One final set of social changes relevant to the decline in voter participation relates to the degree to which citizens pay attention to events in the political realm. This is not a single trend, but multiple related trends that likely interact and reinforce one another. The first of these is a widening gap between young and old in levels of *political knowledge*, or what political scientist Henry Milner (2002) evocatively calls *civic literacy*. The second is the diminished level of *interest in politics* expressed by younger citizens. The third pertains to patterns of *media use*, in particular the low numbers of young people who read newspapers regularly or pay close attention to politics on television.

On all three counts, the empirical evidence for a role in declining voter turnout is persuasive. As Table 12.6a shows, young people in New Brunswick are less familiar with basic political facts, in this case the names of the premiers of three provinces, New Brunswick, Nova Scotia and Alberta. Only 17% of those under 30 were able to name at least two of the three, compared to 58% of those 60 and over, a striking difference. Also noteworthy are differences in political interest and media use: only 15% of the younger group express a high level of interest in politics compared to 33% of the 60 and over group; and just over a quarter (28%) read the newspaper 3 or more hours per week, compared to nearly two-thirds (64%) of older respondents. Lest it be assumed that young

Table 12.5a: Attachment to community by age, New Brunswick, 2003

	Age					
	18–29	30–39	40–49	50–59	60+	Total
Strong attachment (%)	45.4	66.4	63.9	73.0	72.5	65.8
Moderate attachment (%)	31.9	19.0	23.0	20.5	20.7	22.6
Weak attachment (%)	22.7	14.6	13.0	6.5	6.8	11.6
(N)	(141)	(137)	(230)	(215)	(251)	(974)

Source: Author's calculations based on 2003 NBSCS

Table 12.5b: Attachment to community and voter participation, New Brunswick, 2003

	Voted in 2003 (%)	(N)
Strong Attachment	90.0	(629)
Moderate Attachment	79.8	(208)
Weak Attachment	66.7	(99)

Note: The attachment to community scale is based on two questions asking respondents how attached they felt to their local community and how attached they felt to New Brunswick. Possible responses were very attached, somewhat attached, and not at all attached. Responses were combined and recoded to produce a three-point scale.

Source: Author's calculations based on 2003 NBSCS

Table 12.6a: Attention to politics by age, New Brunswick, 2003, and Canada, 2000

	Age					
	18–29	30–39	40–49	50–59	60+	Total
Able to name at least 2 of 3 provincial premiers (%)	17.0	41.0	46.5	50.5	57.5	45.2
High level of political interest (7 or more out of 10) (%)	14.9	21.2	30.6	28.4	32.5	26.9
Read newspapers 3 or more hours per week	27.9	36.2	42.6	45.4	63.8	45.6
(N) (%)	(141)	(137)	(229)	(215)	(243)	(964)
Watched at least 1 leaders debate in 2000 (%)*	30.6	40.9	44.9	52.6	66.4	46.9
(N)	(684)	(628)	(735)	(567)	(682)	(3296)

Source: Author's calculations based on 2003 NBSCS; *Author's calculation based on 2000 Canadian Election Study

Table 12.6b Attention to politics and voter participation, New Brunswick, 2003

	All Ages Voted in 2003 (%)	(N)	18–39 only Voted in 2003 (%)	(N)
Premiers identified				
None	75.2	(137)	61.3	(62)
1	84.1	(372)	75.2	(117)
2 or 2	89.7	(435)	83.5	(79)
Newspaper reading (hours per week)				
None	79.4	(107)	65.9	(41)
2 or less	82.7	(387)	72.7	(128)
3 or more	89.0	(438)	80.5	(87)
Political Interest				
Low (0–3)	76.9	(225)	56.3	(71)
Moderate (4–6)	85.8	(443)	78.5	(135)
High (7–10)	92.3	(260)	92.0	(50)

Source: Author's calculations based on 2003 NBSCS

people, if not avid newspaper readers, must supplement their political diet with politically oriented TV programming, the same table contains a telling comparison from the 2000 Canadian election study: only 31% of Canadians aged 18 to 29 reported watching one of the leaders debates in the election campaign compared to 66% of those over 60.

At the same time, knowledge, interest, and media use all show moderately strong relationships with voter participation. The figures on the left-hand side of Table 12.6b show a difference in voter participation, in the 2003 New Brunswick provincial election, of 10% to 25% between those who fall into the high and low categories on the knowledge, newspaper-reading, and political-interest scales. It should be added that previous research, using election study data for the 2000 federal election, has found stronger effects on voting than those in Table 12.6b; that same research has also revealed that political attention variables tend to have a greater impact on voter participation among the young than the old (Howe 2003, 2006). Thus, the right-hand column of Table 12.6b shows voting differences (again for New Brunswick in 2003) for those under 40 years of age only. In all cases, the voting gap between those in the high and low categories on the political attention variables is larger for the under 40 group than it is for the sample as a whole. Together, the results in Tables 12.6a and 12.6b suggest that waning attention to politics is indeed playing a significant role in declining turnout among young New Brunswickers.

If political attention variables help explain the age gap in voter turnout, they also shed light on an important demographic characteristic of young non-voters that has been noted elsewhere. It has been observed that the drop in voter turnout among young voters over the course of 1990s was most heavily concentrated among those with low levels of formal education (those with only a high school diploma and high school dropouts) (Gidengil et al. 2003, 10). Since low levels of education are associated with diminished levels of knowledge and interest in politics, as well as inattention to politics in the media, it is not surprising to find these variables playing a role in the reduced turnout levels of young New Brunswickers.

If these empirical findings are fairly clear-cut, the challenge with this particular dimension of voter disengagement lies in thinking through the larger implications. One critical view would be that the political attention variables are not really very helpful because they probably are as much symptoms as causes of disengagement among the young. Like the act of voting itself, they are part of a broader syndrome of disengagement with multiple manifestations that still stands in need of explanation (Johnston and Matthews 2004, 10). This is a useful criticism because it challenges us to dig deeper to search for the root causes of political inattention among the young. In doing so, it becomes clear that one critical issue is which of the three political attention variables—knowledge, interest, or media use—is considered the principal starting point for processes of waning political attentiveness.

Consider first the possibility that changing patterns of media use have led the way, producing changes in political knowledge and interest in their wake. Such an interpretation would lay heavy emphasis on changes in the media environment that have gradually unfolded over time and reduced the exposure of young people to political information. The first critical development would be the advent of television many years ago, which saw newspaper reading, a rich source of political news and information, gradually yielding ground to TV viewing. The effects were not necessarily drastic or immediate, however, since most viewers, in the early days of television, would have watched at least some news programming, if only due to a lack of program choice in the era of one or two channels. But as time has marched on, channels and viewing choices have proliferated, due to the advent of cable TV and later satellite, so that nowadays viewers can easily spend an evening in front of the television without encountering any news programming. This is not to mention the rise of other electronic diversions, such as video games and the Internet, that preoccupy many young people and allow them to avoid encountering any political content. As a result of these ongoing changes, young people are less likely to encounter political news and information, rendering them less knowledgeable about politics and less interested in the subject. On this interpretation, young people are not actively turning away from politics; their inattention is primarily an unfortunate by-product of a changing media environment (Wattenberg 2003, 164–167).

A quite different interpretation emerges if it is supposed that political knowledge is the initial catalyst for processes of disengagement: young people lacking a foundation of civic literacy find much of the political news and information they encounter difficult to digest or fully comprehend, and consequently they come to feel that politics is uninteresting and make little effort to seek out more information via the media. In this causal scenario, our sights naturally turn to the school system and the question of whether or not young people are being adequately equipped with a basic understanding of politics in their years of formal schooling. Is their formal education providing them with the civic literacy needed to take up the challenge of self-directed citizenship—keeping informed of political developments, grasping their significance, acting upon their own political preferences and ideals—upon graduation? If suspicion is cast on the education system, the question also arises as to whether there was ever a "golden age" of civics education when students were better prepared for the citizenship challenges that lay ahead, and, if so, what was done differently back then? These questions remain inadequately researched, but given the vast gulf in levels of political knowledge between young and old nowadays, the idea that shortcomings in the education system play a role in disengagement should not be discounted.

Another distinct interpretation arises if it is assumed that political interest is the critical starting point for processes of political inattentiveness. This is perhaps the most straightforward account: young people, for one reason or another, are not interested in politics and therefore make little effort to keep abreast of political developments in the newspapers and on TV, and therefore know little about politics. It is also the account that lends itself most readily to a *political* interpretation, as the follow-up question naturally arises: if young people are not interested in politics, is it something about the political system that has turned them off? The next section of the paper explores some possible answers to this question.

In doing so, however, it is not assumed that there must be some clear and identifiable element of the political system that is responsible for the declining political involvement of young people. This section has outlined some important social trends, largely removed from the political realm, that explain with varying degrees of success why young people are less inclined to participate in elections nowadays. The New Brunswick data, in keeping with findings elsewhere, suggest that one relevant factor is the changing values of younger generations, which include a relatively weak sense of civic duty and heightened individualism. Another important dimension is the reduced attention to politics among the young, as manifested in their media consumption habits and levels of civic literacy, patterns that can potentially be attributed to changes in the media environment and/or shortcomings in the education system. Bearing in mind these largely apolitical accounts, we now turn to consider more explicitly political factors to see how they can enhance our understanding of voter disengagement.

Explanations for Declining Turnout: Political and Institutional Factors

A number of hypotheses relating to the political and institutional sources of voter disengagement have been advanced. Some are more readily substantiated with empirical data than others. Together they add up to an important alternative perspective that usefully complements those interpretations that emphasize societal trends.

Uncompetitive Elections

One simple and popular political explanation for declining voter turnout is lack of electoral competition. Close elections bring people out to the polls and Canada has experienced a series of uncompetitive elections in recent times. The argument seems to have some applicability at the federal level, where the elections of 1993, 1997, and 2000 were won handily by the Liberals, with no opposition party managing to mount a serious challenge for power. Since the outcome was a foregone conclusion, many people did not bother to vote.

This changed, of course, in 2004. Based on pre-election polls, the election was billed as the closest in many years. The prospect of a minority government gave supporters of the smaller parties ample reason to feel that their votes might have some real influence on the election outcome and subsequent government policy-making (as indeed turned out to be the case). And yet turnout fell below the record low of 2000, to 60.9%. While turnout did increase in the election of January 2006, another close contest, the rise was modest (to 64.7%). These recent federal results clearly do not provide strong support for the simple version of the electoral competition theory. The theory also runs into problems explaining the recent experience at the provincial level. The New Brunswick elections of 2003 and 2006 provide pertinent counter-examples: in what were much the closest elections in recent history, turnout continued to follow the long steady decline that began some 15 years ago. The same is true of the Nova Scotia election of 2003, a tightly fought race that resulted in a minority government and also produced the lowest turnout in that province's recent history (65.8%).[12]

There is, however, an important variation on the electoral competition argument that can account for the continued turnout decline in the highly competitive elections of recent years. It can also help explain why turnout has declined among the young, but not nearly as much among older people. The argument here starts from the premise that voting is a habit that one either acquires or fails to acquire early in life. The first elections at which one is eligible to vote are quite critical: if one fails to vote in these inaugural contests, this becomes an established pattern that is unlikely to change (Plutzer 2002). This has two implications: first, a lack of electoral competition will have its greatest impact on young voters because older voters are already set in their ways and unlikely to be influenced by the degree of competitiveness in any given election; and secondly, this impact on the young voters of a particular period will have a lasting impact, creating habits of voting and non-voting that a particular generation will carry forward into the future. This reasoning, developed most fully in the writings of political scientist Mark Franklin (2002, 2004), leads to the proposition that turnout in New Brunswick has fallen and remains low today because New Brunswickers under 30 acquired the habit of non-voting due to uncompetitive elections at both the federal and provincial levels for much of the past 10 to 15 years.

This is a more complex and intriguing account of the relationship between electoral competition and voter participation. It is also one that can be tested quite readily. If this modified version of the theory is correct, there should have been a spike in turnout among the youngest voters in the close electoral contests of late: the 2003 and 2006 New Brunswick elections and the 2004 and 2006 federal elections. In the New Brunswick case, there are no readily available studies of earlier elections that would permit comparisons of turnout in particular age categories to the more recent contests. For the 2006 federal election, relevant data are not yet available publicly. For the 2004 election, however, there are some available sources. There is, first, the Elections Canada study based on its sampling of voters list records for the 2004 election. The study found that participation among first-time voters was a few points higher than among second-time voters (38.7% versus 35.4%), an anomalous result that can potentially be linked to the heightened effects of renewed electoral competition on the very youngest voters.[13] Survey data are consistent with this account. The turnout figures in Table 12.7 are based on the 2000 and 2004 Canadian election studies. Age groups are defined so as to distinguish first- and second-time voters in each election; larger age categories are used for older groups. The results point to a considerable jump in voting in 2004 among young voters—about 15 percentage points for first-time voters and about 6 points for second-time voters.

Table 12.7: Voter turnout by age, 2000 and 2004 federal elections

	First-time voters 18–21	Second-time voters 22–25	26–35	36–45	46–55	56+	Total
Turnout 2000 (%)	56.5	61.5	74.1	84.9	89.7	93.0	82.7
(Unweighted N)	(131)	(158)	(507)	(686)	(540)	(833)	(2893)
Turnout 2004 (%)	71.9	67.0	78.5	86.2	89.9	94.7	86.4
(Unweighted N)	(119)	(144)	(443)	(692)	(663)	(1057)	(3120)

Note: Age is approximate only, as it is based on birth year. First-time voters in 2004 are those born between 1983 and 1986; first-time voters in 2000 are those born between 1979 and 1982. Second-time voters in 2004 are those born between 1979 and 1982, and in 2000, those born between 1975 and 1978. Unavoidably, some of oldest voters in these younger groups may be misclassified, i.e., they may have been eligible to vote in one additional election, depending on the month in which they were born.

Source: Author's calculations based on original data for 2000 and 2004 Canadian Election Studies. National weights have been applied to the turnout calculations. However, unweighted Ns are reported, as these are more relevant to margin of error estimates (weighted Ns are inflated for younger age groups).

If these results lend some support to the proposition that electoral competition bears heavily on the participation of young voters, several caveats should be added. First, the numbers in Table 12.7 represent estimates only based on surveys with relatively small sample sizes in the younger age categories (between 119 and 158 respondents) and highly inflated estimates of voter participation, both overall and within particular age categories. These imprecisions render firm conclusions suspect. Moreover, it is important to recall that whatever the effects of heightened electoral competition in 2004, it remains the case that, according to Elections Canada's study, turnout among first-time voters was only 38.7%. If turnout among young voters is to be bolstered significantly—above 50%, say—more than close elections will be required. Finally, and perhaps most critically, the 2004 election differed from 2000 in that Elections Canada, recognizing the problem of declining participation among the young, made special efforts to get young people out to the polls: first, by ensuring that their names were included on the National Register of Electors (a significant problem in 2000), and secondly through advertisements designed to encourage young people to vote. These additional efforts, rather than intensified electoral competition, may account for the spike in participation among young voters in 2004.

The Voting Age

While a more plausible account about the role of electoral competitiveness in declining turnout can be constructed by invoking the concept of habitual voting, this does not work as well when the broader international experience is taken into account. Voting has been declining in many places around the world; in most cases, low participation rates among young voters are a principal cause (Wattenberg 2003). Yet many of these countries have not experienced a prolonged period of reduced electoral competitiveness in recent times. Competition between parties varies a great deal from place to place and fluctuates considerably within countries over time. There is simply no steady and consistent downward trend in electoral competitiveness that could explain why young voters have simultaneously withdrawn from electoral politics in many countries.

Franklin's recent work provides another hypothesis based on the premise of habitual voting that helps to explain this consistent global pattern. He suggests that the lowering of the voting age from 21 to 18—a change that took place in many established democracies in the late 1960s and early 1970s—was an ill-advised move that resulted in more young people failing to develop the voting habit. The key idea here is that 18 (or a year or two older, depending on election timing) is an unsettled age for many people, a time of leaving high school, finding a job or embarking on post-secondary education, and moving away from home for the first time. These conditions make it less likely that 18-year-olds will vote. By 21 (or, again, a year or two older) people are often more settled in their lives and therefore more likely to vote (Franklin 2004, 63). What this argument amounts to is an innovative blending of life-cycle and generational accounts of voting proclivities: when we take into account habitual voting, factors relevant to the life-cycle pattern of voting—people voting less at a young age for a variety of practical and temporary reasons—can have a lasting impact and thereby turn a life-cycle pattern into a generational one.

This explanation is broadly consistent with trends in voter participation in Canada. While the focus in recent debates has been on low turnout among the youngest voters, those under 25 or perhaps 30, it should not be assumed that the problem is confined to this group alone. The definitive longitudinal analysis of voting turnout at the federal level in Canada, which uses survey data for elections dating back to 1968 to track voting patterns over time, indicates that generational differences in voter turnout extend to older cohorts as well. Turnout among those born in the 1960s, for example is about 12 or 13 points lower than among those born before 1945; even among those born between

1945 to 1959, it is 2 to 3 points lower than among the pre-1945 group (Blais et al. 2004). Since anyone born in 1952 or later would have been affected by the 1970 drop in voting age, Franklin's hypothesis may help explain at least some portion of these long-standing intergenerational differences. Of course, other factors must also be at work, since the most recent cohorts (those born in the 1970s and 1980s) vote considerably less than older cohorts also affected by the lowering of the voting age. Uncompetitive elections of the 1990s would seem to fit the bill. A theory organized around the concepts of habitual voting, the voting age, and electoral competition in different periods could potentially explain a good deal about current levels of voter participation in different generations.

At the same time, however, it is difficult to assess the real significance of the voting age factor. One challenge in assessing the theory is that most countries changed the voting age around the same time and lowered it to the same age, 18. Thus, there are not many counter-examples that can be used to test whether or not keeping the voting age at 21 or lowering it at a different point in time actually resulted in a different outcome. And many other factors have also been changing in the period since the voting age was lowered, including ones noted in the previous section—changing social values and norms, the media environment, and so on. But theories about habitual voting and the factors that affect participation among young voters in their critical first elections are worth bearing in mind. The last section of this chapter will suggest what might be done to enhance the likelihood that young people will vote at their first opportunity and thereby develop the habit of voting.

Dissatisfaction with Government Performance and Democratic Institutions

Other explanations of a political or institutional nature for declining turnout among young Canadians have also been advanced. The most popular of these is the idea that younger citizens are voting less because of various forms of dissatisfaction with government. Sometimes this refers to dissatisfaction with specific government policies, such as the program cuts in areas like education and welfare that most governments undertook during the 1990s. It can also refer to more general assessments of government competence, honesty, and integrity, issues that surface intermittently and have certainly been in the spotlight recently as a result of the sponsorship scandal that has embroiled the federal Liberal Party. Or, more broadly still, it is sometimes thought that the object of disaffection is not the political players but the rules of the game itself—a parliamentary system hamstrung by stringent party discipline, an electoral system that produces significant distortions between votes and seats, an appointed upper house in Ottawa that does little to enhance our democratic

Table 12.8a: Dissatisfaction with government by age, New Brunswick, 2003

	Age 18–29	30–39	40–49	50–59	60+	Total
People running government are smart people who know what they are doing —disagree (%)	18.7	14.0	24.4	21.3	27.5	22.2
Trust federal government to do what is right only some of time or almost never (%)*	40.9	38.7	55.1	62.7	58.8	53.4
Trust provincial government to do what is right only some of time or almost never (%)*	48.2	40.1	52.0	51.4	49.8	49.1
Dissatisfied with democracy in Canada (%)	15.4	18.1	21.8	23.0	22.4	20.8
Government does not care what people like me think (%)	52.2	53.6	54.4	57.1	60.7	56.2
Many people in government are dishonest—agree (%)	59.7	47.8	52.5	49.3	50.4	51.6
(N)	(132)	(136)	(221)	(209)	(238)	(936)

*Other response options were: "almost always" and "most of the time."

Source: Author's calculations based on 2003 NBSCS

life. While some would suggest that criticisms of government are overdone and that citizens sometimes have unrealistic expectations, the widespread discontent in recent times with at least some aspects of the structures and performance of government is undeniable.

And yet, surprisingly enough, this discontent does not appear to play a significant role in declining voter turnout among the young. The survey data do not point to heightened dissatisfaction among young respondents on a variety of measures used to assess how people feel about the performance of government, the competence and integrity of decision-makers, or the democratic system itself. As Table 12.8a indicates, young New Brunswick respondents are less likely to express skepticism about whether those running the government know what they are doing, and they are less likely (or no more likely) to express low levels of trust in the federal and provincial governments. Similarly,

Table 12.8b: Dissatisfaction with government and voter participation, New Brunswick, 2003

	Voted in 2003 (%)	(N)
Competence		
People running government know what they are doing—agree	84.8	(723)
People running government know what they are doing—disagree	87.7	(203)
Trust—federal		
Trust federal government most of time or almost always	84.2	(436)
Trust federal government some of time or almost never	86.8	(492)
Trust—provincial		
Trust provincial government most of time or almost always	85.7	(481)
Trust provincial government some of time or almost never	85.4	(445)
Satisfaction with democracy		
Satisfied with democracy in Canada	87.0	(738)
Dissatisfied with democracy in Canada	81.5	(178)
Government cares		
Government does not care what people like me think—disagree	86.2	(407)
Government does not care what people like me think—agree	84.9	(516)
Honesty		
People in government are dishonest—disagree	88.7	(444)
People in government are dishonest—agree	83.0	(458)

Source: Author's calculations based on 2003 NBSCS

young New Brunswickers are less likely to display negative attitudes than older citizens when asked about their degree of satisfaction with "the way democracy works in Canada,"[14] or their concurrence with the statement "government does not care what people like me think." The only question to which those under 30 gave answers more critical towards government is that asking whether people in government are dishonest. None of the age differences on these items, however, is particularly pronounced.

Meanwhile, as Table 12.8b demonstrates, the gap in voter participation between those who are dissatisfied with government on these various measures and those who are content is minimal—6% at most. On reflection, this is perhaps not a surprising finding: after all, people who are unhappy with how government is handling the nation's affairs can use the ballot box to try to bring about change. It is not obvious that dissatisfaction with government must breed voter apathy and this basic empirical evidence would suggest that, in fact, it does not.[15]

It might be added, however, that the relationship between dissatisfaction with government and voter withdrawal may be more complex than is allowed for in this individual-level analysis. Even if young people themselves are not politically malcontent to any exceptional degree, the political discontent that is "in the air" could have affected them nonetheless. It was noted earlier that many younger Canadians have largely tuned out from politics, registering relatively little interest in, or knowledge about, the political world. While this suggests indifference rather than discontent, it could be the case that negative attitudes towards government are playing a role. The hypothesis here would be that young people, vaguely aware of the prevailing contempt toward government, elect to ignore the world of politics, so much so that they themselves do not develop negative attitudes. Thus dissatisfaction in the population at large ends up manifesting itself in indifference and apathy among the young. This is a more complex account that would require further research of a different nature to verify and substantiate. In short, if there is a link between rising democratic discontent and declining participation, further digging will be required to uncover it.

Depoliticization
At the same time, it is important to be sensitive to other possible explanations for the apparent indifference of young people towards politics in recent times. In particular, it is reasonable to speculate that there has been a process of depoliticization over the past twenty years, which has affected young people especially, and has led to a deep skepticism about the role and importance of government. Factors contributing to such attitudes would lie in the realm of both ideas and political realities. These would include: the notion that became popular throughout Western democracies, from the 1980s on, that governments in the post-war period had allowed themselves to become overextended and needed to scale back operations; the spending cutbacks of the 1990s and the renewed emphasis on private enterprise and individual self-reliance and initiative; the end of the Cold War, heralded as the "end of history" by one prominent commentator to signal the victory of the liberal democratic model of government and the end of the ideological bipolarity that had structured and animated political debate for much of the 20th century (Fukuyama 1992); and the rise of globalization and the attendant idea that national governments increasingly face significant external constraints on their domestic autonomy. These elements of contemporary political discourse all point to a receding role for government and the ebbing of political division and debate in the face of new realities. Young people, coming of age in this era, may have come to conclude that politics and government are simply not as critical to their lives as

older citizens were led to believe.

Testing this particular proposition is difficult to do with existing survey data. While there has been ample measurement on various surveys of satisfaction with government, there has not been much probing of attitudes relating to the overall salience and significance of government; and in any event, the relevant attitudes are very broad and diffuse, and consequently would be difficult to capture through survey questions. Methodological challenges notwithstanding, this represents an area where further investigation is warranted, to see if apolitical attitudes are in fact a distinguishing trait of younger generations that can help to account for their greater levels of indifference towards electoral politics.[16]

Administrative Factors

Not to be overlooked in discussing political and institutional factors that affect voter turnout are the detailed rules and regulations around the administration of elections that can facilitate or inhibit voter participation. Research has shown that these can and do have a considerable effect.

In the Canadian case, the administrative factor that has received the greatest measure of attention is the new approach to voter registration adopted at the federal level in 1997. In place of the old method of assembling a fresh voters list for each election through door-to-door enumeration, Elections Canada adopted a permanent voters list. A database of eligible electors, updated on an ongoing basis through data-sharing with other government agencies, is now used to compile the preliminary voters list, with revisions taking place in the run-up to an election. Most provinces, New Brunswick included, now maintain their own permanent databases to generate preliminary voters lists in preparation for provincial elections.

Many concerns were voiced in the 2000 federal election about systematic omissions from the permanent voters list. Certain categories of electors were particularly likely to be excluded, or to have incorrect information on their voter's card, and to therefore be in the position of having to make extra efforts in order to be properly registered to vote. Among the acutely affected groups were young people, in part because the youngest among them represented new voters who would not have been on the list for the previous election, and in part because of their high degree of mobility and relatively frequent changes of address. According to one trenchant study of the new voter registration regime (Black 2003), the effects on voter participation in 2000 were considerable, with young voters among the most acutely affected groups.

In considering this dimension of elections administration and its potential effects on participation, it is important to note that New Brunswick has not altered registration procedures to the same degree as some other jurisdictions. At the federal level, door-to-door enumeration now takes places only in selected areas where voter coverage is thought to be relatively poor, a procedure referred to as targeted revision.[17] In New Brunswick, a full province-wide enumeration is still carried out in order to verify the information contained in the database of electors and make changes as necessary. Therefore, problems of the exclusion of certain demographic groups, among them young people, should not be nearly as significant in New Brunswick as they appear to have been at the federal level in 2000.[18]

The permanent voters list is the only significant element of the administration of Canadian elections that has changed in recent years, and therefore the only one that can reasonably be linked to declining voter turnout. This is not to say, however, that voter registration is the only administrative factor that affects participation. A 2003 study for Elections Canada of voter turnout in 61 countries found that voting is about 10 points higher in countries that allow voting by mail, voting in advance, and voting by proxy, compared to countries that provide none of these options (Blais, Massicotte, and Dobrzynska 2003). It has also been found that in Canadian federal elections, turnout has been about 6 points lower in elections held in the summer or winter months (Blais et al. 2004, 223), while in provincial elections, springtime elections have produced the highest turnouts (Studlar 2001, 310–312).

That these types of administrative details can make a difference to participation is in keeping with the finding that many Canadian non-voters do cite practical obstacles—a simple lack of time, for example, or being away from their riding on voting day—as reasons for not voting (Pammett and LeDuc 2003, 17). These self-reports do not necessarily provide the full picture—presumably at least some who are dissuaded from voting by minor procedural obstacles are also people who do not feel strongly motivated to vote for more substantive and significant reasons (e.g., a lack of political interest, a weak sense of civic duty)—but it does seem clear that the effort involved to get out and vote can tip the scales for at least some voters.

All of this points to what is undoubtedly already an important objective of those in charge of the administration of elections: facilitating access to the voting process to the greatest degree possible. Some specific changes that might be made in this regard are noted in the recommendations section that follows.

What Is to Be Done?

This review of competing explanations for declining voter turnout among young voters in New Brunswick and elsewhere canvasses a wide range of possible explanations and underscores the complexity of the issue. According to some of the theories considered here, society has been changing gradually and inexorably in a variety of ways over the past thirty years; younger generations have been particularly implicated in these changes, which have brought with them a reduced proclivity to participate in elections. Other theories discussed above focus more on political and institutional factors that are responsible for declining turnout, as well as some relatively complex accounts that highlight the interplay of a variety of different factors. Out of this survey, there emerges no single account that cuts to the heart of the matter and identifies *the* overarching reason for the disengagement of young people from electoral politics.

At the same time, however, thinking through the implications of some of the theories and the findings from the data analysis does suggest that the range of potential strategies for addressing the issue is relatively limited. In the first place, some of the hypotheses considered above turned out not to have much merit. The social capital account, with its emphasis on associational involvement and interpersonal trust, does not appear to provide much explanatory leverage; nor does the idea that it is their tight adherence to post-materialist values that explains why young people prefer not to vote. There is also no solid evidence that dissatisfaction with government performance or the institutional structure of government is a significant factor behind the declining participation of young voters.

In the second place, among those theories that do have explanatory leverage, some identify no levers that government can reasonably hope to budge. These would include the decline in the sense of civic duty, which is almost certainly embedded in a deeper cultural shift unlikely to be undone by government action or exhortation, as well as the rise of individualism and decline of community spirit, which likewise is a phenomenon deeply rooted in the changing temper of the times. Similarly, a media environment that nowadays affords people greater choice in their reading and viewing experiences, and thus results in reduced exposure to political news and information, is not something government can readily address. Nor, for that matter, is the competitiveness of elections, which is largely a function of the waxing and waning fortunes of political parties and is therefore beyond the control of public authorities.

If, then, consideration is limited to causal factors that seem to make a significant difference and can reasonably be targeted by government, there are relatively few to reflect on. The most notable ones are: civic literacy and attendant patterns related to attention to politics; the voting age; and voter registration and other administrative factors.

The first significant potential reform, relating to civic literacy, would be the adoption of a more systematic approach to civics education in the New

Brunswick school system. The most obvious objective of such an initiative would be to enhance young peoples' knowledge and understanding of the political system, giving them a firmer grounding that would enable them to grasp the meaning and relevance of real-world politics as it unfolds. There are, however, a number of additional effects that might also be achieved through a dedicated civics curriculum and which could have equally important effects on the political engagement of young New Brunswickers. These benefits are more speculative, but it nevertheless seems prudent to consider them in reflecting on the structure and delivery of civics education. They would include:

- Paying attention to politics in the media. This would entail a civics curriculum that encourages regular newspaper reading, viewing of politically oriented programming on television, and the use of the Internet to acquire political information.

- Reversing the depoliticization of younger generations. Civics education should impress upon students the significance and vitality of politics and government; in concrete terms, this means supplementing the somewhat sterile "how a bill becomes a law" approach with genuine political discussion and debate (Gidengil et al. 2004, 182). While this can run up against concerns about partisanship in the classroom that would have to be managed and addressed, it probably does represent an important component of an effective civics curriculum.

- Enhancing political interest. This would go hand in hand with giving students a sense of the real world importance of political issues and would help create the motivational foundation that is needed for students to continue their engagement with the political world once they leave their studies behind.

Another reform that might be considered is changing the voting age. The discussion above suggested that lowering the voting age to 18 may well have contributed to lower participation levels, enduring because of the phenomenon of habitual voting. While this might seem to point to the wisdom of raising the voting age back to 21, this clearly is not in the cards either in New Brunswick or most other places where voter turnout is a concern, and instead another idea has been gaining ground: lowering the voting age to 16. This seems counterintuitive at first blush: if reducing the voting age from 21 to 18 was ill-advised, why would it now make sense to lower it further still? The logic, however, derives from the life circumstances prevailing at different ages.

At age 18, young people are entering a new stage of life, a time of considerable flux and uncertainty. At age 16, most young people are at a relatively stable stage of life, attending high school and living at home with their parents. Moreover, the fact that they are still in school provides an opportunity to organize educational activities at election time designed to inform students about the voting process and encourage their participation (Franklin 2004, 213–214). In the absence of such activities, lowering the voting age could be a counterproductive move; but with the requisite measures in place, this might prove an opportune way to instill the habit of voting in new voters.[19]

Interestingly, there is already an initiative underway in Canada that largely mimics this model. In the federal elections of 2004 and 2006, mock elections were held in many high schools across the country, organized by the non-partisan group, Student Vote. In 2004, roughly a quarter of a million students in 1,100 schools cast ballots in these elections, which were held with the co-operation of Elections Canada and were designed to resemble the real voting experience.[20] It is possible that these mock elections could serve as an effective way of initiating young citizens to the voting process. The test will lie in the voting habits of young adults a few years down the line: will those who participated in the recent mock elections actually go out and vote in greater numbers when the first real opportunity comes along? In addition to this initiative, there are also others taking place elsewhere to consider. A number of jurisdictions have either lowered the voting age (e.g., Cambridge, Massachusetts, to age 17 for local elections; several German states, to age 16, again for local elections) or are considering the idea (e.g., some American states; the United Kingdom). The cautious approach would be to wait until some assessment can be made of the impact in places that do adopt this reform to see if there is merit in lowering the voting age here in New Brunswick.[21]

Finally, there are administrative procedures that should be given some attention. There is, first, the matter of voter registration. In light of some of the concerns that have surfaced in instances where only targeted or selective enumeration has been used to make corrections to a list generated by a permanent register of electors, it would be advisable to retain the current New Brunswick practice of province-wide door-to-door enumeration. To move towards a more limited revision approach would likely accentuate the voter participation gap between young and old. In addition to keeping the registration procedure as is, there are administrative changes that might be made to enhance access to the voting process and thereby improve participation rates. Since New Brunswick and other jurisdictions in Canada already have in place many of the relevant procedures (advance voting, voting by proxy, and so on), most of these pertain to technological innovations that might be deployed to make the voting process even more accessible than at present. The most notable example would be enabling voters to use the internet for voter registration purposes and potentially even voting itself at some point down the line, ideas that are popular with many Canadians (Pammett and LeDuc 2003, 55). Clearly the technological issues and challenges involved in such an initiative would have to be closely examined by those with experience and expertise in these matters, but this does seem something worth pursuing. This also might prove to be a way of helping to reduce the age gap in voter turnout, given the differences between young and old in internet use and familiarity (though these differences are gradually diminishing over time).

Fixed election dates—another change being proposed by the Commission on Legislative Democracy—might also be designed with voter turnout considerations in mind. Selecting a fixed date in the spring or fall would ensure that the lower turnouts associated with winter and summer elections are avoided. Other provinces adopting fixed election dates seem to be taking this approach, as BC has opted for a fixed date in May, and Ontario for a date in October.

Meanwhile, however, it must be recognized that these proposed measures to help address declining turnout would not necessarily bring voter participation back up to earlier levels. There are many factors behind this disquieting trend, some of them intractable and intertwined, and it is therefore difficult to be confident about the precise benefits of any given initiative or change. Since Canada as a whole, and many of the individual provinces, are currently engaged in considerable soul-searching about the state of democracy, with concerns about voter turnout a consistent theme across the country, it is to be hoped that a variety of solutions will emerge in different places, the effects of which can be tested and compared. Given the complexity of the matter and the range of possible factors involved, careful monitoring of this sort is probably going to prove the most effective way of determining the relative efficacy of practical solutions to the pervasive problem of declining voter turnout.

Notes

1. The 2003 New Brunswick Social Capital Survey was funded by the Social Sciences and Humanities Research Council of Canada (SSHRC). The fieldwork was conducted by the Institute for Social Research (ISR) at York University. The principal investigators were Don Desserud, Joanna Everitt, and the current author.

    Data for the 2000 Canadian National Election Study were made available by the Institute for Social Research (ISR) at York University. The principal investigators were André Blais, Elisabeth Gidengil, Richard Nadeau, and Neil Nevitte. Data for the 2004 Canadian National Election Study were accessed on the Canadian

Election Study website; principal investigators were André Blais, Joanna Everitt, Patrick Founier, Elisabeth Gidengil, and Neil Nevitte. Fieldwork for both studies was conducted by ISR and both were funded by SSHRC and Elections Canada.

The 2002 Study of Voters and Non-Voters was made available by Elections Canada. The fieldwork was conducted by Decima Research and the principal investigators were Jon Pammett and Lawrence LeDuc.

The original investigators (current author excepted), the study sponsors, and the distributing agencies bear no responsibility for the analyses and interpretations presented here.

2. The initial turnout estimate for 2004 was 60.5%. The 60.9% figure is a revised figure, after the removal of duplicates from the final list of electors (Kingsley 2004).
3. Adjusting for duplicates on the list of electors for the 2003 New Brunswick election produces a revised turnout figure of 73.6%. See the technical note on the website of the Chief Electoral Officer, "Changes in the Enumeration Process and Voters' Lists," http://www.gnb.ca/elections/03prov/03changes-e.asp, accessed 7 July 2004. An adjusted figure for the 2006 New Brunswick election is not yet available.
4. The statistical reliability of the results is +/−4.3%, 19 times out of 20, "when generalized to the entire Canadian voting age population" (Elections Canada 2005, 4).
5. For sample size reasons, in the analysis that follows based on this survey the two younger age groups are grouped together as an 18 to 29 category.
6. The survey asked about membership in 14 different types of associations: service clubs, labour unions, professional or business associations, voluntary associations, neighbourhood associations, churches, ethnic organizations, recreational associations, parent's groups, women's organizations, conservation, environmental or animal rights groups, political parties, political action groups other than a political party, and any other groups or organizations.
7. These findings mirror what has been found in more in-depth investigations using survey data for the Canadian population. See Johnston and Matthews (2004) and Tossutti (2004).
8. For example, an Ipsos-Reid survey just before the 2004 federal election pegged support for the Green Party at 8% among those 18 to 34 and 4% among those 55 and over (figures are taken from the poll released on 25 June 2004, in the Public Affairs section of the firm's website at www.ipsos.ca).
9. Respondents were asked to indicate which of four goals—fighting crime, giving people more say in important government decisions, maintaining economic growth, or protecting freedom of speech—was most important to them, and which was the second most important to them. Those picking "giving people

10. more say" and "protecting freedom of speech" as the two most important goals were classified as post-materialists.
10. This research is based on data from the American National Election Studies of 1980, 1984, 1986, and 1988. It finds that over-reporting of voting, expressed as the percentage of non-voters who indicated they did vote, ranges from about 10% among groups unlikely to feel much pressure to vote to just over 40% among groups likely to feel the most pressure—a substantial difference (Bernstein, Chadha, and Montjoy 2001, 35).
11. This is a viewpoint associated with rational choice school of thought, prominent in recent political science theory. For a critique (but also a useful summary) of its application to voter participation, see Green and Shapiro (1994, 47–71).
12. A broader investigation of the effects of the margin of victory in provincial elections has, however, found a small, but statistically significant, impact. Looking at all provincial elections from 1945 to 1998, Donley Studlar (2001, 312) reports that an increase of 10% in the margin of victory has been associated, on average, with a 2% decrease in turnout.
13. Elections Canada does caution that the difference between the two groups of young voters falls within the margin of error for the study (Kingsley 2004).
14. The survey did not ask about satisfaction with the way democracy works in New Brunswick, which would be a preferable measure, particularly for assessing the relationship to voter participation in provincial elections.
15. The same result appears in American studies of voter turnout. See, for example, Popkin and Dimock (1999).
16. A more extended discussion related to these themes can be found in Whitaker (2002).
17. See the description provided by Rennie Molnar of Elections Canada (2002, 84–85).
18. What does appear to be a significant issue in New Brunswick, however, is the problem of duplicate entries in the database of electors, which has the effect of artificially deflating official turnout levels (for details, see note 3 above).
19. However, we might note that a question about lowering the voting age was posed on the 2002 Elections Canada Survey of Voters and Non-Voters and it was *not* a popular idea: 76% of respondents disagreed with the statement "The voting age should be lowered to 16 to encourage young people to participate." Interestingly, younger respondents were just as likely as older ones to reject the idea.
20. Further details can be found at www.studentvote.ca.
21. Preliminary assessment of the experience in some German states where the age has been lowered is promising, as 16- to 18-year-olds have been voting in somewhat higher numbers than those who are slightly older (Aarts and van Hees, 2003).

References

Aarts, Kees, and Charlotte van Hees. 2003. "Lowering the Voting Age: European Debates and Experiences." *Electoral Insight* 5(2):42–46.

Bernstein, Robert, Anita Chadha, and Robert Montjoy. 2001. "Overreporting Voting: Why It Happens and Why It Matters." *The Public Opinion Quarterly* 65(1):22–44.

Black, Jerome. 2003. "From Enumeration to the National Register of Electors: An Account and an Evaluation." *Choices* 9(7): 3–43.

Blais, André. 2000. *To Vote or Not To Vote: The Merits and Limits of Rational Choice Theory.* Pittsburgh: University of Pittsburgh Press.

Blais, André, Louis Massicotte, and Agnieszka Dobrzynska. 2003. "Why is Turnout Higher in Some Countries than in Others?" Ottawa: Elections Canada.

Blais, André, Elisabeth Gidengil, Neil Nevitte, and Richard Nadeau. 2004. "Where Does Turnout Decline Come From?" *European Journal of Political Research* 43(2):221–236.

Clarke, Harold D., David Sanders, Marianne C. Stewart, and Paul F. Whiteley. 2003. "Britain (Not) at the Polls, 2001." *PS: Political Science and Politics* 36(1):59–64.

Cross, Bill. 2004. *Political Parties.* Vancouver: University of British Columbia Press.

Cross, Bill, and Lisa Young. 2004. "The Contours of Political Party Membership in Canada." *Party Politics* 10(4):427–444.

Elections Canada. 2005. "Estimation of Voter Turnout by Age Group at the 38th Federal General Election (June 28, 2004)." Final Report. Available at www.elections.ca/loi/report_e.pdf.

Franklin, Mark. 2002. "Learning (Not) to Vote: the Generational Basis of Turnout Decline in Established Democracies." Paper presented at the 2002 convention of the American Political Science Association, Boston.

—. 2004. *Voter Turnout and the Dynamics of Electoral Competition in Established Democracies Since 1945.* Cambridge: Cambridge University Press.

Fukuyama, Francis. 1992. *The End of History and the Last Man.* New York: The Free Press.

Gidengil, Elisabeth, André Blais, Neil Nevitte, and Richard Nadeau. 2003. "Turned Off or Tuned Out? Youth Participation in Elections." *Electoral Insight* 5(2):9–14.

—. 2004. *Citizens.* Vancouver: University of British Columbia Press.

Green, Donald P., and Ian Shapiro. 1994. *The Pathologies of Rational Choice Theory.* New Haven: Yale University Press.

Howe, Paul. 2003. "Electoral Participation and the Knowledge Deficit." *Electoral Insight* 5(2):20–25.

—. 2006. "Political Knowledge and Electoral Participation in the Netherlands: Comparisons with the Canadian Case." *International Political Science Review* 27(2):137–166.

Howe, Paul, and David Northrup. 2000. "Strengthening Canadian Democracy: The View of Canadians." *Policy Matters* 1(5): 3–104.

Inglehart, Ronald. 1977. *The Silent Revolution: Changing Values and Political Styles Among Western Publics.* Princeton, NJ: Princeton University Press.

——. 1990. *Culture Shift in Advanced Industrial Society.* Princeton, NJ: Princeton University Press.

Institute for Research on Public Policy. 2002. "Transparency, Disclosure, and Democracy: Assessing the Chief Electoral Officer's Recommendations." Transcript of an event held on February 27.

Johnston, Richard J., and J. Scott Matthews. 2004. "Social Capital, Age, and Participation." Paper presented at the Youth Participation Workshop held at the annual meeting of the Canadian Political Science Association, University of Manitoba, 3 June.

Kingsley, Jean-Pierre. 2004. "Chief Electoral Officer's keynote speech." Delivered at the Centre for Research and Information on Canada (CRIC) Research Seminar on the Political Engagement of Canadian Youth, Ottawa, 1 October. Retrieved 15 November 2004 from the "Statements and Speeches" section of the Elections Canada website, at www.elections.ca.

Milner, Henry. 2002. *Civic Literacy: How Informed Citizens Make Democracy Work.* Hanover, NH: University Press of New England.

Nevitte, Neil. 1996. *The Decline of Deference.* Peterborough: Broadview Press.

Nevitte, Neil, André Blais, Elisabeth Gidengil, and Richard Nadeau. 2000. *Unsteady State: The 1997 Canadian Federal Election.* Don Mills, ON: Oxford University Press.

O'Neill, Brenda. 2001. "Generational Patterns in the Political Opinions and Behaviour of Canadians: Separating the Wheat from the Chaff." *Policy Matters* 2(5):3–45.

Pammett, Jon H., and Lawrence LeDuc. 2003. "Explaining the Turnout Decline in Canadian Federal Elections: A New Survey of Non-Voters." Ottawa: Elections Canada.

Plutzer, Eric. 2002. "Becoming a Habitual Voter: Inertia, Resources, and Growth in Young Adulthood." *American Political Science Review* 96(1):41–56.

Popkin, Samuel L., and Michael A. Dimock. 1999. "Political Knowledge and Citizen Competence." In *Citizen Competence and Democratic Institutions*, ed. Stephen L. Elkin and Karol Edward Soltan, 117–146. University Park, PA: Pennsylvania State University Press.

Putnam, Robert D. 2000. *Bowling Alone: The Collapse and Revival of American Community.* New York: Simon and Schuster.

Studlar, Donley. 2001. "Canadian Exceptionalism: Explaining Differences over Time in Provincial and Federal Voter Turnout." *Canadian Journal of Political Science* 34(2):299–319.

Tossutti, L.S. 2004. "Youth Voluntarism and Political Engagement in Canada." Paper presented at the Youth Participation Workshop held at the annual meeting of the Canadian Political Science Association, University of Manitoba, 3 June.

Voogt, Robert J.J., and Willem E. Saris. 2003. "To Participate or Not to Participate: The

Link Between Survey Participation, Electoral Participation, and Political Interest." *Political Analysis* 11:164–179.

Wattenberg, Martin. 2003. "Electoral Turnout: The New Generation Gap." *British Elections and Parties Review* 13:159–173.

Whitaker, Reg. 2002. "The Flight from Politics." *Inroads* 11:187–202.

CHAPTER THIRTEEN

Defining and Redefining Democracy: The History of Electoral Reform in New Brunswick

GAIL CAMPBELL

Introduction

THE NEW BRUNSWICK Commission on Legislative Democracy, established in 2003, is part of a broad national movement towards electoral reform. As recounted in Chapter 1, similar contemporary exercises at the federal level and in British Columbia, Ontario, Quebec, and Prince Edward Island have examined many of the questions being addressed by the New Brunswick commission. The commission's mandate, which comprehends electoral, legislative, and democratic reform, is very broad: "to examine and make recommendations on strengthening and modernizing our electoral system and democratic institutions and practices in New Brunswick to make them more fair, open, accountable and accessible to New Brunswickers" (New Brunswick Commission on Legislative Democracy 2003). If the New Brunswick commission is in the mainstream of a current trend towards electoral reform, it is equally grounded in a long history of electoral, legislative, and, indeed, democratic reform in New Brunswick and in Canada as a whole. In undertaking to reform the system, New Brunswick legislators are, in effect, both defining and redefining democracy. Each of the proposed reforms, ranging from a mixed-member proportional representation scheme to fixed election dates, has some links with the past, but also takes us a very long way from the ideas about government shared by those who established the province of New Brunswick in 1784. In determining the best way forward, it is often instructive to look to our own history for guidance. This chapter examines the ways New Brunswickers have defined and redefined electoral democracy over the course of their history. To that end, it focuses on the history of democracy in New Brunswick as reflected in the evolving and enduring modes and systems of representation in the legislature.

The Origins of Legislative Democracy in New Brunswick

Those who established the province of New Brunswick in 1784 sought neither "life, liberty and the pursuit of happiness" nor "liberté, égalité, fraternité." (The objectives of the American Revolution had been stated in 1776, while those of the French Revolution would be defined in 1789–1792.) Rather, their goals were much closer to the goals articulated by the Fathers of Confederation two generations later: "peace, order and good government." The founders most certainly did not equate democracy and good government. On the contrary, they were convinced that "too much democracy" had facilitated, if not actually caused, the American Revolution, by allowing too many men to participate in politics. In the new colony, Loyalist elites sought to establish a government that would be "the envy of the American States" (Condon 1984). And when the first New Brunswick election (1785), under a very liberal franchise, revealed considerable opposition to their slate of candidates (especially in Saint John), lawmakers, wary of the dangers of excessive democracy, moved quickly to pass the most restrictive franchise in British North America (Garner 1969). Voting, then, was not a right, but rather a privilege accorded those men who, as the owners of land, had a tangible stake in their society. Yet in a society where land was cheap and plentiful, a significant proportion of adult men owned land and could therefore vote (Campbell 1990). The earliest definitions of democracy in New Brunswick neither included nor excluded women, but rather ignored them, then moved towards exclusion rather than inclusion.

The definition and redefinition of democracy between the introduction of the £25 freehold franchise in 1791 and today's universal adult suffrage has involved much more than suffrage reform and is a process well worth examining. In stressing pork barrelling and parochialism, vote buying and inherited loyalties, earlier analysts of the history of electoral politics in New Brunswick have told a contradictory if colourful story (Doyle 1976; Fitzpatrick 1972). Yet New

Brunswick, the first colony in British North America to introduce the secret ballot, has not been a laggard when it comes to democratic reform. During the decade leading up to Confederation, New Brunswick had developed a healthy and diversified economy. As responsible government became entrenched, a well-established party structure also emerged (MacNutt 1963; Campbell 1986). Saint John had a unique, broadly based franchise, which was extended to all the city's freemen (men licensed to work in the city). A thriving centre of manufacturing and trade, it would enter Confederation as Canada's third largest city, after Montreal and Quebec (Acheson 1985).

For New Brunswick, then, becoming part of the new Dominion meant a diminution of status and independence. New Brunswickers, like Nova Scotians, did not give up power lightly in joining Confederation. Colonial negotiators, recognizing their minority status and the necessity of balanced regional representation in safeguarding their democratic rights, redefined notions of democracy to insist on strong regional representation rather than representation by population: hence the negotiation of a guaranteed minimum number of seats for each province and proportional representation in an appointed senate. Until 1974, regional representation on the provincial level was achieved through multiple-member constituencies. Today, as we once again begin to redefine our notions of the way democracy should work, we would do well to look to past reforms and to consider what has been lost as well as what has been gained. Extension of the franchise means extension of democracy by anyone's calculation. But the risk that majority rule will deny a voice to minorities remains. As we seek to address this and other issues, the lessons of the past may offer a useful corrective to what some see as the wave of the future.

The Evolution of the Franchise

The exercise of the franchise is fundamental to the concept of representative government, but in New Brunswick, as in other Western democracies, ideas about who should be allowed to vote have changed significantly over time. During the 19th century, New Brunswick, following a common pattern, both extended the franchise and adopted the secret ballot. Such suffrage innovations set the stage for the emergence of mass politics and the organization of mass-based political parties. The decision to extend the franchise was sometimes a response to pressures from below, but was just as often the result of contests for influence among competing elites. The history of the franchise is central to any understanding of changing definitions of democracy and is, therefore, the most obvious point of departure for any overview of the historical evolution of electoral reform.

Under the 1791 Election Act, which received Royal Assent in 1795, only propertied individuals 21 years of age or over and in possession of a freehold valued at £25 or more were legally eligible to vote (Garner 1969, 55–58). With one significant, though little noticed, modification, the act remained the basis for the New Brunswick franchise until the early 1850s. By the 1840s, some members of the Legislative Assembly had begun to call for franchise reform, while others remained firmly opposed to any liberalization of the franchise. The latter won the day, for the only change of substance during the 1840s closed a loophole that had allowed some women to vote. Women who met the property qualifications were not legally excluded from voting in New Brunswick until 1843, when the word "male" was inserted into the revised Election Act (An Act to improve the Law relating to the Election of Representatives to serve in the General Assembly, passed 11 April 1843). Before that time, some propertied women did exercise their franchise, though it was not customary for women to do so. Thus, in the confirmed cases of women exercising their franchise—44 women in Kings County in the 1827 election and 39 women in Sunbury County in the 1839 election—there is an extant record of these women precisely because their names were struck off the rolls (Klein 1996, 71–75). The 1843 amendment to the Election Act transformed custom into law and redefined the limits of democracy to exclude women on the basis of their gender.

During the following decade, legislators proved reluctant to consider any alternative qualification for voting beyond the £25 freehold. This excluded a rising professional class who were not property holders, and by the 1850s pressure for franchise reform was coming from outside as well as from inside the legislature. Two petitions in 1851, four in 1853, and six in 1854, all from the towns of Woodstock and Fredericton, urged legislators to reform the Election Act (New Brunswick Legislative Assembly Sessional Records: RS24, RG4, PANB). Yet in 1853 a bill that would have extended the franchise to leaseholders, established a voters' registry, and introduced vote by secret ballot aroused so much controversy that it was allowed to die. The newly emerging Reform Party, popularly known as the "Smashers," took up the cause, however, and, in 1855, having achieved power, introduced legislation to extend the franchise to include owners of personal property assessed at £100 or more as well as those assessed as recipients of an annual income of £100 or more. The assessment rolls would form the basis for a voters' register and vote by ballot would replace viva voce voting. The amended Election Act was passed with the proviso that it would not come into effect until 1 January 1857, to allow ample time for the preparation of voters' registers (Garner 1969, 68–9; *Acts of the General Assembly*, 18 Vic., c 37).

New Brunswick was in the forefront of the movement towards the secret ballot and voters' registers. The New Brunswick legislators who had introduced these measures had perceived in them a method whereby corruption at elections might be curbed, if not altogether eliminated. They were among the very first to make such arguments: Australia, which is given credit for introducing the secret ballot, adopted it in 1856, just a year before it was instituted in New Brunswick. Sweden adopted the secret ballot in 1866, Germany in 1867, Great Britain in 1872, France in 1875, and Belgium in 1878 (Rokkan 1962, 75). The Dominion of Canada would follow New Brunswick's example in adopting the secret ballot only after the Liberal victory of 1874. By that time, the so-called Australian ballot was becoming widely accepted as one of the common characteristics of Western democracies. But in 1855, some New Brunswick legislators had expressed serious reservations about whether or not the secret ballot actually represented a step towards greater democracy. John Hamilton Gray, a Saint John member, sounded a note of caution: "He had looked into the working of the ballot in other countries—it was the duty of every member of the House to do so, and not to take it for granted that he knows everything intuitively. The ballot had been adopted in St. John in electing the municipal officers and there it was rather approved of; but in remote settlements, where education is limited ... he thought it would lead to fraud—the simple inhabitants would be duped by designing men" (NB House of Assembly 1855, 59). Other arguments in favour of retaining the traditional viva voce voting system reflect a particular underlying definition of the rights and responsibilities of voters in a democracy. Thus, while James Ryan of Albert County did not oppose vote by ballot, he opined that he had "always thought there was an independence in a man coming to the polls in a man-fashion way; a man that was afraid to vote ought not to have one" (NB House of Assembly 1855, 59). But in the end the majority agreed with Francis McPhelin's argument that the secret ballot would "enable a man to come forward against friend or foe, without affection or fear—it will enable the voter to exercise his right, independently and free." As A.H. Gilmour of Charlotte County put it, "the ballot ... was very much required to secure the rights of voters"(NB House of Assembly 1855, 70–71). This redefinition of voters' rights, in offering the voter anonymity, erased his specific identity even as it protected him from coercion.

Voters' registers, which became common throughout British North America only in the 1860s, proved more controversial than the secret ballot. In critiquing what he considered the ill-conceived notion of a voters' register compiled from the assessment rolls alone, John Hamilton Gray pointed out that New Brunswick's 1855 bill "did not even require that the burdens should be borne to give the franchise. It was not necessary that the taxes should be paid, only that the party should be assessed.... To vote it is not requisite you should pay your taxes. Swell the burdens of the state, but pay no portion of the load" (NB House of Assembly 1855, 74). Proponents of the measure, on the other hand, argued that, if rigorously enforced, the use of a voters' registry, compiled from the assessment rolls and revised annually, would serve to prevent those who were legally ineligible to vote from contriving to exercise the franchise.

Yet Gray's concerns about the integrity of voters' lists based on lists compiled at other times and for other purposes were not unfounded, as the Ontario example has demonstrated. Studies examining the practice in that province in both 1867 and 1891 have analyzed the various ways voters' registers were manipulated, with men who had relocated or died not only included on the lists, but apparently casting votes as well (Kerr 1970; Forster, Davidson, and Brown 1986). New Brunswick's innovative voters' register, then, could not be expected to eliminate corruption or illegal voting. At the same time, one group of illegal voters would, indeed, disappear, for the introduction of a voters' register did virtually eliminate the practice, common in the rural areas, of allowing men who were long-time community members but did not meet the property qualification to vote on sufferance and by convention. Returning officers, with a clear law before them, would become much more cautious in bending the rules for such men. A democratizing tendency that had long operated by custom to broaden the franchise in rural areas was thereby reversed. Thus the Election Law of 1855, which also introduced an assessment franchise, threatened to disfranchise as many men as it enfranchised in rural counties (Campbell 1990).

In adopting an assessment franchise, New Brunswick was participating in a suffrage reform movement that was international in scope. But in this case, the little colony was scarcely in the vanguard of that movement. Pennsylvania had introduced a taxpayer suffrage as early as 1776. Other states soon followed suit. By the 1840s the United States had adopted universal white manhood suffrage. France adopted manhood suffrage in 1848, Prussia in 1849. In England, the Reform Bill of 1832 abolished local franchises and created a national system that enfranchised all leaseholders of property of a stipulated value—most of them for the first time. At the same time, it should be noted that borough franchises had long been established by local practice. A few were very generous. Thus the Reform Bill of 1832 also disfranchised voters in the more democratic boroughs, some of which had had an assessment franchise for centuries (Pole 1966, 272–273, 494; Rokkan 1962, 75).

The New Brunswick assessment franchise established in 1855 was, at best, a modest reform. Even so, it represented a redefinition of who should participate in democracy, and not all legislators agreed that such a redefinition was required or even desirable. James Ryan declared that "he would oppose any departure from confining the franchise to landholders, and thought that when it went beyond that, there would be no stopping place from universal [manhood] suffrage.... It would be much better," in his view, "to leave the elective franchise in the hands of those who have a stake in the country, than to extend it to those who could have none, as in the case of those having only personal property" (NB House of Assembly 1855, 59). John Ambrose Street, the representative from Northumberland, also feared that the proposed franchise would "degenerate into universal [manhood] suffrage." Patrick McNaughton, of Gloucester County, disagreed. While he certainly "could never consent to commit the representation of a country into the hands of Tom, Dick, and Harry," he was voting in support of the reforms, which he did not think would lead to universal (manhood) suffrage (NB House of Assembly 1855, 65). As proponents of the bill pointed out, professionals and the wealthier artisans were, after all, the men most likely to benefit from this extension of the franchise. In supporting the proposed changes, James Brown of Charlotte County admitted that "some of our farmers may not see the expediency of these reformatory measures," but, he asserted, "that does not argue against them." Abner McClelan, one of the two Albert County members, agreed. He welcomed the reforms, although he recognized that a franchise based on personal property would benefit people in towns and cities rather than those in the country. The people of McClelan's own county, like the majority of New Brunswickers, would be little affected by this extension of the franchise (NB House of Assembly 1855, 52–72). The new Election Act, then, represented but a tentative first step in franchise reform.

Some legislators would have been prepared to go much further in redefining democracy. Francis McPhelin, of Kent County, had "never believed in the doctrine that broad acres gave a man more common sense than his neighbour, or that great wealth imparted intelligence, or better fitted a man to serve the public interests. He thought every British subject was entitled to equal privileges, and he knew no reason why a man should be punished because he is poor" (NB House of Assembly 1855, 70). James Brown agreed, arguing that "every man who is bound to obey the laws ought to have a voice in making them." A.H. Gilmour also saw "the true principle" as "universal [manhood] suffrage." He "could not understand how it could be unconstitutional to allow a poor man to vote" (NB House of Assembly 1855, 71). Such legislators could not command a majority in 1855, however. New Brunswick would follow the lead of England, not France or the United States, in limiting the extension of the franchise.

Contesting the Franchise and Bicameralism

The transition to responsible government in the years that followed brought no radical transformation in New Brunswick politics. Dubbed "Smashers" by their opponents, the Reformers, having achieved the ascendancy, proved cautious in their legislative program. Nor did they make any move to change the general structure of government, which was based on the British model. On the contrary, they reaffirmed that structure not only by maintaining it on the provincial level, but by replicating it on the federal level at Confederation. Accepting the notion, articulated by the British colonial secretary in 1862, that "in a popular Assembly the numbers, and the practical energy, and the immediate desires of the community find a real expression ... [while] an Upper Chamber is generally intended to represent not only the settled principles and what on a large scale is called the traditional policy of the country; but also to a certain extent, its property, experience, and education" (quoted in Kitchin 1972, 65), the Fathers of Confederation established a bicameral federal legislature. This action implied a general satisfaction with and confidence in the parliamentary system.

Thus, New Brunswick, like Quebec, Nova Scotia, Prince Edward Island, and Manitoba, entered Confederation with a bicameral provincial parliament. Only Ontario rejected this historical precedent in establishing its new provincial government, deciding on a unicameral legislature for reasons of expediency rather than on any ideological or philosophical grounds: legislators there sought to avoid potentially powerful political opposition to cabinet decisions and to save the cost of maintaining an upper house (Kitchin 1972, 61). In New Brunswick, the new provincial government was the mirror image of the old colonial government. The elected Legislative Assembly was balanced by an appointed Legislative Council. The Executive Council, or cabinet, was drawn from members of both houses. In 1791, the Legislative Assembly was made up of 26 representatives from eight counties. As the population grew, new counties were carved out of the old and also allotted representatives. By 1870, the members of the Legislative Assembly, now numbering 41, were elected from 15 multiple-member constituencies comprising the province's 14 counties and the city of Saint John. The members of the Legislative Council, like the members of the federal Senate, were lifetime patronage appointments, selected by the government then in power, but, once appointed, councillors, like their federal counterparts, enjoyed a high degree of independence.

In the years that followed, perhaps as much because of the councillors' ungrateful independence as because of their partisanship, the Legislative Council fell out of favour with successive governments. When Andrew Blair was called upon to form a government in 1883, he immediately promised to abolish the upper chamber, something that Premier James Murray, his immediate predecessor, had also spoken of doing. But to achieve this goal, the legislation had to be approved by both houses, and the council did not prove keen to abolish itself. Two years later, the Blair government determined on a less ambitious course, announcing in the throne speech that a bill would be introduced to "change the constitution of the Legislative Council" and suggesting that the council might be willing to accept a bill "providing for the election of members to the Council, from time to time." When the leader of the opposition accused the government of reneging on its promise to abolish the Council, Blair reminded him that the Council could not be abolished unless the councillors themselves supported the move, and they clearly did not (Gordon 1964, 67–69). Pragmatism, not ideology, underlay attempts to abolish New Brunswick's Legislative Council. In the mid-1880s, the appointed Legislative Council, or upper house, acted as a check on the democratizing tendencies of the elected assembly. Nowhere was this clearer than in the council's opposition to suffrage reform.

An 1885 bill introduced by the recently elected Blair government suggested commitment to an ideological continuum that still identified land as the key criterion in determining voter eligibility. The measure, introduced with little fanfare and in response to little apparent agitation, would have given the vote to tenants, farmers' sons, occupiers of real estate, and widows and spinsters having property (Clarke 1979, 65; New Brunswick Legislative Assembly 1885, 109). Approved with minor amendments, the bill passed in the lower house in 1886, but foundered in the Legislative Council, where it was amended to such an extent that the government allowed it to die (New Brunswick Legislative Assembly 1886, 76). Women suffragists, who had not agitated for the bill, may never have realized that they had been just one step away from the franchise at this early date (Clarke 1979, 65). The earliest arguments in favour of woman suffrage, then, did not violate the principle of a property-based franchise. More significant in some ways, the government of the day had shown themselves willing to grant some women the franchise.

Yet the bill had, after all, represented a compromise position, with different legislators supporting it for very different reasons. The proponents of women's suffrage among them, seeing this unexpected opportunity slipping through their grasp, were loath to give up. In the Legislative Assembly, A.E. Killam of Westmoreland County continued to press for the enfranchisement of propertied women, introducing a measure designed to give voting rights to unmarried, propertied women in 1887 and, when that failed, appealing for the full enfranchisement of the ratepaying women of the province in 1888

(Clarke 1979, 66). The failure of the 1885 bill in the Legislative Council had made Premier Blair more cautious, however, and he began to rethink just what the limits of democracy should be. While he had been willing to extend those parameters to include propertied women, it had never been his intention to extend the franchise to women on the same terms as men. Now, with his government moving inexorably towards universal manhood suffrage, Blair was clearly alarmed at the possible implications should the measures Killam and others were advocating be adopted. He warned against the extension of the franchise to single and widowed women property owners: "In all probability before many years manhood suffrage [will] be adopted and if we now confer the suffrage upon women owning property we would be embarrassed when we come to do away with the property qualifications of male voters, as we would scarcely feel like giving the franchise to women universally as soon as they came of age" (Blair, quoted in Clarke 1979, 123). Blair's opposition to female suffrage escalated in direct proportion to his growing commitment to universal manhood suffrage.

Ironically, the Legislative Council had played the role an upper house is designed to play: it had given Premier Andrew Blair the opportunity for "sober second thought." In 1889, the Blair government moved to amend the Election Law to introduce universal male suffrage; it made no reference to women's suffrage in the bill. When A.A. Stockton of Saint John County proposed an amendment to include propertied widows and spinsters, he was persuaded to withdraw his amendment on the grounds that the universal manhood suffrage bill would surely lose if women's suffrage were attached to it. The Electoral Franchise Bill of 1889 stipulated residency within the province as the only prerequisite for males aged 21 and over who were British subjects. It also eliminated property qualifications for candidates, substituting a deposit of $100, to be forfeited should they receive less than half the number of votes garnered by the lowest successful candidate on the ticket. Only when the bill had passed did Stockton again move a resolution that voting rights be conferred upon propertied widows and spinsters. Killam, pointing to a "strong" women's movement in a number of counties, supported the resolution, while William Wilson of York County, perhaps in response to that same "strong movement," went even further, with an amendment which would have given the franchise to all women, married or single, over the age of 21 (Gordon 1964, 141; Clarke 1979, 66). But the legislators were by no means ready to extend to women the same privileges they had just extended to men. Observing that the women themselves were not clamouring for the franchise, Blair argued that "It was not the duty of the legislature to march in advance of public opinion.... Better that the laws should be behind than in advance of public opinion" (Blair, quoted in Clarke 1979, 65).

DEFINING AND REDEFINING DEMOCRACY

The Electoral Franchise Bill redefined democracy in New Brunswick by opening the doors wide to include an entire new category of voters: men without property and without a significant income. The passage of the Franchise Act, scheduled to come into effect on 1 January 1890, significantly enlarged the electorate, and Blair wasted no time in calling an election. As he explained, the present assembly, elected under a more restricted franchise had "ceased to be representative of the people" and he wanted the newly enfranchised to have the opportunity to select representatives to whom they could "entrust their political interests" before another session of the legislature was held (Blair, quoted in Woodward 1976, 22). With the Opposition entirely unprepared for the election, Blair's government won a strong majority.

Universal male suffrage had been achieved with an appointive Legislative Council still in place, for in the end Blair's government had neither abolished the council nor moved towards election of councillors; rather, Blair chose to appoint councillors to fill some vacancies, in the hope that these patronage appointments would at least support his bills, and perhaps eventually would also prove willing to vote themselves out of existence. But despite the passage of the Franchise Act, this ploy did not prove entirely successful. In 1888 a frustrated premier noted that "the Government has shown an earnest desire to abolish the Legislative Council and had appointed men to that body whose record in the Lower House on the subject should have been ... a guarantee that in the Council they would vote ... for abolishing the Council." The Government could not be blamed if these men "had abandoned their principles" (Blair, quoted in Gordon 1964, 126–127).

Yet abolition would soon occur. By 1890 there were five vacancies on the council. Although Robert Young, a senior legislative councillor, had promised to introduce a resolution to abolish the council if Blair filled the seats before the upcoming election, the Premier, distrusting the long-time council member, refused to comply with his request. Nonetheless, Young did introduce the resolution, which lost by a very narrow margin. Seizing this opportunity, Blair packed the council with appointees who had privately signed assurances that they would vote to abolish the council. This they did, although they amended Blair's bill to delay dissolution until after the next election. In response, Blair called the election two years before the end of his mandate (Gordon 1964, 177–182).

The abolition of the Legislative Council, which had come to be viewed as a thorn in the flesh of successive administrations, was certainly a major accomplishment for Blair. Having worked towards this goal for nearly a decade, he considered it "one of the greatest reforms inaugurated by any government in the history of this province." It was, without doubt, one of the most radical reforms ever undertaken, for it redefined the structure of democracy as practised in the province. The system of checks and balances was thereby altered. Yet this reform was never construed as ideologically motivated. Among other things, it was touted as a cost-cutting measure and, because the bill abolishing the upper house was to take effect only upon the dissolution of the current provincial parliament, the premier called the early election "[to save the taxpayers] very considerable expense." Most voters and assembly members supported the abolition of the Legislative Council, although a few worried about the concentration of power in the elected assembly (Woodward 1976, 24). Such a concentration of power would reach its apogee in 1987, with the election of the McKenna government, which held every seat in the Legislative Assembly. By this time, few would spare a thought for the kind of "loyal opposition" a Legislative Council might have been able to provide, however.

While it is easy to understand why successive New Brunswick provincial administrations wanted to rid themselves of the Legislative Council, there is equally good evidence to demonstrate that, in some cases at least, the council served the function that the late Senator Muriel McQueen Fergusson saw as the Senate's major role: its members, because they were not elected and, under the terms of their appointment could not easily be removed, were free to act in a non-partisan way, to offer the advantage of "sober second thought" (Muriel McQueen Fergusson Papers). The council's review of municipal bills, its amendments to statutes, and its consideration of railway and company bills had served the interests of the province. Much legislation passed since the abolition of the council would have benefited from a judicial review by a non-partisan senior chamber (Gordon 1964, 196). Therefore, perhaps reform would have been a better solution than abolition. But reform in the direction of elected councillors would not have solved the problem. Indeed, it might well have exacerbated it, a consideration that should give us pause in thinking about the kind of reformed federal Senate that might best serve New Brunswick interests. Whatever the advantages or disadvantages of the Legislative Council, it is undeniable that if Premier Andrew Blair had been successful in his early attempts to abolish it, the man who became one of the most vocal critics of women's suffrage would have headed the government that first introduced the measure—for propertied widows and spinsters—for the bill had passed in the assembly in 1886. Instead, Blair introduced universal manhood suffrage at the expense of women's suffrage.

Votes for Women

That the introduction of universal manhood suffrage in 1889 represented a significant redefinition of democracy was not lost on the women of the province. Using the only legal means they had to influence their government, they took up their pens to sign petitions demanding the vote. In 1894, petitions containing 10,000 signatures in favour of women's suffrage were submitted to the Legislative Assembly. Armed with such ammunition, women's supporters in the assembly introduced two franchise bills in 1895. But although the margin was small, both bills were narrowly defeated (15 to 14 and 19 to 15). Premier Blair was among those opposed: his definition of parliamentary democracy did not extend beyond the public sphere, where women, in his view, should have no place. Instead, "in other spheres, probably not less important and not less beneficial to mankind, women would ever be the most efficient workers" (Blair, quoted in Clarke 1979, 114).

The ballot was a privilege that should, in Blair's view, be reserved for men, whose obligations, duties, and contributions as citizens extended beyond those of women. It was a view shared by H.A. Powell of Sackville, who asserted during the 1895 debate on female suffrage, "If a woman is to be given the right to vote ... then she is logically bound to perform road work, to pay poll tax, school and municipal, and to perform constable duty when required. If she is entitled to a full share in the making of the laws she is certainly liable to do her share in enforcing laws" (Powell, quoted in Clarke 1979, 128). In short, the right to the ballot was now connected to the obligation to perform military service, police duty, and jury duty, and to hold public office when required. But times were changing and so were definitions of democracy. In the same debate, A.A. Stockton argued, "If there is one citizen in the land who ought to be given the right to vote, it is a denial of justice if a law is not passed giving him the right to vote." H.R. Emmerson of Albert County supported this view, reminding his colleagues that "democracy functions on the principle that government derives its just powers from the consent of the governed" (Stockton and Emmerson, quoted in Clarke 1979, 132–133). But New Brunswick would not be in the vanguard of those provincial legislatures granting the vote to women, for more legislators shared the premier's views than those of Emmerson. And although suffrage bills would be introduced again in 1899, 1908, 1909, 1912, and 1913, the 1895 divisions would be the closest women would come to victory until after World War I. In 1894, J.D. Phinney of Kent County had declared, "If legislators do not lead public opinion they are forced forward [by it]" (Phinney, quoted in Clarke 1979, 142). So it was in New Brunswick.

By 1909, supporters of women's suffrage in the legislature, hoping to achieve at least some measure of reform, had reverted to an earlier and more modest definition of the parameters of democracy. And they did win some converts among their more conservative colleagues as a result. Daniel MacLachlan of Northumberland County, a man who subscribed to the "old fashioned idea … that a man and wife are one, that their interests were common and that the man represented that interest in public," found himself nonetheless able to support the limited franchise proposal then before the house, that would have extended the franchise to propertied single women, on the grounds that such a change would go no further than "to extend a measure of justice to those women deprived of the protection of a husband" (MacLachlan, quoted in Clarke 1979, 122–123). Others, however, fearing that such a measure represented the thin edge of a wedge that would be used to lobby for further franchise extension, defeated the proposed measure. Thus, the extension of the male franchise did not open the door for women: quite the opposite. At the same time, educated women, with or without property, began to argue that they were more qualified to exercise the franchise than many male voters. And anti-suffragists increasingly found it necessary to seek further justification for their stance against allowing any woman access to the vote.

In seeking such justification for their opposition to female suffrage, some legislators actually redefined electoral democracy in negative terms. In the 1909 debate, former Premier James Murray of Kings County expressed the view that women voters, by participating in the "mob and excitement" about the polling station, could not escape sharing man's depravity (Murray, quoted in Clarke 1979, 119). In the same debate, Dr. Alphonse Sormany, a member of the legislature from Gloucester County, warned that, should she be granted the franchise, the woman voter would soon sink to the level of her male counterpart, selling her vote "for a drink or a dollar" (Sormany, quoted in Clarke 1979, 119). In the 1913 debate, John Sheridan of Kent County claimed to have it "on good authority" that "more divorces had resulted in the United States from political differences in the homes, due to the fact that women's suffrage was in vogue than from any other cause" (Sheridan, quoted in Clarke 1979, 118). Nor were opponents the only ones to define democracy in negative terms. In the 1895 debate, H.R. Emmerson, a strong supporter of women's suffrage, had claimed that women would bring a much-needed "broom of regeneration" to the legislature (Emmerson, quotes in Clarke 1979, 120).

By 1917, British Columbia, Alberta, Saskatchewan, and Manitoba had all granted women the provincial franchise. Western women were also the first to gain the vote in the United States, where Colorado and Wyoming granted women the franchise in the 19th century. In May 1917, New Brunswick women seemed to have public opinion on their side. On the day Dr. William Roberts, the Liberal minister of health, introduced a private member's bill calling for the full enfranchisement of women, seven or eight delegations of women from around the province were on the steps of the legislature; support came, as well, from all 19 branches of the province's Woman's Christian Temperance Union, the Local Council of Women, and the 25 societies it represented. Ella Hatheway, of the Saint John Women's Enfranchisement Association, reported that "women flocked in such numbers to the halls of the legislature that we had one hall itself and the MPPs went to the gallery" (Hatheway, quoted in Clarke 1979, 105–106). Yet, in the end, the government missed the opportunity to ride the crest of the wave and that bill, too, was defeated. Public opinion and the example of other provinces signalled that a revision of the legislators' vision of democracy was required if the government wished to maintain support, however. "Forced forward by public opinion," Liberal Premier Walter Foster promised that his government would introduce a suffrage bill to enfranchise all women, at the next sitting of the legislature. On 21 March 1919 that promised bill was introduced; less than a month later, on 15 April, it was quietly passed into law.

The story of the campaign for women's suffrage demonstrates the weakness of the system, and the very great challenges involved in achieving electoral reforms that are designed to benefit those members of society who are the most vulnerable, who wield the least political, legal, or economic power. It is a reminder of how our definitions of democracy can shift according to expediency as well as ideology, and of how such definitions can be adjusted and readjusted to exclude some groups even as they become more inclusive of others. In gaining the vote, women got the right to help choose their legislators, but they were denied the right to participate in making the laws. Indeed, this issue proved a potential stumbling block during the debate on the Bill to Extend the Franchise to Women, with John R. Campbell, a Conservative representing Saint John City, inquiring whether it was "the intention of the Government to go so far as to give women the privilege of becoming members of the House" (New Brunswick Legislative Assembly 1919, 124). Although he was assured that "such was not the intention," this may not have been the response he was looking for. Certainly this response and the general tenor of the discussion irritated Frank Potts, a fellow Saint Johner and fellow Conservative, who commented that "he did not know whether the Bill should be passed as a joke or not." Claiming that "the Government brought the measure in, not because it wanted to but because public opinion compelled it to take action," he argued that "by refusing women the right to be members of the House it was excluding the class best qualified to clean house. On school boards and other public bodies women had shown themselves well qualified to conduct public business. There were many women who could do better as law makers than many of the men he saw on the opposite side of the house." He expressed the hope that the government "would not give a half-hearted measure, but would give women a chance to sit in the House" (New Brunswick Legislative Assembly 1919, 125). But Potts' view did not carry the day. Although they were granted the vote in 1919, women would not be granted the right to run for election to the Legislative Assembly until 1934.

Nor did New Brunswick achieve universal suffrage with the enfranchisement of women. First Nations men and women living on reserves did not gain access to the provincial franchise until 1963, following the 1960 revision of the Indian Act, which had granted them the federal franchise. Moreover, for First Nations people the vote did not carry with it the potential for increased leverage, for in no riding did they constitute a significant proportion of the electorate. Four years later, during Canada's centennial year, New Brunswick's opposition Conservative Party began agitating for an extension of the franchise that would involve a further redefinition of the parameters of the eligible electorate, to include young people between the ages of 18 and 21. Henry Irwin of Charlotte County made the standard argument in favour of the measure, reminding his colleagues that at 18 young people became subject to the responsibilities of an adult if they broke the law and were also considered old enough to undertake the responsibility of serving their country in the armed forces. Yet, as he went on to point out, although society classified them as adults in these two fundamental ways, neither most provinces nor the federal government "permitted them the right to express their views with respect to these responsibilities" (New Brunswick Legislative Assembly 1967, 377).

But New Brunswick would not lead the way in lowering the voting age. In an era when the baby boom generation was just beginning to come of age and at a time when the Liberal government's policy of administrative centralization had recently dismantled the traditional structures of local government, the measure proved too controversial and the risk too great. The Robichaud government's bold Equal Opportunity program, implemented between 1965 and 1967, was designed to address issues of economic disparity within the provinces. However, the decision to abolish county government in favour of transferring financial and administrative responsibility for the provision of education, justice, public health, and social welfare from the local to the provincial level had brought accusations that the provincial government was arrogating too much power to itself. About to call an election, the Liberals were unprepared to expand the electorate. Thus this milestone in the history of electoral reform would not be reached until 1971, the year after the Conservatives gained power.

By that time, the issue was no longer controversial; indeed, Gerald Clavette, a Liberal member from Madawaska, predicted that "the lowering of the voting age will not advance the interest of any party or individual" (New Brunswick Legislative Assembly 1971, 1335). The final chapter in the history of New Brunswick suffrage reform came in 2003, with the extension of the franchise to the men and women incarcerated in the province's prisons. This very recent reminder signals the continuing reality that voting remains a privilege rather than a right accorded all adult citizens.

Redefining Constituencies

Those who became eligible to vote in New Brunswick prior to 1973 gained access to a system that was complex and, according to some commentators, confusing. Multiple-member constituencies and, until 1967, what one scholar has referred to as "the peculiar provincial ballot" made voting in New Brunswick a distinctive experience (Thorburn 1961). Depending on the population in their individual ridings, voters elected from two to five MLAs, choosing to do so by using either a pre-printed ballot supplied by one of the political parties or a blank ballot. Entering the polling booth with an envelope provided by the polling clerk, the voter would choose a party ballot, accept it as it stood or delete some names and add others; alternatively, voters could write the names of their preferred candidates on a blank ballot. The completed ballot would then be inserted into the envelope and given to the polling clerk, who deposited it in the ballot box. Familiar as New Brunswickers were with this method of voting by the 1960s, critics argued that, because it was different from the federal system, voters might get confused and spoil their ballots. No such concerns had been expressed when universal manhood suffrage was introduced in 1890 or when women were granted the vote in 1919. And although some have argued that there was more scope for intimidation when parties supplied their own ballots, there is little evidence that the system actually made corruption easier (Thorburn 1961, 135). In the end, however, "modernization" overtook the province: in 1967 the provincial ballot was revised to conform with federal practice, and in 1974 multiple-member constituencies were abolished and the principle of one person, one vote entrenched. There was no intrinsic reason why the first reform should lead to the second, but the two were connected, for the federal system that replaced the old system was clearly designed for use in single-member constituencies.

Moreover, the two reforms had been connected in a report submitted in 1967 by Chief Justice J.E. Michaud, who had been commissioned by Louis Robichaud's Liberal government to undertake a study of the Elections Act.

But while the government had accepted Michaud's recommendation to revise the format of the ballot, his proposal to move to single-member electoral districts was rejected in favour of adding four new single-member ridings encompassing the urban centres of Fredericton, Bathurst, Campbellton, and Edmundston, while retaining the multiple-member ridings. This raised the membership of the Legislative Assembly to 58. The boundary changes introduced in the Elections Act of 1967 brought accusations of gerrymandering from the Opposition benches. "What about single member ridings?" demanded Opposition leader Charles VanHorne. "Where is the principle in this bill? It was in the recommendation of Justice Michaud who prepared a good report, one with which we agree almost wholeheartedly. But where is the principle of single member ridings?... We want single member ridings, where the member will be responsible to ten or twelve thousand people and the people will know who is solely responsible—that member. That is what is contained in the Michaud Report. That is the principle behind it" (New Brunswick Legislative Assembly 1967, 309). The majority of the complaints focused not on the retention of multiple-member constituencies, however, but rather on the secrecy surrounding the committee responsible for designing the changes. When asked to name the members of the committee, Premier Robichaud refused, stating only that there were "six or seven of them" and that "they were extremely competent" (New Brunswick Legislative Assembly 1967, 301). The view of George E. McInerney of Saint John that the task should have been undertaken by an independent commission was echoed by a number of his colleagues (New Brunswick Legislative Assembly 1967, 299). The Conservatives would forget neither the issue nor their frustration over the process. During the 1970 election campaign, the promise to introduce single-member constituencies became a key component in their election platform.

Yet multiple-member constituencies had potential advantages. They gave parties the opportunity to balance the ticket in constituencies of varied populations, allowing for the possibility of a certain level of voluntary proportional representation, with what one scholar has referred to as "more complicated combinations and permutations than in other Maritime provinces—Acadian Catholic, Irish Catholic, Anglo-Saxon Protestant, etc. This ensured that the legislature essentially reflected the population in terms of ethnicity and religion, provided that the voters did not cross party lines to vote on the basis of demographic background" (Dyck 1991, 169). However, while multiple-member constituencies held the potential for certain advantages, this potential was not always realized. Thus, even in Acadian counties, with the exception of Madawaska, where four francophone candidates were regularly elected, francophones remained under-represented (Thorburn 1961, 46). Yet these were not the issues the Conservative government would focus on when, three years into their mandate, they moved to carry out their election promise to institute a single-member electoral system.

Late in 1973, Premier Richard Hatfield struck a commission to redefine New Brunswick's electoral boundaries, transforming multiple-member constituencies into single-member constituencies. Although, by this time, a majority of members in all parties favoured this change, the timing and mandate of the commission generated criticism in the legislature. Curiously, the most common argument in favour of the shift to single-member constituencies portrayed the change as a substitute for the lost system of local government. In explaining his government's position, the premier noted that many rural New Brunswickers felt they had "no effective form of government left." The logic that constituents would be more effectively represented by one MLA than by two or more members was grounded in the view that the latter was "not an effective relationship between the men elected to represent the people and the people themselves" (New Brunswick Legislative Assembly 1973, 2480). Robert Higgins, leader of the Opposition, also favoured "the concept of single-member ridings, based largely on the principle of greater accountability between representative and constituency." However, he pointed out that "there are some members in our caucus who feel otherwise, because of their concern for continued expression of community of interest among the mixes of the peoples of our province." (New Brunswick Legislative Assembly 1973, 2478). Arguing that "a unique New Brunswick experience has developed which has seen the expression of communities of interest through multiple member ridings," and, further, that "even within areas of the province where the population could be considered homogenous, the multiple member riding allowed broader representation of the diversity within what might be considered a single community of interest," Higgins cautioned that "extreme care must be taken to ensure that creation of single member ridings ... do[es] not weaken the political fabric of New Brunswick in such a way that existing communities of interest feel that the new structure will be to their detriment" (New Brunswick Legislative Assembly 1973, 2479).

Neither the Opposition leader nor the other members of his party who spoke during the debate opposed the concept of single-member constituencies. Rather they complained about the apparent contradiction in the terms of reference of the Representation and Electoral Boundaries Commission, which directed the commission in the first phase of its mandate to create single-member ridings and, in the second phase, to determine whether or not single-member ridings were the most desirable form of representation (New Brunswick Legislative Assembly 1973, 2484). They suggested that the order of the two phases be reversed. But the Conservatives, still bitter about the 1967 redistribution, which they viewed as gerrymandering, and anxious that single-member constituencies be put in place before the fast-approaching end of their first term, would brook no changes to the terms of reference, labelling the Opposition amendments a recipe for "delay and procrastination." The warning of Norbert Theriault, of Northumberland County, that, by adhering to county boundaries and creating the same number of seats per county as the number of current county members, the problems of under-representation of some regions and over-representation of others would be perpetuated, went unheeded. Yet in the end Theriault's prediction that in Queens County one member might represent fewer than 4000 people while in Westmorland, another rural riding, as many as over 15,000 people could be represented by a single-member proved prescient indeed (New Brunswick Legislative Assembly 1973, 2488; New Brunswick Representation and Electoral Boundaries Commission 1992, 15–16).

Commentators often portray the end of multiple-member constituencies as a step forward, the end of an "archaic practice." But something was lost as well as gained as a result. Speaking at the end of the fairly tedious housekeeping debate to approve the boundaries of the new constituencies in February 1974, Norbert Theriault outlined some of the positive aspects of the old system:

> Mr. Chairman, I realize from the last amendment to section 20 that this Act does not come into force until an election is called, but I want to say it has been my privilege for 14 years to represent, along with my colleagues, the good people of Northumberland County from Boiestown to Portage River and from Bellefond to Baie Ste Anne. Like everybody else in this House, I don't know whether I will represent anybody after the next election—that is up to the people—but I want to say very seriously that as a French-speaking New Brunswicker elected for four successive elections by an area which is roughly 70 per cent English-speaking, it has been a great education for me. I have learned … of the feelings and the desires of people of different ethnic and religious groups who are separated by 100 miles of geography, and all I can say is that that privilege has been afforded me and allowed me to be a more full person in the sense of wanting to serve all the people of my county.
>
> I would miss this very very much, and that is why I have often wondered in my own personal mind—not my political mind—about the desirability and the validity of single member ridings. I am concerned, and I hope that what the Premier has said about the old county boundaries and the comradery that existed in the various ridings, not only in

Northumberland County, will continue, because that is even more important than being elected. (New Brunswick Legislative Assembly 1974, 2594)

Theriault thus identified what was lost in the move away from multiple-member constituencies. With only riding representatives, the single-member system leads to a focus on local issues, fosters competition between regions, and neglects the broader issues.

The 1973 Representation and Electoral Districts Boundaries Commission had worked within restrictive guidelines: county boundaries, historically the basis for representation in the New Brunswick legislature, were to be respected and the number of members allocated to each county was to remain unchanged. Thus the commission's ability to adjust boundaries in such a way as to ensure a fair distribution of voters per constituency was limited, precluding the possibility of addressing anomalies resulting from widely differing county populations. This cautious approach is not, in itself, surprising, given the significance of the shift from multiple-member to single-member constituencies. What is surprising is that between 1975 and the appointment of the Representation and Electoral Boundaries Commission in 1991, electoral districts were not redrawn. New Brunswick had fallen far behind other provinces in redistributing seats, and, as a result, the tasks assigned the 1991 commission were "to make recommendations on the number of electoral districts, the average number of voters per constituency, the appropriate allowable variation in voter population between districts and the best way to ensure New Brunswick's aboriginal people representation in the Legislature" (Mellon 1992, 107; New Brunswick Representation and Electoral Boundaries Commission 1992, 7).

The first task was the more straightforward of the two: the commission recommended eliminating four seats, for a total of 54 seats, with a range in enumerated voters from a minimum of 8,000 to a maximum of 12,000 per constituency (New Brunswick Representation and Electoral Boundaries Commission 1992, 15–16). The select committee of the legislature charged with considering the commission's *First Report* recommended a few relatively minor modifications: increasing the number of seats from 54 to 55 to accommodate a seat for the Fundy Isles of Grand Manan, Deer Island, and Campobello and decreasing the average number of voters in each of the other electoral districts to 9,411 rather than 10,000, with an allowable variation from the average of 25% rather than the suggested 20% (New Brunswick Representation and Electoral Boundaries Commission 1993, 7–8). The most striking feature of the new electoral map was that it no longer relied on county lines, which had traditionally been the basis of electoral distribution in New Brunswick (New

Brunswick Representation and Electoral Boundaries Commission 1993, 15).

The commission's second task—"to consider the best approach to ensuring that New Brunswick's aboriginal people are given representation in the Legislative Assembly in a manner similar to the approach currently employed in the State of Maine"—proved more complex. The issue was a serious one. New Brunswick's First Nations peoples are by no means apolitical, with voter turnout in band elections ranging from 86% to 93% during the decade from 1981 to 1991. Yet during the same decade, participation rates for First Nations people in provincial elections had continued on a precipitous downward trend, falling from 47% to 28% (Bedford 2003, 17–18). The decline, although more dramatic in New Brunswick than in other provinces, was a nationwide problem, and New Brunswick was not the first Canadian jurisdiction to consider the issue: Canadian and Nova Scotian electoral boundary commissions were the first in the field. But even before the New Brunswick commission submitted its *First Report*, the Nova Scotian commissioners had abandoned their effort, citing time constraints as the explanation (New Brunswick Representation and Electoral Boundaries Commission 1992, 18).

To inform their deliberations on this issue, the New Brunswick commissioners "requested written briefs from aboriginal groups, studied approaches in other jurisdictions and held a public meeting devoted to this discussion" (New Brunswick Representation and Electoral Boundaries Commission 1992, 17). The Maine model did not prove attractive, for the two representatives elected by the aboriginal peoples of that jurisdiction are not allowed to vote in the legislature. In its brief, the New Brunswick Aboriginal People's Council "rejected the Maine model as 'token', a view repeated by others at the meeting the Commission held with aboriginal representatives" (New Brunswick Representation and Electoral Boundaries Commission 1992, 18). The commissioners noted that in the case of a less frequently cited model, that of the Maori people of New Zealand, four seats were dedicated to the Maori representatives who, unlike Maine's aboriginal representatives, are full members of parliament. Since 1975, Maori voters had been given the option of registering on the Maori roll or on the electoral list in their home constituency (New Brunswick Representation and Electoral Boundaries Commission 1992, 18).

The commission received briefs from three aboriginal groups, the New Brunswick Aboriginal Peoples Council, the Mawiw Council of Chiefs (Big Cove, Burnt Church, Tobique), and the Kingsclear Indian Band. Two briefs recommended establishing two native seats, one for the Mi'kmaq and one for the Maliseet. Concerning boundaries, one brief suggested that the boundaries respect those of the two tribes' historic hunting grounds, while another suggested that they match the reserve system. Questions about the makeup and maintenance of electoral rolls, eligibility requirements and election process were also discussed and a number of suggestions made. In rejecting the Maine model, representatives called for more consultation with native groups in formulating a better option. While the non-aboriginals consulted on the issue generally favoured some system of ensuring adequate representation in the Legislative Assembly, a variety of concerns were, nonetheless, raised (New Brunswick Representation and Electoral Boundaries Commission 1992, 18–19).

Recognizing the complexity of the questions involved and the need for more consultation with native groups, the commission recommended that "a Joint Committee of not more than four persons comprising a member or members of the Commission and a member or members of the aboriginal community be struck by the Select Committee [of the Legislature]" and that this committee report its findings to the commission within three months. The commission would then review the committee's findings and submit its final recommendations (New Brunswick Representation and Electoral Boundaries Commission 1992, 19). The select committee rejected this recommendation, however, recommending instead "that this Commission not institute further consultations with the aboriginal community concerning their representation in the Legislature unless such consultations were requested by the aboriginal community" (New Brunswick Representation and Electoral Boundaries Commission 1993, 8). The legislature accepted the recommendations of the select committee, thereby washing its hands of the thorny issue of aboriginal representation.

Since that time little progress has been made towards the goal of establishing "better representation for and greater participation of First Nations communities in the electoral process" in New Brunswick. The most recent commission to consider the issue did not, it would seem, follow the recommendation of the 1991 commission calling for more consultation with First Nations. Instead, the 2003 commissioners decided to test the waters with a new proposal, recommending "that the First Nations population vote be centralized into one electoral district, rather than be distributed across the current 10. Miramichi was the selected electoral district based on its already significant Aboriginal population." This would mean that First Nations peoples living on a reserve would constitute 10% of the eligible electors in the designated electoral district, giving them more leverage and, the commissioners hoped, an increased motivation to participate in the electoral process. However, neither the First Nations people nor the non-aboriginal community found this an attractive proposal, and, commenting that it would "respect the wishes of the people," the commission abandoned its attempt to establish "better representation for and greater participation of First Nations communities in the electoral process" (Canada Federal Electoral Boundaries Commission for New Brunswick 2003, 18).

Conclusion

While the earliest electoral reforms in New Brunswick were clearly related to shifting ideologies, electoral reform has, more often than not, tended to be pragmatic in inspiration as well as approach. And pragmatic reforms—those touted as cost-cutting measures, designed to improve efficiency—have been more rapidly, as well as more routinely, implemented. Since cost-cutting measures are invariably more easily drafted and implemented than are more substantive reforms, this is not, perhaps, surprising. Thus, in contrast to their failure to pursue the goal of better representation of First Nations peoples in the legislature, the government's response proved much more timely in the case of the recommendation in a 1996 discussion paper on electoral reform in New Brunswick to move towards the elimination of door-to-door enumeration. In 1998, in the amendments to chapter E3 of the Election Act, enumeration was made optional (New Brunswick Office of the Chief Electoral Officer 2003, 33–34). Although enumeration has not yet been eliminated in New Brunswick, the process has changed. In their rounds made prior to the 2003 election, enumerators started out with voter information garnered in 1999 and 2001.

Unfortunately, this did not improve efficiency. Enumerators were instructed to remove voters from the list only in cases where they "were able to confirm definitely that voters previously listed at an address were no longer there" even though it was recognized that this would mean "the voters' lists would include more voters than are actually in the province." In his report, the chief electoral officer concluded "that most (not all) of the 37,615 voter difference between the final 1999 list and the final 2003 list are duplicate entries" and that "the major effect of duplicates on the voters' lists is to make the voter turnout percentage look artificially low" (New Brunswick Office of the Chief Electoral Officer 2003). Thus, the reported voter turnout was 68.67% in the 2003 election, a significant drop from the 75.59% turnout in 1999. But when the probable duplicate voters are removed from the list of eligible voters, the turnout for 2003 rises to 73.58%, well within the average range for Canadian elections. This new practice of overestimating the number of eligible electors calls into question both the efficacy of this cost-cutting approach to voter enumeration and concerns about the ostensibly serious decline in voter turnout in recent elections.

Historical analysis of electoral reform can offer a useful model for analyzing the ways in which policy makers implicitly define and redefine democracy over time. Historically, the tendency to revisit definitions of democracy has sometimes reflected a genuine shift in societal attitudes. Such an ideological shift can be traced through the evolution of attitudes about who should have access to the vote: a shift measured by the distance between the £25 male freehold franchise of 1843 and the virtually universal franchise of 2004. In other instances, apparent redefinitions offered a clearer justification of traditional attitudes, sometimes exposing the nature of underlying prejudices that acted to delay or stall reform. In the case of suffrage reform, for example, a gender-based discourse is thrown into stark relief by juxtaposing the government-sponsored campaign for universal male suffrage in the 19th century against the largely externally inspired campaign for female suffrage in the 19th and early 20th centuries.

In still other instances, redefinitions of democracy have occurred without comment or even notice when very significant changes in structure or process have been undertaken in the guise of efficiency or as simple cost-saving measures. Such was the case with the abolition of the Legislative Council in 1890. And experience has shown us that reforms intended to streamline the system are more readily made than those intended to redefine our notions of the way democracy should work. The latter include reforms involving hard issues, such as designing a system of proportional representation that will give greater voice to groups that are disadvantaged by the present system. The insights gained through such historical analysis suggest that in contemplating electoral reform, ranging from sweeping or fundamental change to mere tinkering, it is useful to consider how that reform will redefine democracy. Then we may achieve a better understanding of the implications of the decisions that we make.

References

Acheson, T.W. 1985. *Saint John: The Making of a Colonial Urban Community*. Toronto: University of Toronto Press.

Bedford, David. 2003. "Aboriginal Voter Participation in Nova Scotia and New Brunswick." *Electoral Insight* 5(3):16–20.

Campbell, Gail G. 1986. "'Smashers' and 'Rummies': Voters and the Rise of Parties in Charlotte County, New Brunswick." Canadian Historical Association *Historical Papers*: 86–116.

—. 1990. "The Most Restrictive Franchise in British North America? A Case Study." *Canadian Historical Review* 71(2):159–188.

Canada. Federal Electoral Boundaries Commission for New Brunswick. 2003. *Federal Representation 2004: Report of the Federal Electoral Boundaries Commission for New*

Brunswick. Ottawa: Elections Canada.

Clarke, Mary Eileen. 1979. "The Saint John Women's Enfranchisement Association, 1894–1919." MA thesis, University of New Brunswick.

Condon, Ann Gorman. 1984. *The Loyalist Dream for New Brunswick: The Envy of the American States*. Fredericton: New Ireland Press, 1984.

Doucet, Philippe, and Jean-Guy Finn. 1983. "Éléments de réforme du système électoral du Nouveau-Brunswick." *Journal of Canadian Studies* 18(4):132–153.

Doyle, Arthur. 1976. *Front Benches and Back Rooms: A Story of Corruption, Muckraking, Raw Partisanship, and Intrigue in New Brunswick*. Toronto: Green Tree Publishing Company.

Dyck, Rand. 1991. *Provincial Politics in Canada, Second Edition*. Scarborough, ON: Prentice-Hall Canada.

Fitzpatrick, P.J. 1972. "New Brunswick: The Politics of Pragmatism." In *Canadian Provincial Politics: The Party Systems of the Ten Provinces*, ed. Martin Robin, 120–137. Scarborough, ON: Prentice-Hall Canada.

Forster, Ben, Malcolm Davidson, and R. Craig Brown. 1986. "The Franchise, Personators, and Dead Men: An Inquiry into the Voters' Lists and the Election of 1891." *Canadian Historical Review* 67, 17–41.

Garner, John. 1969. *The Franchise and Politics in British North America, 1755–1867*. Toronto: University of Toronto Press.

Gordon, Michael. 1964. "The Andrew G. Blair Administration and the Abolition of the Legislative Council of New Brunswick, 1882–1892." MA thesis, University of New Brunswick.

Kerr, D.G.G. 1970. "The 1867 Elections in Ontario: The Rules of the Game." *Canadian Historical Review* 51: 369–385.

Kitchin, G. William. 1972. "The Abolition of Upper Chambers." In *Provincial Government and Politics: Comparative Essays*, ed. D.C. Rowat, 61–82. Ottawa: Department of Political Science, Carleton University.

Klein, Kim. 1996. "A 'Petticoat Polity'? Women Voters in New Brunswick Before Confederation." *Acadiensis* 26(1):71–75.

MacNutt, W. Stewart. 1963. *New Brunswick: A History, 1784–1867*. Toronto: Macmillan.

Mellon, Hugh, 1992. "New Brunswick: The Politics of Reform." In *The Provincial State: Politics in Canada's Provinces and Territories*, ed. Keith Brownsey and Michael Howlett, 81–112. Mississauga, ON: Copp-Clark Pitman.

Muriel McQueen Fergusson Papers. MC 1372. Provincial Archives of New Brunswick, Fredericton, NB.

New Brunswick. *Acts of the General Assembly*. 18 Vic., c 37.

New Brunswick Commission on Legislative Democracy. 2003. "Mission, Mandate, and Terms of Reference." Fredericton: New Brunswick Commission on Legislative Democracy. Retrieved from www.gnb.ca/0100/mandate-e.asp.

New Brunswick Department of Municipalities, Culture and Housing, Election Branch. 1996. "Electoral Reform in New Brunswick: A Discussion Paper." Fredericton: Department of Municipalities, Culture and Housing, Election Branch.

New Brunswick House of Assembly. 1855. Debates of the House of Assembly for New Brunswick, 1855. Microfilm F71, Provincial Archives of New Brunswick [PANB].

New Brunswick Legislative Assembly. 1885. *Synoptic Report of the Proceedings of the Legislative Assembly of the Province of New Brunswick for the Session of 1885.*

—. 1886. *Synoptic Report of the Proceedings of the Legislative Assembly of the Province of New Brunswick for the Session of 1886.*

—. 1919. *Synoptic Report of the Proceedings of the Legislative Assembly of the Province of New Brunswick for the Session of 1919.*

—. 1967. *Synoptic Report of the Proceedings of the Legislative Assembly of the Province of New Brunswick for the Session of 1967*, vols. 1–3.

—. 1971. *Synoptic Report of the Proceedings of the Legislative Assembly of the Province of New Brunswick for the Session of 1971*, vols. 1–5.

—. 1973. *Synoptic Report of the Proceedings of the Legislative Assembly of the Province of New Brunswick for the Session of 1973*, vols. 1–8.

—. 1974. *Synoptic Report of the Proceedings of the Legislative Assembly of the Province of New Brunswick for the Session of 1974*, vols. 1–5.

New Brunswick Legislative Assembly Sessional Records. 1851/Petitions 461, 463; 1853/Petitions 22, 63, 85, 104; 1854/Petitions 104, 114, 115, 183, 217, 420. RG4, RS24, Provincial Archives of New Brunswick, Fredericton, NB.

New Brunswick Office of the Chief Electoral Officer. 2003. *Report of the Chief Electoral Officer, 35th General Election, June 9, 2003*. Fredericton, NB: Office of the Chief Electoral Officer. Retrieved from www.gnb.ca/elections/pdf/2003/ProvRpt.pdf .

New Brunswick Representation and Electoral Boundaries Commission. 1992. *Towards a New Electoral Map for New Brunswick: First Report*. Fredericton: Representation and Electoral Boundaries Commission.

—. 1993. *A New Electoral Map for New Brunswick: The Final Report*. Fredericton: Representation and Electoral Boundaries Commission.

Pole, J.R. 1966. *Political Representation in England and the Origins of the American Republic.* London.

Rokkan, Stein. 1962. "The Comparative Study of Political Participation: Notes Toward a Perspective on Current Research." In *Essays on the Behavioral Study of Politics*, ed. Austin Ranney. Urbana: University of Illinois Press, 47–90.

Thorburn, Hugh G. 1961. *Politics in New Brunswick*. Toronto: University of Toronto Press.

Woodward, Calvin A. 1976. *The History of New Brunswick Provincial Election Campaigns and Platforms, 1866–1974*. Toronto: Micromedia Limited.

Copyright Acknowledgments

Statistics Canada information is used with the permission of Statistics Canada. Users are forbidden to copy this material and/or redisseminate the data, in an original or modified form, for commercial purposes, without the expressed permission of Statistics Canada. Information on the availability of the wide range of data from Statistics Canada can be obtained from Statistics Canada's Regional Offices, its World Wide Web site at http://www.statcan.ca, and its toll-free access number 1-800-263-1136.

Chapter 10 by Don Desserud, "Fixed-Date Elections under the Canadian Parliamentary System," adapted from "Fixed-Date Elections under the Canadian Parliamentary System," from *Electoral Insight* 7:1 (2005): 48-53. www.elections.ca. Reprinted by permission of Elections Canada.

Figures

Figure 9.2a: Stewart Hyson, "Deviations from Provincial Mean, 1995," from *Electoral Boundary Redistribution by Independent Commission in New Brunswick, 1990-1994, Canadian Public Administration* 42:3 (1999): 178-179. Reprinted by permission of Institute of Public Administration of Canada

Figure 9.3: Government of New Brunswick, "Country Boundaries in New Brunswick," from *Maps of New Brunswick*. Date Retrieved: March 1, 2005. http://www.new-brunswick.net/new-brunswick/maps/nb/nbmap.html. Reprinted by permission of Government of New Brunswick.

Figure 9.4: Statistics Canada, "Regional Health Authority Boundaries in New Brunswick," adapted from "New Brunswick Health Regions," from *Health Indicators*, Vol. 2002, No. 2, Catalogue 82-221. www.statcan.ca/english/freepub/82-221-XIE/01103/images/jpg/nb.jpg. Reprinted by permission of Statistics Canada.

Figure 9.5: Elections Canada, "Federal Electoral District Boundaries in New Brunswick, 2004," *from Federal Representation 2004* (2004). www.elections.ca/scripts/fedrep/searchengine/search_by_maps.asp. Reprinted by permission of Elections Canada.

COPYRIGHT ACKNOWLEDGMENTS

Figure 9.6: Office of the Chief Electoral Officer, "New Brunswick's Provincial Electoral District Boundaries, 2004," from *Provincial Electoral District Maps* (2004). www.gnb.ca/elections/03prov/03provmap-e.asp. Reprinted by permission of the Office of the Chief Electoral Officer of New Brunswick (OCEO). The OCEO is not responsible for any errors or inaccuracies in reproduction.

Tables

Table 5:1: Michael Laver and Norman Schofield, "Summary of Conventions by Country," from *Multiparty Government: The Politics of Coalition in Europe* (Oxford, England: Oxford University Press, 1990): 64. Copyright © Oxford University Press, 1990. Reprinted by permission of Oxford University Press.

Table 6.2: Inter-Parliamentary Union, "Cross-National Gender Representations by Electoral System," from *Women in National Parliaments* July 31(2004) www.ipu.org/wmn-e/arc/classif310704.htm. Reprinted by permission of Inter-Parliamentary Union.

Table 7:1: Kenneth Carty and William Cross, "Percentage of Women Candidates, Elected 2004 Federal Election," from Can Stratarchically Organized Parties Be Democratic? The Canadian Case *Journal of Elections, Public Opinion and Parties* 16:2 (2006): 93-114. Reprinted by permission of Taylor & Francis Ltd. www.tandf.co.uk.journals